CU01460922

COAL WAS OUR LIFE

An essay on life in a Yorkshire former pit town

ROYCE TURNER

Coal Was Our Life

Sheffield Hallam University Press
Learning Centre
City Campus
Pond Street
Sheffield S1 1WB

Designed and typeset by Design Studio, Learning Centre, Sheffield Hallam University

All rights reserved. No part of this publication may be reproduced, stored in a retrieval system, or transmitted in any form or by any means, electronic, mechanical, photocopying, recording, or otherwise, without prior written permission of the publishers.

©2000 ISBN 0 86339 892 8

Sheffield Hallam University

ABOUT THE AUTHOR

Royce Turner is the author of two other books on economic and social change, *The Politics of Industry*, 1989; and *Regenerating the Coalfields*, 1993. He edited a third, *The British Economy in Transition*, 1995. He has studied at the Universities of Sheffield, Manchester and Liverpool, and taught at the Universities of Warwick and Liverpool prior to Sheffield Hallam University. He is the author of numerous articles of social commentary as well as articles on political economy and political sociology. He previously worked in the steel industry. Barnsley is his home town.

For Joyce and Ted, who were there

Cover photograph by Andrea Wigfield

CONTENTS

Introduction

This book was written as a portrait of how life has changed in towns and villages once dependent on coal. It sought real life stories from real life places, in West and South Yorkshire. As such, it avoided the theoretical and the overly-academic. Walking on the streets of Featherstone, or Castleford, or Grimethorpe, life does not feel theoretical and overly-academic. Life feels different from that. Less of a gaming exercise. More of a survival exercise.

The reasons for writing this book are simple. The social conditions, the way of living, the local economies, the values — at least among some sections of the community — have changed so dramatically in mining areas that they need to be documented. Mining towns and villages were never rich. But they did have a social stability. People did have a regular source of a reasonable income. There were structures in place which bolstered that stability: family and friendship ties; the union; the fact that you could nearly always get a job, if you wanted one.

When the coal industry was closed down, that stability was destroyed. Once redundancy monies were spent, incomes dried up. Mining villages were not the kind of places to attract inward investment and, at least in West and South Yorkshire, not places where there had been a high emphasis on education. Creating a new world from the ashes of the old was not going to be easy. And, along the way, there were going to be casualties.

The objective of this work is to describe how life is in the late twentieth and early twenty-first centuries in the former pit towns. It is based on discussions with people, largely in Featherstone in West Yorkshire, but also in other mining towns and villages in Yorkshire. There are real characters here, though their names have been changed to protect their identities. The work seeks an audience wider than the simply academic. Because the story, from hope to despair, from regular money to scratting about for survival, from fierce pride to social dislocation, is a story worth telling.

In any case, other works have addressed the sociology of changing conditions in former mining areas from an academic perspective and, in some cases, done an excellent job. Warwick and Littlejohn, for example, with *Coal, Capital Culture,* visited four mining communities in West Yorkshire in the 1970s and 1980s, carrying out extensive interviewing [1].

They looked at the mineworkers' strike of 1984/85, and at women's' support groups. They analysed the roles being played by men and women, and addressed commonly held attitudes seen in the past to be characteristic of mining communities. On household decision-making, for instance, they discovered that the idea that 'women are dominated by their male partners, is on the face of it.....clearly refuted'. Women still did most of the housework, nevertheless. But far more women were now involved in paid work outside the home.

Perhaps the most important point that they made, however, related to what they called 'local cultural capital'. This, they argued, was about the strength the community drew from social networks 'based in kinship, friendship and neighbourliness in household and community settings'. These were the networks that held the place together in a 'period of change'; a change which saw the local economy destroyed. They were the strength of the towns and villages.

There were other academic works and many of them were excellent in their own sphere. Some, like Warwick and Littlejohn's, assessed whether or not the 'stereotypical' image of a mining community was still sociologically accurate. Others addressed the changing position of women, concluding that patterns were shifting within the old, patriarchal, structures [2]. Some looked at whether former mineworkers were becoming 'entrepreneurs', fulfilling new roles as minor capitalists within an 'enterprise culture' which Mrs Thatcher dreamed of constructing, an 'enterprise culture' in which 'every man was a man of property, every man a capitalist' [3]. It wasn't a culture that was going to be easily embedded in a place where every man had been a union man, and every family, more or less, had rented their house from the council or from the 'board'. Still other academic work looked at the efforts at economic regeneration. How many new jobs had been created? What kinds of jobs were they? Who was working in them?

But some things were not there. Some things, like the drug epidemic and the crime epidemic to pay for it, were left untouched. Sometimes, the problems themselves were not there when the research for the other, earlier, works had been completed, at least not to the extent to which they subsequently developed. Warwick and Littlejohn, for instance, completed the bulk of their primary research in 1987.

And, moreover, the academic works were addressed to an academic audience, like all academic works are. That is the way that discourse advances, and there is no criticism of it here. But this book is intended for a wider audience; to be read by that much wider body of people who want to know what is happening in the world, in society.

In an industry which had seen such large-scale and rapid decline, an industry which had dominated in the localities it was situated in - economically, politically, culturally - there was a lot for people to look at. A lot for academics to assess and examine. Change; reaction to change. Britain saw its stock of mines reduced drastically. In 1983, British Coal had 191 pits, employing 207,600. By 2000, 17 pits remained, with a total employment of just less than 8,500. What was left was just a shadow of a once great industry. Places synonymous with coal mining - Barnsley, Mansfield, South Wales - saw its complete end or, in a few cases, saw its virtual end, with one or two pits continuing, using a quarter of the labour that they once had, eking out a survival in an uncertain economic world where closure could come at any time.

There was plenty to look at. And there was plenty that was never really seen. That was why this book was written. Training and Enterprise councils would issue figures about how many 'training placements' they had provided; local authorities would circulate glossy brochures about how many multi-agency partnerships they had established; regeneration agencies could boast about how many call-centres had been set up on brand new, shiny, industrial estates.

But what was gone was spirit. It cannot be quantified. It cannot even be adequately defined. With their ideas on 'local cultural capital', Warwick and Littlejohn came near, as near as can be in an academic sense. There may be training places and 'employment opportunities' and self-employment starter packs and new priority areas. But it was an unquantifiable spirit that held these places together. A spirit which had developed over generations, based on collectivism, kinship, advancement by co-operation rather than individuality. The social institutions that characterised the places were all symbolic of that: the Co-op; the miners' welfare; the club trip; the union. The spirit that those trying to foster an 'enterprise culture', where the engine was individual effort and the motivation was individual gain, never quite understood. The purpose of this book is to describe that spirit, as best it can be described, and look at how it infused the community. And to describe, now that it is gone, the consequences of its departure, the ruptured society, the way that a collective community confidence has transmogrified into a series of survival strategies played out by individuals, many of them marginalised. It is the story of a working class community which suddenly has its world destroyed.

NOTES

1. Dennis Warwick and Gary Littlejohn, 1992 *Coal, Capital and Culture. A sociological analysis of mining communities in West Yorkshire*. Routledge, London.

2. See, for example, Sheila Allen, 1989 'Gender and work in mining communities', paper presented to BSA conference, Plymouth, March; Sheila Allen, V.Carroll and C.Truman et al, 1987 'Women in mining communities', paper presented to BSA conference, Leeds, April.

3. Gareth Rees and Marilyn Thomas, 1991 'From coalminers to entrepreneurs? A case study in re-industrialisation', in Malcolm Cross and Geoff Payne (eds) *Work and the Enterprise Culture*. Falmer, London; and R.Turner, 1990 'Mrs Thatcher's Enterprise Culture', *Social Studies Review*, Vol 5, No. 3, January.

Coal Was Our Life

STARTINGS

This is the story of Featherstone, a small former mining town of 14,000 people in West Yorkshire. It could be the story of many mining towns across Britain. It is the story of Featherstone's change from a town where coal dominated economically, culturally, politically, through to an era where coal had gone. Above all, it is a story about people, about how lives have changed, about how people cope with change when the world that they know is taken from them.

Featherstone was the setting for another book, *Coal is our Life*, which was published in 1956 [1]. Featherstone was concealed in that work as 'Ashton', but everybody knew it was Featherstone. There seemed little point here in keeping up a see-through disguise. *Coal is our Life* was a seminal work. Not, in itself, primarily a work about the coal industry, more about the cultural, social and economic *impact* of the coal industry, a social anthropological study of what it was like to live in Featherstone. It outlined the life of a miner and his family in the mid-1950s.

This book returns to the same town more than 40 years after the original study. It is an essay on life in the late 1990s in the former mining communities: what you are likely to do for a job; what you are likely to do when you're not at work; what the aspirations are of the younger generation. Featherstone is the same place. It is, at the same time, a different world. Undoubtedly, there are elements of continuity with the past: people still frequent the same pubs and clubs, drink beer, play bingo. Some men work at the pit, commuting the few miles to the surviving Prince of Wales colliery, or the thirty mile return journey to the Selby coalfield. But the elements of continuity are overlain by a new sense of insecurity and an 'identity' crisis which is reflected individually and collectively as

Featherstone gropes towards a post-coal future. It is the new world which will be explored here. The good parts and the bad.

The original study examined the characteristics of the mining town and the people who lived there. It looked at the nature of the miner's work, and how that affected his lifestyle, his relationships, and the social relations between other people in the community. It examined conflicts between miners and management at work. There was plenty of conflict. There was also mutual respect.

The first book also examined the nature of trade unionism and the wider ramifications associated with rising the ladder of success within the then very influential National Union of Mineworkers (NUM). Where there was success, this could lead on to other positions of responsibility for the individual concerned: perhaps as a local politician, or as a magistrate. In the late 1990s, the idea of trade union membership as a vehicle for social mobility sounds anachronistic. To be thought of as an active and committed trade unionist might actually stop you progressing. But in mining areas, throughout the post-war era, the trade union had a crucial social role beyond the more narrowly-focused industrial relations remit of most labour organisations. That social role was wide-ranging. It encompassed exerting social discipline through to dispensing advice to individuals on a whole range of issues unrelated to work. The 1956 study also looked at the leisure activities pursued by the miner and his family: clubs, pubs, bingo, the miners' welfare, sport. It noted the way that, just as work life was divided because no women worked as miners and few men engaged in domestic housework such as cooking and cleaning, social life too was divided. Men did certain things and women did other things. They were almost separate worlds.

Coal is our Life revealed a community in which a very strong moral and social code obtained. It was a code which governed relationships between men and women, behavioural patterns in a variety of settings and environments, a code which influenced aspirations and expectations. Like religious codes, it worked to make life slightly easier by removing the need to make decisions about particular events or which life direction to follow.

The social code governed the minor intricacies of life, through to the important life decisions. It was a code which was shot-through with altruism: you looked after those who couldn't look after themselves; you helped, if you could, your friends and family. Some pits, for example, including Featherstone's Ackton Hall, would have pit shops which sold whatever the miner needed: army shorts, for example, at Ackton Hall, and dudleys for carrying water. It was common that any profits from the pit shop would be used to benefit the community. Profits from the shop at 'Big K' in west Yorkshire — the biggest pit in Britain — are still used to provide annual holidays in Blackpool for retired miners and their families, and to put on a Christmas party, even in the late 1990s.

The moral code was also one which provided for community sanctions on those who transgressed it. It forbad swearing by men in female company, for example. Swearing was reserved for the pit or the pub, if the company was all male. Breaking this rule could often initiate a fight, if the offender ignored requests to tone down the language. The code governed the age at which people would get married and, to a large extent, it influenced the prospects for that marriage. Ideally, you should get married young. The woman should have kids fairly early on. Men and women might lead virtually separate lives, with the men, if not at work, in the club or at the allotment. But separation, divorce, even in relationships that were not working, was rare. And if anybody did separate, it would be the talk of the street for weeks.

What is perhaps so remarkable, in retrospect, is the extent to which this was a world of certainties. Certainties with limitations but, nevertheless, certainties. Both men and women 'knew their place'; both men and women knew what was expected of them. Both men and women knew what was coming their way, in terms of a job, a marriage, a level of prosperity or lack of it, a position in society. This was an ordered world.

It wasn't like this in Britain in the 1980s, or the 1990s, in mining areas or in many other places. If you lived in a mining town, certainty was replaced by insecurity: if you were in work, you might lose your job at any time. And if you weren't in work, you might not be able to see where you could find it. Mining towns and villages were notorious for their lack of alternative employment. There might be a clothing factory, where women would work, but often there was little else. The angst of insecurity always hits the working class first of all, as all social ills do.

The 1980s and 1990s saw a creeping insecurity which, at least to start with, appeared to be confined to youth and those with what well-paid, suited economists call 'few transferable skills' but, as time wore on, bit deeply into the confidence and the psyche of the British middle classes. It wasn't going to have any political impact until it hit the middle classes. And once it did, their confidence in the Conservative government ebbed, allowing for the rise of the newly 'modernised' Labour Party in the late 1990s, which, after divesting itself of any vestige of socialism, was no longer seen as a threat by the reasonably well-off.

Insecurity hits hardest where there have been certainties. The man certain of the strength of his relationship with his wife is more devastated when she leaves him for another man than the man who knew for years that his wife had been having a string of affairs.

Featherstone had been a town of certainties, as were so many other mining communities, for generations. Ever since Ackton Hall and other local collieries opened in the 1860s, for most men it was a near certainty that they would become mineworkers. And for women, it was a near certainty that they would become miner's wives.

Ackton Hall worked its last shift in 1985. Virtually in the centre of town, its three shaft, extensive pit top winding gear had dominated the sky-line for more than a hundred years. Its very structure symbolised grit, hard work, a macho, somewhat monolithic, culture, a blackened world into which men descended, day after day, night after night. And when they got there, there was no difference between night and day.

When it closed, it employed 600. Only a year prior to closure it had employed 1,100. Two years before that, 1,530 people had worked there. At the time, Geoffrey Lofthouse, MP then for a neighbouring constituency, summed up the new situation facing Featherstone depressingly well:

'What is Featherstone without its pit?

'There will be total desolation. If we cannot get the money [from government for regional aid] to float new firms then Featherstone will be dead' [2].

And, as Featherstone entered its new world of disorder and uncertainty, there was a certain resonance and poignancy in the farewell words of Ackton Hall's manager: 'They have been the best blokes I have ever worked with'[3]. Few of them deserved what was to descend on the town.

Ackton Hall's death had been a protracted one. All along the actions and words of management continued to provide hopes that were all, eventually, dashed.

As late as January 1984, the 'Board', as the NCB (later British Coal) was referred to, was saying:

> 'We plan to turn it into a successful enterprise. All we need now is the co-operation to achieve that objective' [4].

The North Yorkshire Area Director, Michael Eaton, while expressing concern at the pit's performance, added that:

> 'We have got to produce a scheme that will bring a better return to our investment and ensure the long term survival of the pit' [5].

Long term survival.....successful enterprise.... To have hopes raised and then subsequently dashed is worse than to be told, unequivocally, that all is gone, all is lost forever. It is a form of psychological torture. People hang on, just in case. They fret; they worry. They keep a secret hope that there will, after all, be a reprieve. Everything will be all right. Only to be told, in the end, that the world they had built, the world they belonged to, has gone forever.

Five years after Ackton Hall closed, the main centres of employment for women also closed. This was closure town. The smaller of two clothing factories, where all but four of the 90 employees were women, closed in 1990. Locals referred to it as the 'women's pit'. So dominant was coal to the local culture that female employment was characterised by reference to male employment. The factory even used to break for the summer at the same time as the local colliery: the 'pit holidays'. The larger of two clothing factories, employing mainly women, also closed in 1990. And then there was what is often referred to as the 'financial services industry'. This was widely seen to be a growth area in the British economy throughout the 1980s and for at least part of the 1990s, even while factories and pits closed all around. If we no longer made anything, we could still shuffle paper around. But Featherstone saw banking retreat, just as everything else had. On the high street leading to the pit, there once stood four banks. By 1995, only one was left. The last two to withdraw from a declining local economy shut their doors in 1990 and 1995. With the death of coal, there was nothing left to stay for.

Closed Bank, Featherstone, 1998

Likewise, what had been one of the top working men's clubs — the biggest building on the high street — stood vacant and boarded up, a desolate presence from the early 1990s. In 1998, its brooding emptiness symbolised far more than just another failed business. Here was a central part of social life, where people had joked and laughed, cavorted and taken the piss, smoked too many strong cigarettes, drank far too much beer over far too many years. Here was the club at which the NUM's national president had rallied the troops in 1985, stabbing, gesticulating, cajoling, pleading them, invoking every emotion imaginable, not to return to work, not to break the strike, from which he undoubtedly assured them, they could still gain some kind of victory. By the late 1990s, like so much else, it was empty, vacant, redundant, taking up space but ultimately useless.

Working men's clubs were important to Featherstone. They were central to what was, effectively, a male-dominated social life. It was like that in all the mining towns in the north of England. Albert, a 76 year-old former miner who lived in Featherstone and had worked at one of the nearby pits, reminisced, as older men do, about the good times they had had in this club:

> '......we thought it was the best club in Featherstone at the time.....there was always a good turn on....there was snooker, billiards...'

Most of the working men's clubs of the 1950s remain, though one has become an ordinary pub that routinely ignores licensing hours and has a reputation for drugs, and the others are far less popular than they once were. By and large, in the late 1990s, most of the customers are over 40, many in their 50s and 60s. Perhaps the biggest change is that women are as likely to frequent the clubs as men. Not as many women as men, but women, nevertheless. As *Coal is our Life* noted

> 'The Working Men's Clubs are predominantly male institutions. Only one of those in Featherstone admits women as members. The others absolutely forbid by rule the admittance of women into the club except for the concerts on Saturday evening and Sunday mid-day and evening' [6].

Harry, a 66 year-old former winder (winders were responsible for winding men down the pit), told me:

'The leisure side has changed. It was all working men's clubs. There were six in Featherstone. It's all to do with the money that's gone out of the economy. That's why they are now emptier. There were no women in the working men's clubs. For a lot of men in the 1940s and 1950s, leisure was playing snooker and darts. More women started going in the clubs, and there were more club artists. People go out with their wives more now'.

Women are there, but their role is still restricted, even in the late 1990s. In the main working men's club in Featherstone — Red Lane — even in 1998, a sign hanging over the snooker table indicates that 'Ladies not allowed'. If you are a woman, you cannot be a member of the club. And, thus, of course, there are no women on the august governing body, the 'committee'.

Working men's club, Featherstone, 1998

You occasionally come across political scientists who will tell you that things have changed, that a woman's role in a place like Featherstone is now more dominant within the family, and within the community, than it was in the past. That women are less ready to accept a separate and somewhat subordinate role to men. It is true. Things have changed. But the extent to which they have changed is open to debate. More women work, more women are the breadwinners. Nevertheless, the old bonds, of tradition, of the defined social roles which allow certain behaviour but preclude other activities, are still strong.

The pit, the clothing factories, the banks, have all closed. Then there was the shop closures.

Like many pit towns and villages, Featherstone has one main street which acts as its commercial centre, with other, shorter streets containing small terraced housing coming off that. Featherstone's high street had 71 premises in the late 1990s which still were, or had been at one time, retail outlets. Their activities, or non-activities, were indicative of the state of the local economy. Amongst them, there was neither product nor premises which could come remotely near to being classed 'up-market'.

The largest category was the boarded-up shop. There were more premises standing empty than anything else. Eleven out of the 71 premises were in this condition.

Despite the abandoned shops, you wouldn't be stuck for something to eat. The next largest category was the take-away food shop. On the high street, there were two Indians, two Italians, one Chinese and two fish and chip shops. You'd be all right if you wanted a hair cut, too. Spoilt for choice, really. There were six on the high street, the third largest category.

After that, the clothes shop had the highest frequency. There were five. They told a story in themselves. There were no designer labels here. If you wanted to spend a serious amount of money in them you'd find it difficult, if not impossible. One of them sold second-hand clothes for kids. Another sold very cheap women's wear. A third sold 'bankrupt stock' and catalogue returns. At a fourth you could buy wool and socks and other kinds of underwear. One was a sports shop. This is perhaps the only one where you could spend a wad, if you could find an expensive pair of trainers.

Thursday is market day. About five or six stalls are usually pitched in a little precinct. In the centre of it is a sculpture from pit props. It commemorates the deaths of two miners shot by troops in 1893. Coal has gone, but its legacy remains. In Featherstone, you cannot escape it and you cannot forget it, even in the late 1990s. Quite a few of the shops still sell bagged coal. Go on any day you like, and you will see men with bags of coal thrown across their shoulders, struggling with the weight down the high street. In this forgotten world, not everyone has converted to gas.

Usually, in the market, all except one of the stalls sell clothes. Very cheap clothes. The other sells fruit and veg. There aren't many customers. In fact, you wonder how they manage to stay in business.

You can also get yourself a second-hand washer or cooker or second-hand furniture. New furniture is available here also, in a couple of shops, though much of it is 'discount'. But you couldn't get yourself a new fridge or a new washer or a new cooker. You'd have to go elsewhere.

On the high street itself, there are also two churches and two pubs. Intermingled between the open and closed shops, and the never-staffed police sub-station opened in 1990 to counteract drug abuse and vandalism, there is still a speckling of occupied, small, terraced housing. Nearly all these houses would have been occupied by miners, in work, and their families, even just a few years before. Now, the high street is physically dilapidated. Retail business life here is curtailed to that which caters only for those without money. Harry, the former winder:

> *'There are certain things you can't buy in Featherstone....you could in the 1950s....there was a tailors.....there were two menswear shops.....From North Featherstone working men's club, between there and the Red Lane club, there were five butcher's shops, and they all made a living.....now there isn't any at all.... a lot of corner shops have gone ..'*

Peter has lived all his life in Featherstone. He was born in another pit town a few miles south of this, but married a woman from Featherstone. Now in his early fifties, he is early retired — as so many men in this town are — from an administrative job in a nearby town.

> *'The pit closure'*, he told me, had *'devastated local businesses, without doubt'*.

Tom, a former electrician at Ackton Hall, and then a 'pioneer' at the Selby coalfield, said:

> *'....you could buy everything in Featherstone at one time.....there were seven butchers....seven sweet shops....they all made a living. They're all take-aways now'*.

The demise of Featherstone's coal industry was, of course, part of a far wider deindustrialisation that transformed the British economy in the 1980s and 1990s [7]. This deindustrialisation was visited upon Britain's coalfields with particular severity. In 1984, 174,000 mineworkers were employed by the National Coal Board at 172 collieries. By 1994 just 16 of these mines survived in British Coal ownership, employing around 14,000 in total, including administrative workers [8]. There were a few others being run independently. With the closure in 1997 of Asfordby in Leicestershire, the most modern pit in Britain, the Point of Ayr colliery in North Wales, Bilsthorpe and Annesley Bentick collieries in Nottinghamshire, the industry has seen yet further contraction.

The economic landscape of Featherstone and the surrounding area has been changed beyond recognition since 1956. In the late 1950s, as noted earlier, Featherstone was part of the administrative region of the West Riding of Yorkshire. *Coal is our Life* noted at the time:

> 'The West Riding ..... is one of the major industrial bastions of Britain. In this area from the inception of the industrial revolution until the present time, industry has been the keynote of life for its inhabitants. Some towns have become famous for a particular product such as wool textiles or machine tools. Others have supplied the driving power of industry in the form of coal'[9].

If industry was the 'keynote of life' in the 1950s, by the 1980s and 1990s, Featherstone had reached a phase of enforced **post-industrialism**. This manifested itself in a number of ways. Most obviously, across what was the West Riding, much of the 'old' industry — coal, wool textiles and machine tools — has gone or, at least, has been dramatically reduced in size. A vast increase in unemployment is another manifestation, at least in parts of West Yorkshire, though gaining an accurate picture of unemployment is difficult.

Official figures for Featherstone showed 405 males unemployed in July 1996, equivalent to 10.8 per cent of the male workforce. The number of women unemployed stood at 109, or 4 per cent of the female labour force. 10.8 per cent stood only just above the level for Great Britain of 10.2 per cent. Female unemployment in Featherstone was officially **lower** than the 4.3 per cent for Great Britain as a whole [10].

That there is a substantial question mark over the validity of these official figures is probably the politest way of putting it. Official unemployment figures in mining areas are close to meaningless. Study after study has demonstrated that 'true' unemployment in mining towns and villages is substantially higher than that reflected in official statistics. More often than not, this 'hidden' unemployment takes the form of 'incapacity' — through illness — to work.

That there are vast numbers of people desperate to find worthwhile employment is scarcely hidden. The Prince of Wales colliery embarked on its first recruitment drive in 14 years in 1995, advertising in the local paper. According to the press, there were a 'handful' of positions available. They attracted 460 applications. In the end, 17 got jobs. The pit switchboard had been 'inundated' with enquiries from men desperate to find reasonably well-paid work. Other people continued to write in, week after week, asking for jobs. By early 1997, there were 700 applications sitting in a filing cabinet in the personnel office. But there were no jobs for them. By this stage, the pit itself employed only 600, and a third of these were 'contractors' working for companies other than that which owned the mine. Contractors were subject to the least job security of all. They could be 'released' at any time.

It was the same when Morrisons opened yet another of their supermarkets in 1990 in the closest reasonable sized town to Featherstone. They created 350 vacancies: mainly low-paid; mainly part-time but, nevertheless, jobs. As journalists have it, 'Supermarket bosses' were 'staggered' by the rush of applications. The response from people wanting jobs was the 'second highest in the food giant's 91 year history'. They decided to interview 2,300, keeping 700 names on file of people they might call on in future [11].

I talked, in early 1998, with a man who owned a small open cast mine in Great Houghton. Apart from this, and one other open cast mine, both employing about 35 men, and apart from working behind a shop till or bar, there were no other employment opportunities in Great Houghton at all. He told me how he'd had to stop going out for a drink at night in local pubs. He was constantly being pestered by people wanting a job:

> *'If you say that there might be something, you put hope in them....if you say that there might be something in 6 months, they'll knock on your door in 6 months....'*

Great Houghton, a former mining village 5 miles to the east of Barnsley, provides as good an example as any, but they are all much the same. 2,300 people live in Great Houghton. Its adjacent village, Little Houghton, has just over 200 people living there. No one says much about it, but when you notice that the same 3 surnames keep cropping up time and time again, and when you ask and discover that the furthest away anybody marries anybody from is the next village, you realise that many people must be related.

Featherstone and Great Houghton share much in common. Marrying people from the next street is one of them. John was a diesel fitter at one of the closed local collieries. He's in his late

forties and now works in an administrative role in a newish
security business:

> *'It's still happening......this is one of the arguments I've been having*
> *with some people......you're not born to grow up in Featherstone,*
> *marry somebody from 4 doors down, spend the rest of your life with*
> *them.....there's got to more to life than this...'*

So few people lived here, and yet Little Houghton had two pits
until the early 1990s, employing 2,000 people in the 1970s. One of
them had been there more than 90 years, the other over a 100.
Generations of men had tramped down the same country lane that
led to both of them, in the dead of night, or the unearthly hours of
the morning.

Official statistics showed male unemployment in Great Houghton
reaching a peak of 19 per cent in 1987, and falling to its lowest point
in an 11-year period of 10.6 per cent in 1998. Significantly, female
registered unemployment fell from a high point of 14.4 per cent to
3.6 per cent in the same period, demonstrating that the general
trend for higher female participation in the labour market is also
evident in what was traditionally a male-dominated economy. But
there is widespread recognition that the unemployment figures bear
little resemblance to reality. Large numbers of men were 'on the
sick', drawing incapacity benefit, though it was also commonly
accepted that they might be able to work in the right kinds of jobs
in the right kind of circumstances. As Barbara, the leader of the
parish council, and wife of a redundant and now out-of-work
miner, said to me in 1998, 'if you took incapacity into account,
unemployment would be nearer 40 per cent'.

Unemployment was clearly a significant problem in most mining
towns and villages in the 1980s and 1990s, especially among the

youth, who might still be reasonably expected to have career aspirations, rather than the many older men who are 'early retired'. It was, nevertheless, argued forcefully that 'something should be done for those over fifty' and that fifty was too young an age to retire.

Unemployment forces people to change. You have to find other ways to survive. Some people travel further to work. Some opt out all together. Some go into the black economy. John, the ex-diesel fitter, said:

> *'Jobs haven't come to Featherstone since the pit closed....people now have to travel further to work, and a lot of them haven't bothered'.*

With redundancy money all gone, I asked how the ones that hadn't 'bothered' had survived:

> *'By any means they can.....working on the side, there's a lot of that...putting windows in...roofing.....the redundancy money has all gone now, though it provided a cushion for a while'.*

Prolonged unemployment leads to demoralisation. You think that you'll never get a job again, and you might not. You even begin to think that you aren't worthy of a job. Society has no use for you any more.

Take Billy. I'd known Billy for years. I knew him when he was a 'fotty year old bachelor'. It always struck me as a bit odd, but every time we spoke he told me his age. We are all conscious of time passing, but perhaps it preyed on his mind just that little bit more than it did on the minds of others. Perhaps it was because he was still a bachelor. He always told you that as well.

He'd always been fat. He wasn't the most handsome man on earth. He wasn't the most intellectually well-endowed. He wasn't the snappiest dresser. And he couldn't charm you with his conversation.

But he was a good man. An honest man. He'd never do you a bad turn. If he could do you a good one, he would. There were so many men like this. So many honest, decent, people.

I ran into him in 1998, in his home village just south of Barnsley where, like so many others born there, he still lived, unwilling, or unable, to even contemplate living elsewhere.

'Am 56. 'Ave not worked since Grimethorpe pit shut in 1993' he told me, without any prompting, in fact, without me daring to ask if he was working for fear of what answer I might get. After asking me how I was keeping, that he was not working was the first thing he said to me. Not working, so alien to a man who had worked all his life, so alien to a community brought up on the idea of going to work every day, day-in, day-out, was the main pre-occupation in his mind.

He was still a bachelor. He was still honest. He was still fat. He still took the same little alleyway down to the working men's club that he'd been taking for nearly thirty years, only now the shops next to it were tattier than they'd ever been, with more grotesquely offensive graffiti than they'd ever had, and with a higher number of sullen-looking half-kids half-grown-ups sulking about in a nether world. But he wasn't quite as confident as I had remembered him. As another miner, at the time still in work, had said to me years ago, 'at least tha's got a bit of credibility when tha'r a miner'.

Billy's days as a miner were long gone. But he still clung to them. They conveyed a legitimacy. They were a testament to the days when he would make a worthwhile contribution to the economy, to society. And that, really, is all he ever wanted to do. It was a modest aim, but it was an honourable aim. Grimethorpe pit was instantly on his tongue the moment he met you. Billy couldn't, now, see what he could possibly do. He couldn't work in the pits because there were no pits. He could not drive, so he couldn't get to a job elsewhere. He consoled himself by finding a 'social role' as a committee man at the local working men's club. He wanted to carry on making a contribution to the local society. The working men's club — that bastion of working class life, of collectivism, of everybody knowing everybody else, of strict rules, and derided as it might be by some for all these things — allowed him a mechanism through which to do so. He was excluded from work. No one, and he knew it, had any need to employ him. They could employ someone at 18 or 20. Excluded, but still too young and strong to give up. Proud, like so many men were proud. There were so many thousands of other men like Billy in the abandoned Yorkshire coalfield. And you knew, as you talked to them, and because you knew their families, that they never did anything to deserve being abandoned like this in the world.

And then there was Albert. Albert was 76 when I met him in Featherstone in 1998. I saw him across the way in the library. He indicated that he was coming towards me, but that he wouldn't be able to do it very fast. Then I noticed that he was walking with a stick. He told me, after a while, that he had lost his legs when a shell hit his tank in France during the Second World War. Albert was the one who had told me about the working men's club, about how the redundant building had once housed Featherstone's best working men's.

He had worked, prior to the war, at a nearby pit. His job was
shovelling coal back on to the conveyor belt that had spilled off as
the colliers had loaded it. He did this up until being 15 or 16. He
damaged his thumb while doing it. He still couldn't bend it at 76.

In 1939, conscientious objectors had started to come down the pit.
He saw them as 'wanting to get out of the forces'. He himself then
volunteered. To get in, he had to lie. Mining was a protected
occupation, so he told them he was a farm labourer.

One day in France, he was in his tank. A shell must have hit it, but
he thought he was asleep. Then he 'sort of woke up'. He tried to lift
himself, but couldn't. He looked down, and saw that his legs 'were
on, but hanging off'.

When he came back from the war, he had difficulty finding work.
He had tried to set up in business, but losing his legs had left him
prone to ill health. He had to go into hospital for an extended
period. During this time, although he was in hospital, he was
deemed fit for work, and therefore couldn't gain any sick pay or
unemployment pay. He ended up going down the pit again. It was
his only option. He tried to get into the office, but they didn't have
any vacancies, so he ended up down the shaft. He was doing much
the same job as he had done before. Eventually, after a fall, he
believed that he might be a hazard to others, and voluntarily gave
up work there. He had a family to feed, and no other job to go to.
But he might put the others at risk. I realised, sitting in the library,
that Albert was one of the best of men. And the world all these
people knew is collapsing about them.

There have been lots of studies, too many to recount. They all tell
the same story: some mineworkers have found themselves
alternative jobs, usually at lower pay; many have remained

unemployed; huge numbers have re-classified themselves as sick. One study was carried out by Sheffield Business School in the early 1990s. It looked at what had happened after the closure of two collieries near Doncaster, Markham Main and Brodsworth [12]. 40 per cent of the mineworkers had managed to find themselves an alternative job. 25 per cent remained unemployed. Perhaps most importantly of all, however, 23 per cent had been categorised as long term sick. The average age of the mineworkers being interviewed was 39, not the usual age at which people become totally incapable of working. Studies by the Coalfield Communities Campaign in the early 1990s showed 44 per cent of redundant mineworkers at Grimethorpe, near Barnsley, a pit town less than 10 miles away from Featherstone, still unemployed over a year after closure, and 32 per cent officially long term sick. It was much the same story at Parkside in Lancashire, Silverhill in Nottinghamshire, Vane Tempest in the north east [13]. Mining can be a hard job, and has obvious attendant health risks. But another way to view the figures is that becoming long term sick is a rational response to the difficulties of finding a job: sickness benefits are higher than unemployment benefits, or 'Job Seekers' Allowance', as it became known, and minor civil servants do not constantly call you in for interviews to find out why you don't have a job. Why you do not have a job is obvious: there aren't any. Or, to be more accurate, there aren't any for a man in his mid-thirties or early forties, with no qualifications and no experience outside mining, which is the basic situation of most of those made redundant from the coal industry.

The loss associated with pit closures that everybody knows about is the loss of jobs. But it wasn't just any old job. It was reasonably well-paid, better than you were going to find elsewhere. You were working with your mates.

Jim, a former face electrician at Ackton Hall, who now devoted himself full-time to local politics, reflected on the impact on this small town of its closure:

> '*When the pit closed, we lost more then a major employer. For the blokes down the pit, it was like a different town underground. And we'd sort out problems. If a young 'en was causing trouble, I'd see his brother down the pit and say: "if that young 'en a thine comes causing trouble again, I'll knock 'is block off"'.*

Despite the fact that he might have knocked his block off, there was great camaraderie at the pit; a great sense of 'we're all in it together'. You were blunt. You were honest. You had to be. That was the way to be understood. You said what you meant. There were few, if any, subtleties. On that openness, and honesty, you could build the camaraderie. As Arthur, the former NUM branch secretary at Ackton Hall, said:

> '*There was a lot of comradeship....everyone was together....if you cut one, they all bled....the boss cut one, and it was a problem for us all'.*

I wondered how the camaraderie had survived privatisation and defeat in a major strike. I asked Dennis, the branch secretary, if it still existed at the surviving Prince of Wales pit:

> '*....it's the same but to a lesser extent....because of the hostility of the market place...'*

Returning to mining communities in the late 1990s, economic devastation has brought with it social pathologies that they had previously been, if not immune to, certainly resilient towards: drug abuse, family instability, crime. You drive past some of the working men's clubs that were once seen almost as communal property and now they are bedecked with huge rolls of barbed wire, doors and windows barricaded with steel bars. Nobody would have stolen from these places 20 years ago: you would have been seen to be stealing from your own community, your neighbours, people that had as little money as you did.

Life has certainly changed. For men and women, in the 1980s and 1990s, there is a sudden confusion of roles. Betty, in her late fifties, married to a former miner, worked at the miners' welfare hall in Great Houghton. She cleaned the floors and the inside windows and generally looked after the place. She'd seen the changes. We talked in early 1998, after a class of about 20 local people had been in to be taught about working on lap top computers. She summed up the situation as she saw it. Like so many others, she just volunteered the information without any prompting:

> 'There's no pits open, so the men aren't doing anything......the women were in all the time in the past, making meals and doing the ironing......the meals had to be there on the table.......it's not like that now......whoever's in first does the meals.....all except one of the mothers that come here are single parents......they're either divorced or they've never been married'.

Featherstone: place and people

To the north, south, east and west, this was mining country. Across a spectrum of towns, townships, and pit "villages" — in close proximity yet fiercely contesting their independence and sense of identity — this was one of the heaviest concentrations of coal mining in western Europe. In the late 1990s, the legacy of coal was still strong. Pubs in the locality, if not in Featherstone itself, were still called Miners' Arms; older men still sported NUM lapel badges; in working men's clubs you would see pictures of pits and pit-men; RJB Mining, the company that took over the bulk of British Coal's mines after privatisation in 1995, sponsored the local rugby team, and the scarred blue-grey landscape, so symbolic of coal mining, whilst disappeared from Featherstone, is evident in the surrounding area.

In mining towns and villages, the social class system was manifested physically, and so obviously, in the housing. You knew what someone's job was simply by the house that he and his family would occupy. The back-to-backs, and the NCB-owned houses, and the council houses, were the preserve of miners. The more substantial redbrick, sometimes detached, sometimes semi-detached, house, with its garage and gardens to the front and rear, might be occupied by the pit official or manager. Prior to nationalisation in 1947, the mine owners themselves, if local, would live in the finest properties in the area. *Coal is our Life* noted the mix of housing in Featherstone. It listed a mine mansion, suburban semi-detached, council houses, and back-to-backs with communal privies.

In the late 1990s, in Featherstone, the mine owners' mansion has gone, demolished years ago. The back-to-backs have gone too. And, as in many solidly-Labour areas, local authority housing has expanded. Privately-owned suburban housing has also grown. The physical manifestation of social class is, therefore, at least in some ways, less obvious than it was in the 1940s and 1950s. And yet, in other ways, it is perhaps more obvious as the truly dispossessed and excluded have become ghettoised, and have caricatured themselves with their particular form of dress, their style of living: the aggressive tattooing; the big boots; the gaunt look; the searching, but empty, eyes.

But you will not see street-begging in Featherstone or Grimethorpe, or even in much bigger former mining towns like Barnsley. The persistent and sometimes aggressive begging that became such a permanent feature of every big British city in the 1980s and 1990s, with subways and doorways occupied by street dog and beggar asking for 'spare change', did not take hold in mining towns. They were too small. Begging, like prostitution, requires a measure of anonymity. Begging off your neighbours, where you knew everybody and everybody knew you, would be total humiliation.

The local authority and NCB houses — of which, *Coal is our Life* noted that 1,300 were built between 1911 and 1953 — were described in the earlier work as "…..clearly the best in Featherstone from practically every point of view".

In the late 1990s, they are not clearly the best, or anywhere near it. They are seen by many of the local residents as places to avoid at all costs. There are exceptions to this: some of the council estates are neat, tidy, proud, and well cared for by their tenants. That is certainly the case when the estates are compared to similar housing settlements in nearby bigger towns in West and South Yorkshire.

But at least three of the council estate areas are regarded as being places that you must, if at all possible, avoid having to live in. They are caricatured as being full of rough types and no-hopers, who wouldn't work even if they were offered a job. One of the more recent local authority developments, where many of the former back-to-back residents were decanted, has had its name corrupted to 'Vermin Street'. It provides an idea of the esteem in which it is held. A worker in a concrete company on the pit site told me how they 'stick all the scruffy ones down there'. Henry, a 50 year-old worker at Humb Store, the biggest employer in town, said of 'Vermin Street':

'...nearly everybody worked at the pit and when it closed it went to pieces'.

By the late 1970s, many of the NCB houses had been sold to individual tenants. Later, in the 1980s, the ones that hadn't been sold in this way were disposed of to what were, very often, absentee landlords. Most of these houses, many of which had been erected in the 1950s, were in a serious state of disrepair from the 1970s onwards. They were prefabricated, and had been built with a concrete composite with reinforcement. The reinforcement was steel, and eventually it started to rust. Quite clearly, here was one 'privatisation' that had certainly not helped the 'customers' — the tenants. A local authority housing officer explained to me what things were like under the new landlord, how difficult it was, for example, to get repairs done:

'....e in't a good landlord. We always have to be on his back. Generally, people have to complain to us before they get owt done by 'im'.

Things got so bad that, in late 1996, the local authority was going to take the landlord to court to force him into carrying out repairs. At the last moment, with the threat of with legal action, the matter was settled out of court.

The houses were bad. The landlord was bad. The families that lived in them were beset by social and economic problems. On top of that, the residents were struggling to survive in the face of a poor local reputation. It is almost as if the houses are a physical representation of hopes dashed, of a vision for the future turned sour. People had secure employment; brand new, modern, houses; what were seen as good prospects for their kids. Now, forty-odd years later, the houses stand crumbling, and lives have crumbled, too. Old, battered cars sit on oil-soaked drives. If it's sunny, people sit on the door-step for half the day. There's nothing much else to do. Fiona's mum and dad came to Featherstone from Scotland after the pit closed. They were moved into an estate of NCB houses. Dad worked at Ackton Hall. She's a caretaker at Featherstone's youth club. She took the job because her daughter wanted to start going there, but the place had such a reputation for drugs that she thought getting a job there might let her keep an eye on the daughter. Lots of Scots were moved into the 'pit houses' in Featherstone, and a few Geordies too after colliery closures in the north. They used to call it 'Scotties' Corner'. Fiona:

'We used to play on the road. It was beautiful. It was a wonderful place to grow up. Now it's gone to rack and ruin. I think you'd have to put a bullet-proof vest on to go down there. As soon as they sold out, they put anybody in the houses. The landlord doesn't do any improvements. We had to drag him kicking and screaming to come to my mother's house, and she was 80...her window frames were rotting'.

Far from being the 'best' in Featherstone, by the late 1990s, these houses were serious contenders for the worst. As with 'post code discrimination' in inner city areas, just living in the former NCB houses could seriously jeopardise the chance of getting a job. Ralph, in his late fifties, worked at one of the companies that had taken space on the old colliery site. He was involved in training young people to be builders:

'There used to be vandalism, but not now. Not since we've stopped taking the Featherstone lads. We used to take them from the bottom end [the former NCB houses]. There was a lot of trouble with the lads then. There used to be floodlights here. They would come back at night and throw bricks at them. The old pit office used to be at the front of the colliery site. The company in it after the pit had closed used to make football badges for shirts. They moved. Within a month, the

company that owned it had got a client for it. One morning I came here — there was nothing left. Petrol bombs had been thrown through the windows. When a policeman got here, he ran round the back, to see if anyone was trapped. While he was round the back, somebody stole the police car. But, it's not bad now. Not 'round here'.

It was the same in Maltby, another mining community near Rotherham. Sean, a local councillor, took me to the former NCB houses. It was in one of the worst states of disrepair that I have ever

Grimethorpe 1998

seen any housing. Sean told me that it had improved a lot from the way it had been. Many of the houses were boarded up and dropping to pieces. Some of the youngsters had taken to breaking the gas pipes inside and throwing petrol bombs in. They'd completely lost a few of the houses this way. It provided the youngsters with a bit of fun. Sean took me to the derelict houses that had been occupied by his family and friends, where they had looked after the gardens, and been good neighbours and helped each other out. The houses are in rack and ruin, gardens like jungles, without the eerie charm of a jungle. A few yards away is the footpath next to a railway line where the smack dealer had threatened to kill Sean for trying to fight the drug trade.

There are no miners left here, and no ex-miners. They all moved out when miners started to earn decent money in the 1970s. The only people here now are those on benefit. Nobody else wants to be there. They are completely forgotten. Nobody cares and, because nobody cares, the residents don't care.

The 'pit houses' might be in a bad state, but not everything has deteriorated since the 1950s. *Coal is our Life* wrote of air pollution so bad that it would 'reduce clothes, houses and streets to drab uniformity', and of the town being dominated by a huge, black, slag heap. Slag heaps are how the mountains of waste from the coal industry were referred to in mining areas. Spoil tip is the more polite, official term. In the late 1990s, the air in Featherstone is not noticeably different from anywhere else. The reason why is obvious. In the 1950s, and beyond, coal was used to heat almost every household in a town like Featherstone, and in other mining areas. A concessionary coal allowance was, after all, effectively part of the miner's wage. In what was provoked by an effort to overcome the health-endangering London smogs of the 1950s, the Clean Air Act of 1956 empowered local authorities to declare smokeless zones, should they wish to do so. A European Directive, taking effect from 1992, rendered smoke control measures mandatory. Smokeless zones, which meant that only smokeless fuel could be burnt, were introduced progressively in Featherstone from 1978 onwards. Obviously, this reduced the amount of ordinary coal being burnt and consequently reduced air pollution. In any case, the displacement of coal for heating by gas has been a national trend. Outside the former pit villages, where coal is still often burnt, it is something of an irony that the coal fire is now the preserve of the well-to-do in their weekend cottages rather than the staple of the working class family in their small terraces and council houses.

The slag heap, too, has disappeared from Featherstone. Slag heaps were the most ugly physical manifestation of coal mining. Dark, sinister, artificial blue-grey mountains, they haunted mining towns and villages with a brooding physical dominance. Opencasting has removed this monster from Featherstone. It no longer dominates the skyline. What is left is grassed over, and part of it is to become a new industrial estate where the effort to replace jobs lost in the coal industry, and to re-position Featherstone's economy, will be concentrated. So, in environmental terms, Featherstone has improved.

For all the environmental improvements, and for all the expansion of private-sector suburbia, the working class character of Featherstone remains undiminished. Rich people do not live here. Featherstone, like other mining towns, is mono-cultural. You live here if you were born here, if your family are here, if you were a miner here. Nobody comes to Featherstone because it is a pretty and attractive place to live. It isn't. And culturally, it is limited to the provision of the usual outlets in mining towns: there is a bingo club; there are four social or working mens' clubs; there are pubs. There is a relatively new library built in the mid-eighties which, alongside some schools built in the 1970s, some relatively new housing, a small addition to the shopping precinct, and a 'discount' supermarket, represents most of the recent building in Featherstone.

Coal is our Life states that outsiders saw Featherstone as a 'dirty hole'. It's easy to see why. The town was dominated by slag heaps: 'houses and mine-workings crouch under their shadow'; air pollution coated buildings and spoiled any washing put out to dry; and unless there was a dance or a band on at the welfare, the only 'cultural activity' available was to go down to the pub or club. In the late 1990s, Featherstone is less of a dirty hole. But there is still nothing here to attract the visitor, or to entice people to live in the town.

If you compare a variety of 'social indicators' for Featherstone with those for Great Britain, they provide a picture of some aspects of society in the former mining town. Obviously Britain has changed dramatically in many ways since 1956. In the modern world, mass ownership of cars, for instance, is accepted as the norm, as is owner occupation of houses. The number of people with higher education qualifications has increased substantially, and the number of women working has also increased significantly. An approximation of how Featherstone is fairing, economically and socially, can be gleaned by a comparison of some of these social indicators. In several areas, Featherstone fares less well than the rest of Great Britain. According to census figures from 1991, 42.7 per cent of households in Featherstone did not possess a car. That compares with 33.35 per cent of households in Britain as a whole. Residents with long term illnesses in Featherstone, so debilitating that it prevented them from working, stood at nearly 18 per cent in 1991. This compares with just less than 13 per cent for Britain. In terms of housing, too, Featherstone had 55.2 per cent of its housing in owner occupation compared to 67.53 for the country in total, and Featherstone had nearly 40 per cent of its housing rented from the council, compared to only 21 per cent for the rest of Britain. Those in the census-defined social classes 'professional, managerial, technical, and skilled non-manual' numbered only 11 per cent compared to over 14 per cent for the rest of the country. People with higher education qualifications — those above A-level, at diploma or degree level — stood at 3.9 per cent in Featherstone, compared to nearly 11 per cent for Britain. Admittedly, the last two figures come from the 10 per cent census sample for Featherstone, which is not always accurate when extrapolated. Nevertheless, it gives a clear

indication of conditions there. Featherstone's not doing well. You
can see that when you walk down its high street, call into its empty
pubs, walk around the market. And you can even find it in 'official
statistics' which often serve to obfuscate, rather than illuminate,
reality.

The number of people still engaged in mining, despite pit closures
in the 1980s and 1990s, stood significantly above levels elsewhere.
The 10 per cent sample for Featherstone showed 14.1 per cent in
'energy (including coal mining)' — in practice, almost all coal
mining — compared to 0.13 for Britain as a whole [14]. The picture is
one of significantly fewer professionals, significantly fewer numbers
of people with higher education qualifications and, in general
terms, overall less prosperity than elsewhere. The modern world
has not quite passed Featherstone and some other mining towns by,
but it's not fully taken hold either. And where it has, modernity has
sometimes manifested itself in the most negative of ways. Drug
misuse is the obvious example.

Some other trends in Featherstone have mirrored the country as a
whole. In the 1950s, the world of work in Featherstone, for example,
was largely a man's world. *Coal is our Life* noted that for women

> '*the coal industry provides no paid work for them. In an area where
> there is no alternative they have to do without it*'.

This was true generally in mining areas. Dennis, Henriques and
Slaughter refer to Fogarty who had pointed 'to the absence of paid
employment for women in the coal area'. Clearly, another point of
contrast between the fifties and the nineties is the changing role of
the sexes in relation to breadwinning. The 1991 Census indicated
that 46.3 per cent of women of working age in Featherstone were
'economically active'. This compares to just less than 50 per cent for

the country as a whole. So, on that count, Featherstone fits in with
the national trend.

Strikes

The defining moment in the post-war history of Featherstone came
with the 1984/85 strike by the NUM. There had been strikes before,
of course, but not, in recent history, one like this. And the outcome,
in the end, was the crushing of the mineworkers as a force within
trade unionism. The defeat of the miners marked the beginning of
the end of the coal industry, both locally and nationally.
Featherstone has never really recovered.

In the 1970s, the mineworkers had got used to winning industrial
disputes. The 1972 and 1974 national mineworkers strikes are the
obvious comparators to the 1984/85 strike. Both those strikes were
over pay. They were substantial victories for the mineworkers. But
1984/85 was different from 1972 and 1974. First of all, 1984/85 was
not over pay. Secondly, despite NUM President Arthur Scargill's
protestations to the contrary, 1984/85 was a resounding defeat for
the union. Understandably, for one who had staked so much on it,
Scargill himself refused to accept that it was a defeat. At a press
conference in March 1985, after the union had decided to return to
work, Scargill insisted that the 'titanic struggle' that had been
waged by the mineworkers was, in itself, a 'victory' [15]. And he had
a point. There are few other groups of workers who would have
stayed out for so long, and shown such determined loyalty to their
union in the face of unrelenting propaganda from their employers,
from the government, from the press. He himself felt 'terrific, quite
frankly'.

The Times report of what Scargill had told the conference was that:

'In spite of tremendous hardship, his members had remained on strike for a whole year, and the Board did not have a signed agreement that pit closures could be made on economic grounds.

'The board's plan to eliminate 4 million tonnes of high cost capacity during 1984-85 had not been implemented and the threat to close 5 named pits immediately had been withdrawn, Mr Scargill said' [16].

The official line was that the mineworkers went back 'without agreement'. And they went back, at least in public, as Scargill had told them to, with 'heads held high' [17]. In Featherstone itself, the miners gave one last demonstration of defiance. They presented themselves at Ackton Hall on the appointed day of the return to work, and then promptly took the day off en masse in order to 'go back on their own terms'. They were proud, and they weren't going to crawl back to work. Scargill himself led 1,000 mineworkers, accompanied by a lone piper, up a winding, wooded, hill at his home village of Worsbrough, to the gates of Barrow colliery. When they got there, they were greeted by pickets from Markham Main, near Doncaster, seeking to prolong the strike to try to force an agreement on the reinstatement of mineworkers sacked during the dispute. True to his principles, Scargill refused to cross the picket line, leading his men away, back down the winding hill. The press called him the Grand Old Duke of York.

And as they all walked down the hill, they all must have realised, even if only individually, secretly, in their hearts, that very little had been achieved. It was a spirited, courageous fight, in which men had lost their wages for a year, run up huge debts to banks, to building societies, to pub landlords, some of whom had kept providing the best bitter so necessary for solace 'on the tick'. I knew one pub landlord who went bankrupt: he'd kept providing the beer to miners who had very little else to look forward to, in the hope that the strike would end soon, and the miners would pay him back. And they would have done. But the strike didn't end. It dragged on, and on. It was a fight which had put enormous pressure on families, on marriages, on friendships. I saw brothers fight each other in the streets. But, of course, the fights weren't really about trying to hurt each other. They were a form of desperation. They were involuntary spasms by men who had temporarily lost control, by men desperate for a future for themselves and their families.

In the end, the titanic battle which the miners had waged gained them very little. Men started going down the shafts of Barrow colliery again, but it never properly re-opened. It was 'merged' with Barnsley Main in June 1985, a pit closer to the centre of town. Some took redundancy. Some, especially older men, were glad to see the back of it. Some transferred. Like Featherstone, employment for men in Worsbrough had been at the pit, and employment for women at a clothing factory. And like Featherstone, shortly after the pit closed, the clothing factory closed. It hung on for 5 years, but it finally closed in July 1990, after a failed Australian buy-out. Social patterns that had been settled for generations were suddenly disrupted. Men no longer went up the winding, wooded, unlit hill on their night shift. Women no longer gathered in their nylon work wear to sit at sewing machines all day long. Sitting at sewing machines all day long was never fun. But it helped to pay the bills. And it helped you get your small, stone terraced house on one of the streets named after George, Henry or Thomas. I never quite understood why the streets were named after George, Henry and Thomas. And I never thought to ask. It is probably too late to ask now. Most of those who would have known have gone.

The very appearance of Worsbrough has deteriorated since its enforced economic change. There is no point in pretending that it was ever glamorous, or rich, or that, really, there was ever all that much to do. It was like all the other mining villages of South and West Yorkshire. Men would drink in one of the pubs or clubs. They would stand on street corners on summer evenings talking for hours to other men that had gathered. Women would go to pubs and clubs too, but that was rarer, sometimes confined to Saturday night. Women would 'cal', as they did in Featherstone in the 1950s. 'Calin' simply meant talking: in each other's houses; over the garden gate; over the fence. It was often about what other people in the neighbourhood were doing, what was happening in their lives. *Coal is our Life* called it 'gossiping'. Yes, probably it was gossiping.

Worsbrough was tidy and ordered. The church at the top of the hill was neat and well-kept. The Roman Catholic and Church of England primary schools, side by side, were never vandalised. The secondary school was, as a local education officer said to me, 'one of the best schools' in Barnsley, in the 1960s and 1970s. By the late 1990s, it had become

> 'one of our biggest problems. You never knew what the situation would be at the start of everyday. People would knock down walls to get inside to steal, to vandalise. And when the walls were rebuilt, they'd come and take the mortar out before it had chance to dry'.

A line of shops, ranging from butchers to off-licences to general dealers, were rarely in any kind of trouble. Their owners never became millionaires, but they stayed in business. Being broken into was a rarity. In the late 1990s, all the shops that remain have steel shutters, an emblem of insecurity never there prior to the 1984/85 strike. Other shops stand boarded-up, vandalised. The main street, the centre point of the settlement, looks tatty and rundown. It exudes an air of disorder, disharmony, perhaps faint despair.

Years after I had left Worsbrough I bumped into a young woman who came from the same place. She explained to me that she had felt compelled to move. I expressed surprise: surely it wasn't that bad. It was. 'It's areight [all right] if you want to be a burglar or summat like that'. And that was it. It wasn't what I wanted to hear; it wasn't how I wanted to remember it. I wanted to remember it as it was when people thought they had something going for them. It may not just be the demise of Barrow colliery that brought Worsbrough to its knees, and it may not just be the closure of the main centre of employment for women. But it didn't help.

After 1984/85 strike, Featherstone, like Worsbrough, would never be the same again. Within two months of the end of the strike, Ackton Hall had closed. The national unity of the union organisation itself was broken by the emergence of a new mineworkers' union in Nottinghamshire and some other parts of the midlands, called the Union of Democratic Mineworkers. Largely, this represented workers who had not gone on strike in 1984/85. Nationally, the miners' union was virtually broken. As one ex-miner from Barnsley commented to me on Scargill's optimistic interpretation of the outcome, 'if that's a victory, I'd bloody hate to see a defeat'.

Nevertheless, many in Featherstone argued, even 14 years after the dispute had finished, that this was a battle which had to be fought. Harry, the 66 year old former winder:

> *'The strike to keep the pits open was the right thing....I could never understand the economics of closing a pit down'.*

He then went on to detail to me just how much money a closure cost in terms of redundancy money, benefits, pensions. He was right, of course, but ultimately it wasn't the money that really mattered to the government. It had a different agenda. Really, it was all about crushing trade unionism.

The left, and the union movement, traditionally call this kind of industrial battle 'struggle'. And, *Coal is our Life* noted the impact of 'struggle' on Featherstone:

> *'.....there is a long history of acrimonious disputes for which the coal industry is notorious.'*

> *'Common memories of past struggle have undoubtedly helped to bind a community such as Featherstone'* [18].

They did in the past, and they did in 1984/85. If you go through something horrendous together as a community, you never forget.

At least beneath the surface, even if it is not always tangible, the perception in Featherstone that ordinary people are still in 'struggle' persists. In 1993, for example, 100 years after two young miners were shot dead in a lock-out dispute in Featherstone, the event was commemorated with a ceremony at the men's graves in the local churchyard. The cemetery was packed. A play was put on at one of the schools. Whenever I mentioned Featherstone to anybody from the NUM, their usual response was to say 'yes, we lost two men there, you know', as if it was yesterday. John, the ex-diesel fitter in the pit, on being asked where he went to drink in Featherstone, told me, without any prompting, the pub he frequented is where the inquest was held on the two shot miners. Memories of struggle last a long time.

The strike of 1984/85, its pain and its torment, was never forgotten in the coalfields. In April 1998, Ian MacGregor, who had been chairman of the NCB during the conflict, died. A few days later, graffiti appeared near the site of the former Redbrook colliery near Barnsley. Even 13 years after the end of the dispute, someone, still fuelled with anger, had gone and got a bucket of white paint, and covered four red-brick walls with his parting lines to the NCB chairman: 'REST IN HELL. IAN MACGREGOR. BASTARD. 1998. RICH FUCKER.'

Redbrook, Barnsley, 1998

The memories persisted too in Featherstone, and in Great Houghton, and in all the mining towns and villages. In February 1998, at one of the regular meetings called in Great Houghton miners' welfare hall where residents of all the surrounding villages come to express their views and grievances on public transport, jobs, schools, and similar issues, the chairwoman of the meeting, without any obvious need to, raised the issue of the strike:

> '....we were serving 100 meals a day in here. One woman gave all her wedding presents to raffle off for prizes'.

Another woman, who looked after the council housing needs of people in Great Houghton, told me:

> 'A lot of them talk about the strike as if it was yesterday'.

PC Evans, a rotund, moustachioed officer, lived alongside miners and their families in Hemsworth, a few miles from Featherstone. It hurt him that 'they wouldn't play with my kids....they'll never forget....they're like elephants'.

The 1984/85 'struggle' was not just an economic battle. In Featherstone, as elsewhere in the coalfields, it was a conflict which divided man from man. It divided families, friends. It divided, quite literally, pubs. George, a former deputy now in his seventies had been a member of NACODS. This was a union representing overmen, deputies and officials, and had voted against strike action. George recollected:

> *'It was vicious. I'm on about vicious. Night after night, my 'phone was ringing with people trying to cause trouble'.*

> *'We were asked by management for 10 deputies per day, for inspection only. The NUM said "no deputy is going through that gate". Consequently, there was a fight every morning....cars getting turned over.......There was a lot of bitterness. They lost everything. They lost their wives, their families. It was bloody pathetic to see marriages breaking up'.*

And the pubs.....

> *'We used to go to a pub. The NUM men established a demarcation line. The NUM were on one side, officials and NACODS men were on the other. You couldn't cross'.*

Another pub became known as the 'scab' pub. This is where mineworkers who had broken the strike used to meet for a drink. No striking mineworker would enter the door. Even in the late 1990s, this pub is still known as the scab pub. Its identity is marked by the function it performed 14 years previously. Across the road from the scab pub is the pub where the striking miners would gather. During the 1984/85 strike, no 'scab' would have dared enter the door. To have done so would have been to risk serious trouble, for the 'scabs' had transgressed the ethical code which governed social behaviour.

A worker in a company that occupied part of the former pit site recounted in 1996 the story of his father, who had been a miner in a pit village near Doncaster. The young man recalled that his father had returned to work long before the end of the strike. As soon as the miner had broken the moral code that governed behaviour here, none of the rest of his family would talk to him. Not his brothers, who were also miners, not his sisters. After the strike had finished, he took redundancy from the pit, and began to drink himself solidly into the ground. As with most men in mining towns, his tipple was bitter, rather than one of the newer trendy lagers so assiduously marketed by big brewers. Whenever the son had gone out drinking with the father, the father would order two pints for them. Before the son had had chance to pick up his pint, the father had downed his. The father would start drinking in the morning, as soon as the local working mens' club opened, and would carry on all day. Despite the fact that the former miner had been ostracised by the local community, the club allowed him in. He was too good a customer to lose. But lose him eventually they did. One day, he had a pain, was sent to hospital, and died. He had lasted 10 or 12 months after redundancy. Even on his deathbed, his brothers and sisters wouldn't talk to him. He was 43.

Forty-three, but a broken man. The alcohol had killed him, but probably the ostracism too. Isolation, in many ways, is the social counterpart of alcohol. Like alcohol, isolation intensifies emotions, at least the negative emotions. The merely fed-up become the intensely morose after a good dose of either isolation or alcohol. This man had been immersed in both.

In mining towns and villages, the strike breaker was traditionally seen as a moral leper. To have broken a strike was not just seen as disloyalty to the union, or disloyalty to workmates. It was seen as disloyalty to the community as a whole. In Barnsley, the name and address of the first man to break the strike was scrawled in many telephone boxes. We all had to be told who he was. And where he was.

The extent of disapproval of the 'scab' is demonstrated by the NCB's decision to outlaw the use of the term in the pits in April 1985. To call someone a scab could result in your dismissal. So the miners resorted to other mechanisms. They would 'hiss' at scabs; others would refer to them as 'subjects', which is how the police had referred to strike-breakers when they were on picket line duty (19).

In any case, the workers who returned to Ackton Hall prior to the strike were mainly not from Featherstone. John, the ex-diesel fitter in the pit, was adamant. It was definitely not the locals. It couldn't be us:

> *'Most of them weren't from Ackton Hall....it's been proved....they were people who had gone back to other pits....and they'd ask them to do a day at Ackton Hall.....The ones that went back to Ackton Hall didn't live in Featherstone'.*

At Ackton Hall, the strike was solid for several months. Eventually 'they' — the NCB, supported by the police — started to bus 'them' in. Arthur, the former branch secretary at Ackton Hall, explained that it was only two or three that went in, to start with. It was regarded as a cause for particular shame that one of those was the son of a union official at a nearby colliery. He came from a long-standing mining family.

Far from trying to hide, this 'lad' had been gratuitously provocative in his strike breaking. Rather than keeping out of sight in the back of the van that took the strike breakers in, as most of them did, this 'lad' posed in the front ostentatiously, with his feet up on the dash. The only possible explanation that could be advanced for this kind of behaviour was mental illness.

> *'Summat's missing when it's like that....that's what's up....it's t'on'y explanation'.*

What other possible explanation could there be? The 'lad' didn't last long in Featherstone after the end of the strike. His ostentation was soon dissipated. Apparently, he disappeared straight away, never to be seen again other than, one imagines, by his family. I asked John what might happen to a scab in Featherstone.

> *'At the time they went back, something would probably happen to them.....and they would be ostracised afterwards'.*

After the 'lad' had pioneered the strike-breaking, eventually, Arthur told me, 'more and more went in....you didn't really know how many....a lot were never identified'.

However many it was, it was few compared to the number that stayed out. With about a month to go before the strike officially ended, the NCB was claiming that 38 had gone back to work. Everybody agrees that the NCB's figures could not be trusted, though 38 out of 1,100 isn't many anyway. It meant that more than 1,050 had gone for 11 months without a wage packet. Every month that passed, they still had to put food on the table.

And most of the ones that went back were not the hardened souls. They were the 'money grabbers'. The ones who, during normal

times, would work every possible minute of over-time available.
Even for this alone, they were very often not popular. The term
'money grabber' was a term of abuse. Those who were money
grabbers were also seen as being the most parsimonious. They
wouldn't spend their money. They were 'stingy bastards'. As Arthur
said:

> *'You'd think it was those who were the shortest with money that*
> *would have returned to work......it wasn't always them that went*
> *in....sometimes it was them that loved money.....it's a funny*
> *job.....people who love money....the ones that used to live at the pit....'*

The circumspection, bordering on hostility, towards 'money
grabbers' in working class communities is deeply engrained.
Richard Hoggart's wonderful study of working class life in the
1950s and before, *The Uses of Literacy*, had a few comments on this
section of the community and how they were seen:

> *'And there are sharp-eyed little men whom the rest regard with charity*
> *as wrong-headed, who 'never let a penny go'. They take on extra work*
> *at nights and weekends and are always anxious to make an extra bob-*
> *or-two at the hour when others are having a good time. These people*
> *are not usually moving upward or out of their class; they are running*
> *agitatedly around inside it, amassing their unconsidered trifles which*
> *are always about'* [20].

The general sentiment is confirmed in another part of the same
study:

> *'......there is a general dislike of meanness and tight-fistedness — "Ah*
> *'ate mean fowks', and 'E's as mean as muck'* [21]

At only one colliery in the locality was there a substantial return to
work prior to the strike finishing. More than 300 workers were back

two months before the strike ended, and 500 one month before, if British Coal are to be believed. This was the country's biggest colliery, and was differentiated from others both by its size and by the fact that its workforce were commuters in, as opposed to people living on the doorstep in a 'pit village'. Commuting in from Leeds or Wakefield exerts nothing like the same community pressure to hold the line as living in a pit village. In the latter, if you break the strike, you are living alongside those still out. You can feed your kids and they can't. It doesn't do anything for harmonious relationships.

Population change

Apart from people coming from other mining areas at the start of a coalfield development in the middle and late nineteenth century, or where displaced mineworkers would be relocated to areas with longer life mines, especially in the 1960s, Britain's pit towns and villages saw little inward migration. Many of those who came to Featherstone in the 1860s and the few decades afterwards came from Staffordshire. In modern times, some people — though not many — managed to leave Featherstone and similar townships in the West and South Yorkshire coalfield. Few came to settle. There has to be a reason to settle anywhere and, unless you were involved in the coal industry in some way, mining towns and villages in general provided few reasons for anyone to relocate there. *Coal is our Life* noted Featherstone's population in the mid-1950s as being 'nearly 14,000'. That had changed little by the late 1990s. It rose to 14,630 in 1976, though by 1993 had fallen to 13,790 [22]. Despite the demise in mining, Featherstone's population suffered only minor decline. This is possibly, in part at least, because of people's strong attachment to the town. Almost everyone I spoke to in Featherstone laughed in dismissal when I asked if they would ever choose to live anywhere other than Featherstone, this town of only a few streets and little economic activity. For the majority, it was an idea not even worth consideration. The response of Jim, a former electrician at Ackton Hall in his forties, was both typical and unequivocal:

> *'Featherstone is the best village in the world. I love my village. I wouldn't live anywhere else'.*

An unmarried 30 year old woman, long term unemployed after the closure of one of the sewing factories:

> *'No, I've grown up here. You know everybody'.*

For George, the former deputy at Ackton Hall, It was almost beyond his comprehension that anyone should even ask the question.

> *'No! No! We are all loyal to the town. You know coal used to be our life. All we've got is the town now'.*

Harry, the 66 former winder:

> *'No......I have a son who lives in Featherstone......if you asked him the same question, he wouldn't leave either'.*

Fiona, the Scottish miner's daughter:

> *'I love it....we are a little close community...everybody knows everybody'.*

A 24 year old male taxi driver:

> *'Tha'd 'ave to pay me to leave Featherstone'.*

And, if people did leave, they often came back. Harry said to me:

'I've found that people who've moved away....they always come back....they still come back to their roots if they are Featherstone people'.

John, the ex-diesel fitter in the pit:

'I don't want to live anywhere else. I love it....even with all its problems and that, I love it. You can't see what Featherstone's got. It's hidden'.

He explained how, after having to leave the pit, he'd found a job with a company in Leeds and, after a while, they wanted him to work at Milton Keynes. He didn't move there.

'I travelled every day to Milton Keynes for five months'.

His son, in his twenties though never a miner, thought much the same:

'A lot of people I know that left have come back. Even when I was working in London for a few months, I used to come back every weekend....I used to live for weekends'.

And, the son thought, even if you had to work a few miles away in one of the bigger towns, you should 'certainly base yourself in Featherstone'.

In Great Houghton, it was exactly the same. I talked to Barbara, who was in her sixties and married to a man who had worked at the pit all his life until taking redundancy:

'.....if they move, they come back, if they are Houghton people....I've heard it said that we're parochial and we want everything bringing to us, and it's probably true....very few people have moved'.

Viv Nicholson getting married. By permission of the Yorkshire Weekly Newspaper Group.

The corollary to the resistance of migration is the strength of community spirit that mining towns were famous for. Viv Nicholson's *Spend, Spend, Spend* is a tale of dreams, aspirations, hopes, all dashed. A tale of a chance of an escape from a Castleford of pits, and grey-black narrow streets, and crushing, unyielding social and economic certainties. It is also, in many ways, simply a tale of how life was in a mining town in West Yorkshire in the fifties, sixties and seventies. A tale of how the strength of community spirit found expression, a tale of what sociologists call 'community norms', basically a tale of what it was like to live, from day to day, in the small towns of terraced streets dotted across the north of England which, for so many generations, produced the bulk of Britain's energy supplies. It captures the good and the bad, and especially the way that everybody, seemingly, never knows quite how good something is until its gone:

'If you were poorly your neighbour would come in, or you'd send the kids on an errand if you couldn't get up yourself, it was a really good happening and I enjoyed it; up to date it was the best part of my life. Everybody was friendly, you could talk and, you know, you even

seemed to have longer summers. People would stay out till 11 o'clock like they do abroad, and chat and laugh and giggle and smoke and drink a beer with each other, it used to be great. If anyone was going up town they would say, "Do you want owt bringing back, love? Can I do owt for you?" They were all good neighbours.

'It was only a small neighbourhood so you knew everybody, but you didn't know everybody's scandals. If you did, I never heard of it. I don't know where it's gone today but there were a lot of great people in those days. Once a kid got knocked over in our street, I saw it happen, he lived next door to us. It was pathetic, the whole street mourned, not just the parents. There were flowers galore. People really missed you. Many times I just sit and wish these things were back' [(23)].

Probably we all do.

Viv's story even encapsulates the moral code on marriage and divorce:

'The thing was at home when you'd decided to marry then you had to stay with your husband. "You made your bed and you must lie on it", kind of thing' [(24)].

You go back now and you realise just how much more complicated private lives are these days. Neville is the branch delegate at the surviving Prince of Wales colliery. Every pit has a branch delegate. His job is to present the views of local NUM members to periodic meetings of delegates from other pits.

He looks about 36. He has few formal qualifications but, like many who climbed even the bottom rungs of the NUM hierarchy, he can articulate and analyse as well, and better, than many who have been through years of higher education. He laughs, smiles, jokes, points his finger in emphasis. But when you catch his eyes, you can tell there have been traumas. They're etched with the kind of scars that come only from the pain of choice between two difficult options. Dilemma. Those terrible times when you just don't know what to do. But then there's another joke, a ribald dig, your eyes get distracted from his. Many people have worse lives. He tells himself that every night when he walks alone to the Victorian pub that we both knew from our youths and which, he reliably informs me, is now run by two 'puftahs'. People get killed in the pit. He's survived. Things aren't that bad.

He now lives with his girlfriend. She had been his girlfriend for seven years prior to moving in together. His wife had never known about her. He went to Cuba on business, as NUM men sometimes did, and when he came back decided not to live with his wife. They had been arguing a lot. His ex-wife thinks that he lives alone. His girlfriend thinks that he has nothing to do with his ex-wife. Both are wrong. He gets by because he bought himself a mobile 'phone, so neither of his women know where he really is. Modern technology has its uses. Even in the moribund coalfields.

Amongst many in the coalfields, there is a resistance to move, and there is a lack of anyone coming in, even in the late 1990s. Barbara and her family are a classic example. Barbara, wife of an early-retired miner, lives in the same house she was born in more than 60 years ago in Great Houghton. Her son lives next door. He's single, and 40. Living next door gives him his independence, and it also allows him to go round to his mum's house for meals and cups of tea. After months of unemployment, he has found a job as a gardener with the council. One of Barbara's two daughters is on her way to social escape: after working in shops and behind bars she became a mature student and eventually got a degree in social science. She's training to be a school teacher. But it won't be a physical escape. She will stay in the village. Barbara is very proud of her, and talks a lot about her success and her prospects. But Barbara's daughter is an exception. Barbara's other daughter is a bit older, and far more of a classic example of normal lifestyle here. She is a housewife, and is married to an ex-miner. The ex-miner is 42 and was disabled at the pit, preventing him from working there or anywhere else. The older daughter works part-time cleaning in a doctor's surgery. They live in a council house.

Nobody comes, and nobody goes. There is another reflection of population inertia: Featherstone has remained an almost completely white settlement. In 1956, obviously, Featherstone was all white. In fact, whilst the authors of *Coal is Our Life* touched on every other aspect of life in Featherstone, race was not mentioned at all. There was no need for it to be mentioned. Post-war immigration on a large scale was only just at its very beginning in Britain. Yet whilst most of Britain's major cities, and a good number of its small and medium-sized towns, have seen the nature of their populations undergo dramatic change through immigration from what was often termed the 'New Commonwealth', this didn't happen in Featherstone, and it didn't happen in any of the pit towns and villages of the West and South Yorkshire coalfield. The 1991 census records only 10 men meeting the categories 'black Caribbean, black African or black other' in Featherstone, and 6 women. 41 men fitted the category 'Indian, Pakistani or other Asian,' and 24 women. The Chinese made up the biggest ethnic minority group, with 45 men and 27 women. There is little doubt that most of the Asians and Chinese were associated with the take-away restaurants in Featherstone and nearby towns.

In any case, the Asians and Chinese live in their own social world in Featherstone: by and large, they are not integrated. Tom, the former electrician at Ackton Hall and 'pioneer' at Selby, told me:

> '....you don't see much of them socially...you see a few of the young Chinese occasionally, playing snooker'.

There was usually very little to come to the coalfields for, in the way of jobs or cultural facilities. You were only ever there if you were born there, or needed to be there. There had to be a reason. The extent of the recognition of this locally was brought home to me one night in the "striking miners'" pub.

Most nights in this pub, there are few customers, though from Thursday night onwards, it increases in popularity. It once had a more important social role than simply being a drinking house. After the closure of the local miners' welfare, it was where the miners' union had held its committee meetings. Important decisions had been taken in here: whether to strike, or call off a strike, accept or reject a pay offer. Now, it has the occasional turn, and the occasional pub quiz, even the occasional male stripper for the 'ladies' nights', but it will never again be as important to local society.

Apart from its quasi-political role, here was a pub which was always packed, in the fifties, sixties, seventies. Packed with miners and their sons and the occasional woman. The miners liked to drink, so this was a prosperous business. In fact, it was doing so well, it even had its own annual trip to the seaside. This was unusual for a pub.

And the 'club trip', as the annual jaunts to the seaside organised by working men's clubs were called, were important. It might be the only chance you had to take your kids to the seaside. There was spending money for the kids and, on the way back, plenty of booze for the grown-ups. Like being in a trade union, like the municipal Labourism that would provide you with your house, it was another example of collectivism: if we all worked together, we could achieve more than working as separate individuals. John, the ex-diesel fitter in the pit, explained:

'That pub had a trip, but it's not a club....but it was such a busy pub...there were loads and loads of kids on the trips....they used to get £3 spending money each.....that might be £15 in a family'.

£15 was seen as quite a bit of money. The club trip still existed in the Featherstone of the late 1990s, but it was not as popular or as important. More cars mean that families can get away on their own. But it is a remnant of collectivism in an age of enforced individualism, nevertheless. And it is still taken deadly seriously. On the wall in this pub is a small notice. 'Benefits' — ie a bit of spending money — are available on this trip, it reads. But they would not be available for children not attending, unless they had a 'medical certificate'.

The decor in the Victorian pub has remained untouched for generations. This particular night, in late 1996, there are about five men sitting down, drinking beer. Some of them play dominoes. Two wear flat caps. All, except one, are in their early fifties. And all of the men in their early fifties are overweight, with fat beer bellies. I bought two pints of beer, one for the far too smartly dressed bloke that I had entered with. Being smartly dressed might not have been the thing to do. It attracted the wrong kind of attention.

'Get 'ere', came a more than slightly aggressive call from the youngest of the five men. He looked fairly mean. It seemed best to comply.

'What *tha* doing in Featherstone?' he quizzed me.

'Just passing through', I attempted. A weak response, but one which I hoped would defuse his curiosity sufficiently.

'Fuck off', came the rapid, staccato, response, killing dead the notion I had optimistically entertained that he would be naive, or disinterested, enough to accept my bland answer to his question. 'Nubdi [nobody] passes through Featherstone'. And, of course, in his blunt, down-to-earth fashion, he was right. Nobody does pass through. And, if you do, you're going nowhere fast.

'Ziggy', as I later came to learn was his name, was covered in tattoos. On the side of his neck, a swallow and a large rose. The second finger of his left hand was half missing. Half of his ear was missing, apparently bitten off in a fight. He had still managed to find room to squeeze a little tattooed blue star on the bit of the lobe that remained, however. And this slight deformity hadn't dulled his sense of humour. One of the five middle-aged men went to the bar. Ziggy cupped his ear, shouting, 'dunt get me a drink, 'av got half 'ear'. On the front of his neck, another tattoo, in big letters — 'mother' — and the name of a pub — it looked like 'Strafford Arms' — was emblazoned in big letters. His forearms, the backs of his hands, and even the palms of his hands were covered similarly. On the inside of his wrist was the word 'Nazi'. Ziggy had never been a miner, though he came from Featherstone. He was probably too young to have had any serious involvement with the coal industry. He looked a maximum of 30, so he would have begun looking for work in the very early 1980s. By this time, whilst coal mines still existed in the area, the industry was in decline and no longer recruiting.

So, instead of working in the coal industry, Ziggy had become a 'brickie'. He advised us, without our soliciting his advice, that this was not an occupation that we ought to pursue:

> *'Dunt iver be a brickie* [don't ever be a bricklayer]'.

He had begun work that morning in Wakefield, but had had to stop because it had started raining. Consequently, he wouldn't be getting paid for the day. So he had decided to spend the day drinking instead. He presented this decision as if it was one in which he had little choice. If there was no work, and you had money in your pocket, you drank. It was a law of nature. Like night follows day.

And Ziggy knew how to survive, no matter what the economic climate. That day, he'd come across a 'wacker', which must have been a machine used for something or other in the building trade. It was knocked off, from what I could tell. New, it would be worth £2,500. He'd got it for £150, and sold it to the boss of the construction company he worked at for £300. He was pleased with himself, because he'd made £150 that day, despite not working. 'I might look a rough fucker', he said to me, his face pushed close to mine, 'but I've got a business head on me'.

Ziggy might not be typical. But Ziggy represents one strand of modern life in former mining communities. And whilst Ziggy always existed, with less exotic names, Ziggy is more common now than he ever was. In the past, men here did not have the time to become Ziggy. Their world was too ordered. To be tattooed was fine and, in fact, part of the 'community norm'. Most men had a small tattoo somewhere. Very often this was a blue swallow on that slight bulge in the hand between the thumb and forefinger. The blue swallow was almost a badge of identity.

But to be covered in garish, attention-seeking tattoos would have been seen as making a social statement about your attitudes and values. And the statement that it was making would have been seen as rebellion and indifference as to who cared about that rebellion. This embodiment of anti-authoritarianism would have invited mistrust and antagonism in the rest of the community. After all, the

whole ethos of mining communities was a respect for social order,
even a respect for those in the local social hierarchy. More often
than not, this was manifested in respect for, and loyalty to, local
union branch officials. Years ago, it was reflected in a deference —
perhaps a deference enforced by social and economic circumstances,
but still a deference — for the pit manager. As George, the former
deputy, said to me:

> *'The manager were the boss of the pit, and the boss of the village 'en
> all'.*

And, whilst men often drank during the day, especially if they were
on shift work and couldn't drink in the more 'normal' evening
session, there were few who would drink themselves into a state of
inebriation just for the sake of it. There were too many
responsibilities. Too many children to feed. The world was too hard
a place. And, importantly, the miner, psychologically, saw himself as
a 'provider'. A provider for his wife, and provider for his family.
Richard Hoggart rightly argued, in 1959, that there was a certain
gradation in the degrees to which drinking was acceptable and
tolerated. Drinking by women was tolerated at the weekend, but
they weren't expected to drink as much as men. It would be
understood if a widower drank more than most; after all, he had
no wife, and his home comforts might be lacking. Similarly, regular
drinking by a couple without children was considered acceptable:
the money they spent on drink was not depriving kids of their
bread. But:

> *'A husband with a family should drink "within reason", that is,
> should know when he has had enough, and should always "provide"'*
> *(25)*.

Once the family had been provided for, it was acceptable to drink. But drinking had to be done with at least some sense of responsibility. All life was about a sense of responsibility. About not going over the edge.

NOTES

1. N.Dennis, F.Henriques and C.Slaughter, 1956 *Coal is our Life*, An analysis of a Yorkshire mining community. London: Tavistock.

2. *Pontefract and Castleford Express*, 11 April 1985.

3. *Pontefract and Castleford Express*, 18 July 1985.

4. *Pontefract and Castleford Express*,26 January 1984.

5. *Ibid* .

6. *Coal is our Life*, page 142.

7. See, for instance, J.Allen, 1988 'Towards a post-industrial economy?' in J.Allen and D.Massey (eds), *The Economy in Question*, London: Sage Publications in association with the Open University Press; M.Campbell, 1990 'Employment and the Economy in the 1980s and Beyond,' in M.Campbell (ed) *Local Economic Policy*, London: Cassell Educational; T.Caslin, 'De-industrialisation in the UK,' in H.Vane and T.Caslin (eds) *Current Controversies in Economics*, Oxford: Basil Blackwell.

8. R.Turner, 'De-industrialisation, economic regeneration, and social capital,' 1996 *Teaching Public Administration*, Vol XVI, No. 2.

9. *Coal is our Life*, page 11.

10. Unemployment Bulletin Figures for July 1996. Regeneration Department. City of Wakefield Metropolitan District Council (CWMDC).

11. *Pontefract and Castleford Express*, 28 June 1990.

12. Sheffield Business School, 1993 *Responding to the decline of the coal industry,* Longitudinal Study. A research study for Barnsley and Doncaster Training and Enterprise Council. Final Report. November.

13. See: N.Guy, 1994 *Redundant miners survey, Grimethorpe, Silverhill, Vane Tempest, and Parkside,* February and March. Barnsley: Coalfield Communities Campaign.

14. 1991 Census. Crown Copyright.

15. *The Times,* 5 March 1985.

16. *The Times,* 4 March 1984.

17. *The Times,* 5 March 1984.

18. *Coal is our Life,* page 14.

19. *Pontefract and Castleford Express,* 25 April 1985.

20. Richard Hoggart 1957 *The Uses of Literacy. Aspects of working-class life, with special references to publications and entertainments.* Chatto and Windus, London. page 71.

21. Above. Page 80.

22. City of Wakefield Metropolitan District Council (CWMDC), 1994 *Population Bulletin* 1993. Wakefield: CWMDC Planning Department.

23. Vivian Nicholson and Stephen Smith, 1977, *Spend,Spend,Spend,* Jonathan Cape. London. page 10.

24. As above, page 49.

25. Hoggart, page 20.

WORK

Many argue that work — the job you do, the industry you're in —
shapes identity. What we do conditions our life in other directions.
This was certainly the dominating theme of *Coal is our Life*. Your life
was a particular way because you were a miner, or because you
were married to a miner. It influenced every thing you did. You
were in a trade union because you were a miner; you drank in
particular places because you were a miner; you married particular
people because you were a miner. You behaved in particular ways
because you were a miner's daughter, a miner's wife, a miner's son.

It's pretty much common sense, really. The life of one of Versace's
supermodels is going to be different from the life of a typical 1950s
woman in Featherstone, because the circles the women moved in
would be different, the amount of money they had to spend would
be different and, obviously, the images they presented to the outside
world would be different.

The job-as-identification is not restricted to mining. It's the same if
you're a lawyer, a journalist, a steelworker. Huge tomes have been
compiled about the impact of fishing, for example, on cultural
identity, on the local economy, on the family [1]. It's the same with
truckers. They inhabit a secret world. They all dress the same. They
look similar. They go to the same places, where nobody else goes.
You go to their 'truck stops', in the middle of vast industrial estates,
and they have middle-aged women dressed in purple sequinned
dresses singing Sandy Shaw classics from the sixties, and younger
women dancing and taking their clothes off for lorry drivers clad in
short canvas jackets, drinking beer and eating free pie and peas. The
owners of truck stops like to look after the lads. You'd never know
it was happening if you were outside the truckers' world. As the

owner of a trucking company, one of the biggest employers in Featherstone now that the pit has gone, said to me:

'...lorry drivers are funny...they meet and talk in cafes all day....it's like a village on the road...'

If it is true that occupations impact upon how we see ourselves and are seen by others, and it probably is, it is worth examining the 'new' economic structure in Featherstone. What did people do in Featherstone for a living once the local pit, and the surrounding pits, had all gone? If people were no longer miners, miner's wives, miner's sons, what were they now?

The Pit Site

The location of industry and commercial activity can be divided into that on the former colliery site which — in the terminology fashionable amongst economists and 'management consultants' — can be categorised as small and medium-sized enterprises, and that elsewhere in the town, mainly on the roads leading out of Featherstone to other nearby, smallish, ex-mining towns. Amongst the latter were some relatively big employers.

The pit site itself was occupied in 1997 by 12 companies. The largest of these, in employment terms, had 17 workers. The smallest had two. Most of them employed a handful of workers only. Total employment on the entire site amounted to 84. Back in 1984, prior to the big strike, 1,100 people had worked at the pit. More than a thousand people, coming and going, every day. Cars turning up and being parked. Banter, shouts, jests, arguments. Pits were massive employers, relative to the size of the towns that they were often situated in. You go there now and it's virtually silent. There is the background hum of the traffic on the nearby main road, and the occasional noise from a concrete-spinning lorry elevating or contracting its cone-shaped concrete carrier, but there's very little apart from that. The loud, boisterous, noisy world has given way to deathly quiet.

Fryston, 1999

An employer with more than a thousand workers, in a town with a population of only 14,000, represents a pretty big economic sector, even if not all the workers came from the town itself. People overlooked this unusual juxtaposition of the big employer in the small town. It didn't frequently happen. An industrial or commercial organisation employing this many would normally be situated in the middle of some conurbation, drawing its workers from a large nearby population. Pits were often, by contrast, among what were just small towns. Sometimes their setting was semi-rural. Go to Fryston, near Castleford, and you'd think you'd hit some frontier outpost in the wild west. There is one narrow road in, and to come out you use the same road. There are two rows of miners' cottages. There are now no shops, no pubs. The only commercial activity there seems to be is the collection of scrap. Some blokes have piled up old radiators and exhaust pipes on the back of an old, beat-up lorry. There are lots of horses. Some tethered, some being ridden by youngsters across an expanse of greenery in the centre which once contrasted so vividly with the blackness of the pit. There is no pit. But the horses are fun to ride. Like so many panned-out gold mining towns in America and Australia that have become 'visitor attractions', Fryston, and Featherstone, after the end of coal are like a ghost towns too. But here there are no tourists.

The companies that had replaced the pit on the colliery site had quite a bit in common. No less than four of the 12 were associated, in some way, with concrete. You were either making concrete, or turning concrete into bases for houses, or transporting concrete from one site to another, or humping concrete about. Whatever the demand is for concrete, it can be satisfied here: footings for housing; giant loads for multi-storey car parks; small bits for garden sheds; T-beams for house floors. Concrete is pretty important. And, from what I could see on the faces of some of the workers, pretty fucking boring.

There is no sophistication to the way your average concrete company is run. Concrete is concrete. People can have fancy titles like 'Northern Area Manager' but, basically, your Northern Area Manager will sit in a portakabin and make telephone calls about bags of cement.

But it doesn't stop you philosophising. In fact, philosophising is probably a form of intellectual escapism from concrete. One NorthernAreaManager used to have a clothes shop in Doncaster. He'd had big ambitions, you could tell. Start a small business, turn it into a chain of menswear shops, diversify into other sectors, launch a flotation on the stock market, collect a 'beautiful wife' and a 'beautiful car' on the way. You need possessions. You need status. Instead, he'd ended up sitting in a portakabin, making telephone calls about bags of cement. He's in his mid-forties or early fifties. He's thin, and reasonably well-dressed. You can tell that if he had any more money, he would have been better dressed. But being a NAM doesn't pay as much as it sounds it might pay to the average person in the street. In fact, it doesn't pay that much at all, really. But you can't let on. It would destroy your image. To an academic who comes to interview you, you're a philosopher; to the boys back home, you're a lad about town. He has a good facial bone structure, and a mop of now grey hair. You imagine that in his youth he would have been very good looking. A kill for the ladies.

He knows what's good, and what's bad, about Featherstone. Or at least he thinks he knows and that, perhaps, is all any of us know.

The good things. Team work. 'There are certain guys in the yard now....who can cultivate a very, very, high team effort...' His words are measured and slow, as if to emphasise the amount of thought that has gone into formulating this statement. He attributed the high capacity for effective team work to the legacy of coal. In the pit, workers had to work as a team. Your life might have depended on it.

So team work has survived. So, too, according to the almost well-dressed, small time philosopher, had some of the 'bad' aspects associated with mining. Being told what to do, they didn't like: '.....they are exceedingly loathe to accept authority'.

Bolsheness affected the whole working atmosphere, the nam explained. He told me how he would like to have 'better relations here'.....between management, meaning himself, and workers.

'HQ are currently looking at ways of developing better relations'. It sounded, just for a minute, as if we were talking about the secret service. The philosopher could have been James Bond. Deep in his heart, he knew he should have been. He was suave enough. He shouldn't have ended up selling concrete.

He went on to tell me about his personal philosophy that 'people are a company's greatest asset'. Yet here, they weren't sufficiently motivated. They'd take their time to do things. And they were bolshe. I didn't say anything, but it did occur to me how on earth you might motivate people whose sole working task was to heave bags of cement about from one part of the yard to another. Nevertheless, these workers clearly had to share the blame for the condition of their existences. They weren't accepting authority. He left me with the parting thought that this company also has sites in the midlands and south of England, but 'it's harder to impose any kind of work discipline on people here than it is in other areas'.

The importance of team work was stressed to me by five concrete workers and their 'general manager' at a discussion in a makeshift canteen at another plant. This was a big place, yet employed only six people. It was somehow symbolic. You could have extensive, and modern, capital equipment, as you had here, but you didn't need many workers.

The concrete workers here worked in teams. They made concrete T-beams, used for house floors. On another day, the company's owner had been positively apoplectic about the prospects for the T-beam which is, apparently, quite an innovation as far as housing foundations go.

'There are 150,000 flats or houses built in Britain every year. 18,000 take T-beams from us. In 1990, the company sold 600,000 metres of material, now it is selling 1,500,000', he beamed.

Given the team work, if one member is off, the others have more work. They don't like it if someone keeps taking time off. They told me about one ex-miner who had previously worked there. He was into 'drugs', mainly cannabis apparently, and failing to turn in. Eventually, he was pressurised to go. According to their tales, he was making far more money selling drugs than he did from working. He had thousands in the bank. He had money in his mother's bank account, in an effort to hide it. They were probably exaggerating. I was a visitor. It made a good story.

The subject moved on to ex-miners in general, and what they had been like when they had worked at this factory. There had been a few there in the past, though none of the current workers had ever worked in the pit. There was a consensus of opinion that ex-miners were unsuitable for this kind of work. They 'didn't want the work'. It was too hard, and too pressurised. It was believed that, generations ago, working in the pit was hard work but, 'it's all machinery now', Here, the work that's available has 'got to be done today'. Miners didn't think like that. They were used to a situation in which they could leave it for the day shift, or for the night shift, or for someone else to do.....In this job, that couldn't be done.

I couldn't help thinking that they were generalising a bit too much on the basis of one or two ex-mineworkers. And yet, two of these workers came from Featherstone itself, and had grown up in mining families. Another, from Doncaster, was the son of miner. Still, I thought to myself, they must be over-generalising.

Working at this concrete plant involves, just like the pit did, dust and noise. The men said, and it was obvious anyway, that this was hard work. But they had 'good breaks' and it was clear that, providing their wage packet was fat enough, they were quite happy to be grafters. They told me, and this was clear too, that nobody disabled could do the job, and nobody with any kind of hearing impediment. Someone of, say, 18 years old, would not be suitable, as 'they wouldn't have the stamina'. What you needed, according to them and also according to the company's owner, was someone between about 25 and 40, strong and fit. More than one of them spoke of how they had lost weight after coming to work on the T-beams, because of the physical effort involved. One said that he had lost a stone. Another, the youngest, said that he had lost two and a half stones. One of the others said that although he had lost weight, it came back later as muscle. The hard nature of the physical work involved was offered as the reason why one of the workers had to drink so much milk. He was the fattest at the table, with a fat podgy face, and drank milk continuously. Straight from the bottle. I suspected that, secretly, he really liked milk and had been obsessed by it since he was a child. I suspected that he would have drunk it in copious quantities even if he had been unemployed. But the 'hard work' provided a wonderful excuse for such excessive consumption.

What I wondered was what happened to you after 40. After all, reaching 40 is pretty swift. A bit of an electraglide. And I wondered what you did if you were not strong, and fit, and not muscular, and if you were, perhaps, a little bit deaf. If you had worked at the pit, in days gone by, and became less fit as the years rolled on, less strong, a bit disabled, you would still have had a job. You would have been moved off the arduous tasks, moved off the face, but you would still have a job. You wouldn't have earned as much, but you would still have turned up every day, and there would still be a wage packet at the end of the week.

Two of the concrete companies represented new investment in Featherstone. One was the concrete T-beam producers, which had located in Featherstone in 1995 as part of a general expansion. The other 'new' investment — in the sense that it came from outside Featherstone — was the philosopher-lady killer's company, which had been on the pit site six years. The latter company had re-located from nearby Castleford, so there was no real net creation of jobs.

The other two concrete companies had always been in Featherstone, though on a different site. One company was a subsidiary of the other, with one of the firms dealing with the 'big boys' and the other dealing with your small builder or DIY man. Only seven people worked at the two plants and only one — the plant supervisor — was based there all the time. The rest were mainly truck drivers, coming and going as they needed.

All in all, across four concrete companies on the pit site, there were only eight 'new' jobs that had been created for the locality. It's something. It's hardly going to replace what's been lost.

And even then, the jobs are hard to come by. The world, now, in Featherstone, is harsher, if that were possible, than it ever was. To work in an 'industrial capacity', to 'work in concrete', you have to be strong, and fit, and under 40. Otherwise, nobody wants to know you. I wondered. I wondered what on earth you do if you are over 40, and not quite as strong as you were when you were 25, or even when you were 35. Perhaps you looked elsewhere on the site, to the engineering sheds or to the pallet recycler who, probably because his business was on the margins of legality, refused to speak to me.

Four other companies on the site were engineering companies, which is a catch-all term to indicate that these companies would mend machines, or cut metal, or cut plastic. Basically, if you worked at the site where they used to cut coal, you would now stand there with a welding gun, cutting sheets of metal or plastic. Or you might be watching a clanking, old, grey, oily machine. And if you didn't do that, you'd heave bags of cement around.

The people that ran the engineering businesses were all noticeably proud people. Proud of their achievements. Proud of their companies. Proud of their products.

One company, established on the colliery site since 1992, carried out fabrication-welding-site-erection-maintenance-mending-machines-on-site etc. I had to ask what 'fabrication' meant, because it seemed such a catch-all term. 'Fabrication' means welding steel work; 'site erection' means erecting platforms, moving machines, modifying machines.

The Boss told me, taking time before he said it in order to summon up every last sinew of pride within his body, that this was 'the best company of its kind in the area'. He gave out a deep breath after saying it. When you are really proud, there is effort involved.

He had been born and bred in Featherstone. His father had been a miner. When it came to the Boss leaving school, his father, who rarely spoke to him or, seemingly, anyone else in the family, broke his taciturness one evening over the tea table.

> *'What's tha gunna du then, lad? Tha can du owt tha wants except gu dahn pit'.*

So the Boss ended up in engineering, starting out working for somebody else but eventually joining a partnership that owned four companies in the locality.

Ten people worked in this little shed on the pit site, including the Boss and the young woman who answered the telephone, did the filing, made the tea.

The Boss was proud of his company. He was very proud that it was providing work for ten families, and especially proud that six of those were from Featherstone.

Social scientists often ask whether ex-miners have found employment and, if they have, doing what. Amongst the companies inhabiting the pit site after the demise of the colliery, ex-miners were conspicuous by their absence. There were five ex-British Coal workers employed across the four companies in this small engineering sector, but only one had actually been a miner. Two had been welders in workshops on the surface; the two others had also worked on the surface as a plater/welder and a plant operator. Out of 43 employed in total in the engineering shops on the pit site, one ex-miner is not a very promising statistic.

Yet the absence of ex-miners in the engineering sector is hardly surprising. By and large, it is a sector that needs workers with specific skills and, apart from those that had worked in the engineering side of the coal industry, there aren't that many within that industry that would have those skills. They might fare better in the concrete sector, you would think. But amongst the 28 workers employed there, there were no ex-miners at all.

The biggest engineering company was into steel fabrication, and also into constructing buildings from steel, which probably amounts to the same thing. Their main business was fitting anti-vandal guards to earth-moving machinery. So, if you had a JCB and you didn't want the vandals to come and smash it up, they'd come and put steel shutters all around the driving cab. They were diversifying into making a 'road grader' for roads in Ireland, which seemed to involve attaching some extra piece of contorted steel to a tractor. Apparently, an ordinary JCB was too big for this job. It all related to roads in Ireland being narrower than roads in Britain. They were laying great hopes on this one. If it came off, it could be the biggie.

Of course, it was pretty certain that it wouldn't be the biggie. In fact, what will probably happen is that they will continue to fit vandal guards day-after-day, week-after-week. And the people who work there will continue to turn up at the redundant pit site, day-after-day, week-after-week. Their souls probably deserve redemption now, but they must have done something terribly wrong in a past life.

Not a single worker at the vandal guard engineering shop came from, or lived in, Featherstone. Nor was that unusual. While the vast majority of workers came from the nearby locality, no more than about 10 or, at the very most, 15 of the 84 workers on the pit site actually came from Featherstone.

Outside of concrete and engineering, there were four other companies. None of them employed anyone who had previously worked in coal.

The biggest of the four rented out portakabins to building sites. They employed six, three to repair and maintain the mobile sheds. None of the workers came from Featherstone. I met one in the yard. He said he was an electrician by trade. I think he was 40, or maybe a little bit more. But he was a young 40, at least in his expressions and outlook. A few lines on the face. A few around his eyes. But he had seen life in his younger days, in the 1970s, you could tell. At 40, you can be young or old. It's more to do with a state of mind rather than your physical condition. You can have a weather-beaten face, but still be young. Or you can have a cherub baby-face, and have been hidden away and, because you haven't really lived, youth continues to elude you. Youth brings with it a dynamism, and you can't have a dynamism unless you have lived.

The hairstyle of the man in the yard had been fashioned in the early seventies, when he was a lad-about-town, and it hadn't changed since. It was a poor Rod Stewart, coloured in various hues of reddish brown. I asked him what he did and, basically, it boiled down to any repair necessary for the portakabins. They might need a new window putting in, or a new bit of guttering, or they might need a lick of paint.

Rod Stewart had been there for quite a few months, but he was one of the survivors. The receptionist, when asked about turnover of the workforce, told me that 'staff change quite regularly'. Asked why, she shrugged her shoulders in a resigned recognition that only one answer was possible. 'Money, I suppose'.

I never discovered what the wages were. It would be surprising if any of them took home more than £120 per week. But it was, as she said, 'steady'. As a worker, you weren't under immense pressure. Something might need repairing. You had the time to repair it. You could stroll around. You had time for conversations with inquisitive social scientists noseying around former pit towns. You could take your time. You were not in a cut-throat sector, competing against the Japanese and the South Koreans and the Taiwanese. You could have a fag. Rod Stewart had one in his mouth.

He drove a long way to work — perhaps 25 miles — considering that, as the receptionist had told me already, 'we're not the best payers'.

The overwhelming feeling you get as you walk across the pit yard, from engineering company in one shed to a concrete company in another, is one of nobody going anywhere fast. Things are, to a degree, 'steady'. It was always one of those stock answers that everybody gave you when you asked how they were. 'Steady'. Always 'steady'. But never anything more. No more than steady. Ever.

Another small company on the site employed three people and, amongst these, two of them were the boss and his wife. Anything to do with windows, and they could help you out. They manufactured 'aluminium composite' and timber windows. They bought in PVC, and did things with it. They carried out window repairs. They did 'consultancy work' — I had never realised it was possible with something as mundane as windows — which, apparently, boils down to telling people what is wrong and how to go about making it better.

Former miners have, in the past, been employed at the window company. In terms of their strengths as workers, there was a cross-section, thought the window man, and this was often based on their age and up-bringing.

> *'The older miners tended to be a bit more loyal....[to the company].....they were brought up in a community where you looked after each other....I come from a mining family......my father was a miner.....I've seen the changes.....the younger miner/ex-miner does not have the same sense of loyalty, hard work...'*

The Enterprise Culture and Modernity

The 1980s and 1990s, under the guidance of the Conservative governments of the time, was meant to have seen a new economic era. The tired, old, nationalised dinosaurs were disposed of. Enterpreneurship was the new economic currency. In what was dubbed the 'enterprise culture', a previously latent entrepreneurial spirit was to have come to the fore. Its most concrete manifestation was supposed to be that more and more people would want to start new businesses, become self-employed, become entrepreneurs. Enterpreneurs were to be looked up to, admired, respected. As they amassed their fortunes, or failed to pay back the thousands they had borrowed, they were building the economic future. The more entrepreneurship the more dynamic the economy would become. The more entrepreneurship, the more we would all benefit.

We were regaled throughout the 'eighties with talk of how vast numbers of people were suddenly becoming self-employed, suddenly discovering their latent sense of entrepreneurship. Of course, many of them weren't self-employed at all: they were ordinary workers like everyone else. Being 'self-employed' often simply gave the real employer more power over you. It means they can get rid of you more easily. It means that they don't have to make a national insurance contribution for you. There are loads of people in hairdressing, in construction, in taxi-driving, who are technically 'self-employed'. But they aren't really. The employer owns the stock — the salon, the building equipment, the taxi — and the employer organises and manages the work.

Featherstone itself provides a classic example. In the world of concrete that has replaced the world of coal, if you work for the biggest company, you'll be self-employed . You aren't really, of course. You're pretending to be. Really, you're working for a multi-national company. Most of the people working for this company are drivers. You have to buy a lorry. This costs from £55,000 to £73,000. Now, your average Joe does not have that kind of money. So he borrows it. From the multi-national concrete company. In fact, the multi-national concrete company provides the whole package, from lorry itself through to finance to buy it through to insurance on the finance, through to telling you where to go and when. You are self-employed, though, you understand. You're part of the enterprise culture.

And the enterprise culture was going to bring forth 'new entrepreneurship'. The extent of it on the redundant pit site is fairly limited. Perhaps five companies would meet the definition of being created by people previously working for others that had now branched out on their own, employing perhaps half of the total number of employed people on the site. It's a contribution, of course, though no one could argue with any seriousness that a newly-dynamic 'enterprise culture' had developed in Featherstone. The rest of the companies, small scale as they might have been, were branch plants of national, or even multi-national, companies.

Outside of the colliery site, there were some other small and medium-sized enterprises: a manufacturer of 'anything-in-wire'; a mender of bottling machines; a gear-cutter and repairer; a producer of gaming and scratch cards.

The 'anything-in-wire' company used to be a chip-pan wire manufacturer, until 20 years ago. But 'nobody eats chips now', the man who owned it told me. I suppose they don't. Or if they do, they're oven chips. I can remember when chips were the staple diet in Barnsley.

Nearly all the workers here were and are women. There are usually between 50 and 65 of them. 'Traditionally they were the wives of miners, in fact 100 per cent the wives of miners'.

Their job is to 'form wire into shape with machinery, and to spot weld wire together', and from these bits of wire they make trimmings for microwave ovens, and cooker shelves, and refrigerator shelves. It's a bit boring. In fact, it's a lot boring. One young woman of 16 was caught drinking vodka out of one of those plastic bottles with straws at the top that footballers drink out of when they've won something. She'd passed it off as water for days. You can't blame her, really. You have to get through the day somehow. Another couple of young women, who had previously been barmaids, turned up but lasted only one day. They 'phoned up the next to say that they were not coming back. 'We thought we could talk all day and have a good laugh', they explained. No, you cannot have a good laugh. This is seriously boring.

Equal opportunities legislation is a bit of a pain. He needed women.

> *'The Job Centre send anyone. They don't stipulate. It's against the law to discriminate sexually for a start. But it's light work, we can relate it to a sewing factory. Fellas would be looking 'round all day if they were here. But I have to interview all the blokes as well as the women. I'm wasting their time and wasting mine'.*

This was never a problem in the old world. Men didn't want to work here. They would send their wives here. But it wasn't work for men. Work for men was at the pit.

The mender of bottling machines had one of the few businesses in Featherstone that did appear to have a truly international dimension. His major customers had bottle factories across the world: Australia; Sweden; Cuba. It wasn't clear just how many times he visited Australia, Sweden, and Cuba, and how many times he visited Barnsley, Rotherham, Doncaster. Australia, Sweden and Cuba sound better. This man might have been one who fitted the description 'new entrepreneur', depending on how it is defined. He previously worked in a senior position for a company doing similar things in a much more historically important northern city, and had sought to branch out on his own. But it is not always clear who should, and who should not, be classified as a 'new entrepreneur'. There is, evidently, a difference between running a steady-state business, which brings in a living for your family, and a thrusting, dynamic, risk-taking entrepreneur, that might inject something into a local economy that might otherwise not be there. This business was not in Featherstone for any particular reason, other than that, as so many others had found, premises and land in Featherstone were cheap. Five people, including the owner, worked here, all family. Essentially, it was the owner, his wife, his two sons, and his daughter. It's positive, and it seems to be doing well, but it's too small, and too family-orientated to make anything other than a marginal difference to the local economy.

The gaming and scratch card business did, however, at least on the surface, have some purchase on modernity. After all, we're all gamblers now. Ever since the launch of the National Lottery some time in the 1990s, vast numbers of us line up at shop tills to buy various forms of gambling scratch cards. And there is a certain poignancy about it being located here. Featherstone had always been big on gambling, though traditionally it had been bets on the horses. Like drinking, it had been an escape from the dark hole, the small terrace, the entrapped life. It was big in the 1950s, when *Coal is our Life* came out. There are many tales of men who lost all their weekly wages in betting shops before they made it home on a Friday night. George, the former deputy, told me: 'I've seen people work seven days at the pit, and they didn't get home with the money. Seven days!'

Gambling is still an escape. It is even marketed that way. That is why lottery scratch cards are marketed as 'instants'. For an instant, you escape. You are someone else, somewhere else. You aren't sitting at a sewing machine in a big hall making money for the owner of the company. You aren't humping bags of cement about, hoping to God every day that passes that your kids will find something better than this to do. And marketing — which passes as a discipline in some universities — after all, is about advising organisations on how best to take as much money off people as they possibly can. In Featherstone, like so many other places, people are still trying to escape. It's just that the scratch card, to a degree at least, has replaced the horses.

And when you cast deeper, you discover that this brush with modernity has had little impact on the local economy. Fifteen people worked here, both men and women, but only one came from Featherstone. The others commuted in. It was a recent re-location from a much more prosperous town to the north: the workers came with the company. As ever, the reason for choosing Featherstone to re-locate to was that the site was cheap. As so often the case with businesses in Featherstone, there are no ex-miners here. And most of the trades could be described, at best, as 'semi-skilled': printing; guillotining; making things of one kind or another. 'It's all computerised now'.

The owner of the gear-cutters and repairers was friendly. Like the Boss he had been born and brought up in Featherstone. Now in his early fifties, his father had been a miner. He is keen to share his views with me. He is dressed all in black, but rather scruffily. He wears a black jumper and old black trousers made of some man-made fibre which frays and collects bits of fluff of contrasting colours. Occasionally, he half stands up from his utility chair to re-adjust his trousers, which must have hitched up his leg, or stuck to a part of his anatomy that he wishes they hadn't.

We talked in the small room that passed for an office, and which was elevated from the main part of the building. The main part of this converted chapel is jam-packed full of machines. A handful of men in thin green nylon jackets attend them, or walk between them, or struggle against the incessant noise to talk to someone on a telephone.

It's a living. But you just get the most overwhelming of feelings that you would hate it if you had to do it. And yet, asked about the turnover of staff, the gear cutter told me that 'they tend to come and stay.....I'd like to think that the ones who are here will retire here...' I couldn't help but see this as a nightmare. Is there really no hope for them, other than to turn up, day after day, to attend to machines in this chapel?

The gear cutter had been proud, like the others were so proud, of the company and its achievements. It had been operating for 120 years, though not on this site. Previously it had been in Leeds. It was 'fully operational during the war......working on sights for bouncing bombers....also doing stuff for cinema.....it developed into industrial gearing.....'

The basic job of the gear cutter is to operate three machines, sometimes simultaneously. So, basically, he spends his time moving between machines. The customers for this service were companies — large companies, sometimes multinational — in the region.

Five workers, not including the head man, came here everyday. None of them were from Featherstone. They were all shipped in from the far side of Leeds, and all still lived that way. 'We had to bring them over here, because there are no skilled gear cutters in Featherstone'.

That was hardly a surprise. Gear cutting is a fairly specialised skill. Though you didn't get the impression that it would be beyond the wit of ordinary mortals. Yet the general sentiment — that there was a lack of skilled workers in Featherstone — was a familiar refrain amongst what might be termed by some the 'small business community'. The Boss had told me earlier, for example, that his company was all right for labour supply because it was a small company, but 'if it was a bigger company, and it wanted skilled workers, you'd have to bring them in. 95 per cent of your workers would have to be brought in'.

The owner of another small company on the pit site, that 'machined things for the oil industry', also told me that:

> *'...it's difficult to get skilled workers, but that's a national problem. Unskilled workers can be got easily....which we don't need....we have to look further-a-field than Featherstone for skilled workers'.*

Asked about the age of the workers, the gear cutter said that the oldest was about 58; another 52; another, a turner, about 48. But I did also see a quite fat young man, with a green nylon jacket on and a fresh face, who couldn't have been more than about 28, despite the fact that he had completely lost control of his weight. The gear cutter was aware that there was a need 'to put some youth back in...otherwise the company will die with all the skills'. There were no administrative staff here, all that was dealt with elsewhere. But the gear cutter was very proud of his computer, which he leaned over and tapped from time to time as if to emphasise that, in this antiquated chapel that had been converted into an antiquated factory, this computer was emblematic of his lifeline to modernity.

As I left the chapel, and thought about the scene on the redundant pit yard, what struck me about Featherstone was the complete absence of anything which could be claimed as being representative of a modern economy. Everything that is happening here could have been happening at the very least twenty years ago, and most things that are happening here could have been happening fifty years ago. The firmly held ideological belief of orthodox economists was that the 'old' had to be displaced to make way for the 'new'. They called it 'positive adjustment'. It sounds far more sanitised than redundancy, obsolescence, decay, hopelessness, destruction. Without positive adjustment, capital and labour would be caught up in obsolete businesses and industries. Men would still be working as miners when everybody knew that no one needed coal any more. Capital investment would still be being made in redundant sectors, and if we continued to invest in redundant sectors, we would never as a nation compete with the tiger economies, thrusting ahead with their curries on street corners and child prostitution. The trouble with Featherstone, as with so many other former mining areas, is that whilst the old has certainly been displaced, the 'new' has definitely not emerged. If you have a job in Featherstone in the late 1990s, you will be involved with the 'old'. The likelihood is that you will be attending a machine, taking materials to a machine, mending a machine. You might as well be a machine.

From the perspective of the late 1990s, it didn't look like changing. The gear cutter himself was a pessimist. 'Featherstone would never be the same again'.

Undoubtedly true. Pessimism is tolerable, probably realistic. Because of that it retains an acceptability. But scapegoating, as some people engage in when things aren't going the way they would wish, is futile and, more than futile, sometimes completely wrong in its analysis. It turned out that all the social problems of Featherstone were down to single motherhood.

> '.....*there were lots of unmarried mothers....so someone had the bright idea of putting them all together.....it was all to do with*

permissiveness.....you finished up with a row of unruly kids....with no father....and then they have a load of unruly kids....'

It's far too simplistic an analysis. It ignores economic reality, and blames people for social ills for which they do not deserve blaming. It becomes trite, boring, illogical, when it is combined with the idea that, in the 'old days' everything was solved by a 'clip-round-the-ear' from the salt-of-the-earth-stand-no-nonsense-father-figure.

The engineering and concrete companies on the pit site, together with the gear-cutters, the 'anything-in-wire' company, the gaming card manufacturers, and the repairer of bottling machines, represent more-or-less completely the industrial side of the small and medium sized business sector in Featherstone. Alongside this, there is a very small service sector based at the former miners' welfare hall: painters and decorators, electricians, a gym, a motor repair shop, a taxi company. There are a few other bits here and there. The odd double-glazing firm comes and goes, as they do everywhere. But what is described here is more or less the complete picture of the industrial small business sector. And in this respect, Featherstone is better placed than most former mining villages. Most of them had very little outside of mining. Come the late 1990s, even what they had before was significantly diminished.

Go to Great Houghton, a former mining village of 2,300, five miles to the east of central Barnsley. It has one major street. In the village as a whole, there are about 10 shops, which include three hairdressers, a couple of newsagents, a small post office and a betting shop. Alongside these, there are six pubs or working men's clubs. One indicator of economic decline, among many, is that the drinking places now have few customers. The two main working men's clubs no longer bother to open in the afternoon, because it's not worth their while. At one time, the afternoon would have been the 'session' for the miner on nights. Drinking, like fish and chips, was a 'cultural norm'. The fish and chip shop itself is for sale. The remnants of the industry survive in Great Houghton in the shape of two, short-term, open cast mines. One, the smaller, employed 35 for a maximum period of two years. The other was on the site of one of the two deep mines that were located here until the early 1990s. That site, too, would last only two or three years, and employed a total of 38. Just a few years before, almost 2,000 people were employed at the pits. Outside of these scraps of economic activity, there is nothing else in Great Houghton.

Great hopes were placed on the small business sector in the 1980s and the 1990s. Governments intensified 'business support systems'; training and enterprise councils held 'focus groups' of local small business people; university 'chairs' were created, in small business, and 'entrepreneurship'. We were all going to become small business people, entrepreneurs. Small businesses were going to rule the world. You would meet people in former mining towns in the late 1980s and early 1990s, with sober suits on, salaried and sitting behind desks, composing report after report for other salaried sober suits to read. They would sit there and tell you that the way to economic expansion was through 'building job creation capacity' into the existing small business sector. The truth is not so rosy. Despite the hopes pinned on this sector, by so many politicians and economists, despite the column inches in serious newspapers devoted to its economic growth and job creation potential, the inescapable conclusion is that, in Featherstone, like so many other former mining towns, it is both very small and very weak. It is far too weak to provide the basis for economic recovery. From talking to almost all of the owners, or managers, of the small business sector here, it is obvious that there is very little prospect of any serious expansion. It is not dynamic. It is not robust. It is not, even, really, entrepreneurial. Those pinning their hopes for economic renewal on the small business sector are deluding themselves.

In this respect, Featherstone differed little from other former mining areas. The story across so many of them was of an underdeveloped small business sector, lacking much potential for expansion. The small enterprise sector had often been weak, even before the pits had closed down. There was never much of a culture of small business ownership. In mining towns and villages, by and large, you worked for an already existing employer, usually the pit, but in some places, especially in later years, steel works, or engineering works. Unless you owned the local newsagents, or the fish and chip shop, you were unlikely to be working for yourself.

It's all been officially documented. The Coalfield Communities Campaign, an organisation formed by local authorities in former mining areas, noted that in West Yorkshire, for example

'In the ....coalfield area.....in 1981 small firms accounted for only 1 in 20 persons employed compared with 1 in 11 for the country as a whole'[2]. Study after study has paid testament to the fact that the small business sector has generally been weak and, importantly, difficult to stimulate [3]. There is little tradition of 'entrepreneurship' in mining areas [4]. Not that you need official documentation. You need only to go there.

If entrepreneurship was going to inject dynamism, another way to economic modernisation was going to be through training and re-training. Training of young people, especially, we are told by politicians of all sides, is essential if economic growth, economic 'modernisation', is to be achieved. Training is crucial to the development of skills, and several employers in Featherstone spoke to me about the difficulty of securing good quality, skilled workers.

When the NCB/British Coal occupied the pit site, extensive training of youngsters was an integral part of the operation. Training in the

coal industry was taken very seriously. It had to be. Your life might
depend on it. As the personnel and training manager of the Prince
of Wales colliery told me:

> '*All the training for this and other nearby collieries was carried out at
> a big pit six miles away. They had a special training gallery set up.
> This would have a mock up face, and the workers would also learn
> about haulage, conveyors etc.. It was basically about intense safety.
> Then you would go back to whatever pit you were with and then you
> did CPS [Close Personal Supervision]. Basically, they'd put you with
> an old guy who knew the ropes. In years gone by, he would have
> worked on the face, but would have come off because of his health.
> He'd be buggered. Then, they'd let you loose. You'd be on your own.
> The colliery overman would then deploy you to do various jobs.
> Eventually, say they needed a new loco man, or a new belt man, the
> training manager would call you in, you'd do a course, and take up
> the job'.*

After pit closure, systematic training of youngsters took place at
only one of the organisations on the site. This outfit occupied what
were the major colliery buildings, and had done since the late 1980s.
They were owned by a Sheffield-based, but nationally-orientated,
construction company. They carried out YTS training, teaching
youths in construction skills. About 40 trainees would be recruited
every year. They would do about two years attached to this
particular unit. To start with, they would get basic instruction on
the fundamentals of construction. This would include drain laying,
concreting, scaffolding. Most of the time, the trainees would not be
based here at the colliery site at all. Instead, they would be engaged
in placements with building companies, not usually in Featherstone,
but in nearby towns. At any one time, there would be only five or
six trainees at this site. What was in all this for the construction
company was that they received a payment for every trainee that
achieved a National Vocational Qualification to a certain level. It's

not difficult to reach NVQ 2 or 3. In fact, it's more difficult not to achieve them. It's a question of certificating what was not certificated before. So it's a fair business proposition.

The environment facing pit trainees was one of reasonable financial conditions and employment security. A job was guaranteed. The trainee underground pitman would start, at 16, on the lowest underground rate of pay. Even at that age, he'd earn more than a surface man. As *Coal Is Our Life* noted, mining offered 'complete security of employment in the West Yorkshire and most other coalfields' [5]. Once you were set on, you had a job, though it was not always clear at the outset what that would be. At 18, for example, you might do face training. Once you'd qualified and were working on the face, you'd be entitled to more money. There was no obligation to do it. Face training took 120 days, a third of a year. It used to take 140 days, until this was changed in the late 1980s. It was intensive and competency-based. The risk that somebody might not be properly trained could not be taken. You had to reach a particular competence level otherwise you stayed on the course until you could demonstrate that you knew what you were doing.

The situation facing construction trainees is completely different. Qualitatively far worse, far more insecure. There is no guarantee of a job. Most of them eventually get jobs, perhaps 75 per cent. The money they are on while training, frankly, is appalling. Little more than the dole. Up to 17 years old, it is £29.60 per week. After 17, it increases to £35 per week. A few trainees are sponsored by the Construction Industry Training Board. These are really rolling in it. Their wages go up to £45 per week for the first year, then £55, then up to £65 if they have been on the course for more than 18 months. The two training providers that I spoke to did not think these terms ungenerous. They made the point more than once that these sums were tax-free and, moreover, that some of the trainees got 'backhanders' from the companies where they were on placement.

The quality of training at British Coal, as at so many of the nationalised industries in the 1960s and 1970s, was second to none. You could get day release to study at colleges. The propaganda in the 1980s was that everything the nationalised industries ever did was terrible. It wasn't. The training was good. But there are big question marks over the quality of the training being received by these construction lads. Most of the trainees I saw looked like sullen youths, overall-clad and sulking about aimlessly with sweeping brushes, resentful of something, but not sure what. You didn't get the impression that they were at ease with their position in the world. They were here, it seemed to me, because they couldn't think of anything better to do, and nobody else could think of anything to do with them.

A fair proportion of these sullen trainees were the sons of miners. Had they been born a few years earlier they would have been in the same pit yard, but preparing to go down the shaft rather than skulking about with sweeping brushes.

> *'Quite a few of their parents are out of work. Some of them have the attitude "there's nowt for us now, the government's shit on us", but that's not as common as it was five years ago. Then we used to get parents ringing up saying "you're just using them, like the government did"'.*

It showed on their faces. They looked like those kids that everyone knew and who were always at everyone's school, and who didn't want to be there at all. They didn't fit. They didn't belong. They still don't.

The fastest growing 'industry' in Featherstone in the 1990s is security. There's an old school that's been converted into the centre of operations for a security firm that was formed in the early 1990s. It was a classic case of a small business being created to meet a market need. There is more nicking, so you need more security. And, with 50 people working from this building, it qualified as the biggest employer amongst the 'small businesses'. There's hardly anybody there during the day, just a couple of people to take 'phone calls and do basic administration. It is a world that operates at night. That's when you can go and catch the nefarious types. If I came at night, I was assured, I would see a lot more activity. 'You'd see a lot of blokes at night.....a lot of ex-miners amongst the door lads'.

The security firm is owned by Steve, who started by 'doing the doors' himself after the pit had closed, and is run, on a day-to-day basis, by John, an ex-diesel fitter in the pit. Miners did all right here. It was work they could relate to, felt comfortable with. John took the 'phone calls and made the bookings, ran the parish council in his spare time and, like so many mineworkers, had 'taken a very large drop in money to take this job'.

The company provided three services: 'door lads'; 'static'; and 'mobile'. 'Door lads' are basically bouncers for pubs and clubs. In the 1970s, they were a real rarity on the doors in the pubs and clubs of the northern mining towns. I can hardly remember any, save for special events. But as the 1980s wore on, they were everywhere. In pubs in Barnsley, mid-week nights, there were sometimes more bouncers than customers. Some people whispered about protection rackets. Surely, that cannot happen. Not in little Barnsley. Most of the men doing this kind of work were in their late twenties or early thirties. This company provided the 'door lads' for the pubs and clubs in nearby, larger, former mining towns. There are some women, too, doing this kind of work. They are there to search other women for weapons and drugs, and to follow them into the ladies'. 'Static' is where a bloke is put into a car showroom, or somewhere similar. He sits there all night to guard the place. 'Mobile' is where someone goes around in a car, checking schools and factories.

There is a certain social status to being a bouncer. You're dressed smartly. Your hair is very short. You are hard. People don't mess with you. It gives you a credibility. You have a role. You are proud. If your colleagues are having a spot of trouble in a nearby pub, you run to their assistance. People get out of your way. You always come out on top. You don't brag about your prowess, but people notice it as you exchange pieces of gossip and insider knowledge with them as they enter the pub, indicating just how much 'in-the-know' you are. If they're all right with you, you're all right with them.

I told John about the book that had been published in 1956, and asked him what he thought the differences were between then and now, and why security had become such a 'growth industry'. The theme was familiar, but no less valid for that.

> *'If you go back to when that book was written, you wouldn't need security companies because fathers would have clipped us round the ear'.*

His co-worker, Karen, a woman in her mid-thirties married to an ex-miner who happened, also, to be John's niece, concurred.

> *'Kids didn't knock about like they do now....if you go back to 1970 to 1975, when I was at school, you wouldn't have needed security'.*

As we talk, Steve, the owner of the company, comes in. He, too, used to be a miner. But not your typical miner. Far from it. There is something different about him. It's noticeable, but you can't quite describe it. It's a kind of presence, a kind of dynamism. He is dressed in one of those ridiculous suits that are highly fashionable: black, with a long jacket that is buttoned up almost to the neck. The kind that footballers wear who've got far too much money and don't know what to spend it on and who've got no dress sense. They think that they look wonderful but, really, deep down, you can't help thinking that someone somewhere has signed them up for a panto but not let on. Steve is 41. His chin is strong and covered in a short, very dark, stubble. He has either tried really hard to get rid of it and couldn't or he's left it on in yet a further attempt to increase what he sees as his macho, sexually attractive appearance. You can't tell which. As he sits down, you can't escape the thought that he looks like a middle-weight boxer just slightly past his prime.

But Steve is successful. He's survived the changing fortunes of the local economy. He's a role model for the community. He's well-off and expensively dressed, and many men here would wish that they were in his position.

The bigger companies

Small businesses provided a limited range of jobs for a something less than a couple of hundred people. Mostly, they weren't jobs that called for high skill levels and, by and large, they weren't hugely well-paid. Fortunately for Featherstone, it did not have to rely solely on small businesses for work. On the roads out of Featherstone there were five far more substantial employers. None of them were anywhere near as big as the pit had been, in terms of the numbers employed. In fact, between them, they employed far less than the pit had done in its heyday, though perhaps a couple of hundred more than it did before its final demise.

The biggest employer, with about 600 workers, is Humb Store, a packaging company split into two divisions, corrugated cardboard packaging and plastics packaging. The former makes those cardboard boxes that you see that have stiffened corrugated paper inside. The latter produces polystyrene egg boxes, trays for meat sold in supermarkets, and those polystyrene containers that hamburgers from one of those ubiquitous high street chains come in.

The older of the divisions, the cardboard company, has been in Featherstone since 1963. It was operating while the pit was in existence, though not when *Coal is our Life* was being written. The plastics division is more recent.

No one in the management of the company would talk to me. This was 'on the basis that our Human Resources policies are sensitive and disclosure of them in any form could lead to competitive disadvantages'. It wasn't immediately clear to me what I could do that would lead to 'competitive disadvantage', but they were obviously not going to risk it. When a company has such an importance, their refusal to talk doesn't stop you finding out about it.

This company is widely regarded as being the best possible place to work. It is seen by the community as being secure, here to stay, and as paying some of the best wages in the locality.

Bob is 45. He works as a shift leader. He stressed to me just how good this company is. 'It is a very good company to work for'. There was a heavy emphasis on his words. He, too, like the men who were running the small businesses, was a proud man. Proud of his position; proud of the company he works for. He elaborated further, with a list of the company's positive attributes. It was an equal opportunities employer; they would help you if you had a personal problem; they would give you time off to study; above all, they paid good wages.

> *'It is an equal opportunities company. It's ok to be black, disabled, a woman. They have even installed a lift so that disabled people could become clerical workers there. They allow people time off to study. They are a very human-orientated company. You've got a problem at home? You haven't got a problem'.*

I almost felt like joining up there and then.

Harry, the 66 year-old former winder, had heard much about the company from friends and relatives:

> *'....they are a first class company. Everybody I've spoken to there gives it a good name. They pay proper wages, that's a lot to do with people thinking it's a good firm. They've found that we've a good workforce in Featherstone, if they're given jobs'.*

The trade unionist who negotiated with management on behalf of the workers at one of company's divisions was also complimentary, but a little less sanguine:

> *'If you ask the employees, they will tell you they get treated like shit. But they get decent wages and, as it stands, a fair amount of overtime....to lose a job there, you've got to be really bad....even if you made a mess of the job you wouldn't get the sack.....it's a no smoking site, but there are still people wanting to smoke...then they do get the sack...but that's down to their own stupidity.....you'd have to be guilty of gross misconduct......to get the sack......they are one of the better companies I deal with'.*

Officially, yes, this company did have an equal opportunities policy. It was more in name than actuality. Bob was painting a rosy picture. The trade unionist told me that reality was different:

> *'There are some women on the shop floor, but it is predominantly male.....the women are mainly in the office....I don't think there's a coloured person there....I haven't seen one, to be honest'.*

The absence of former mineworkers seen in the small business sector was replicated here. Bob, the shift-leader told me that 'there are some ex-mineworkers here, but not many'. The trade unionist: 'yes, there are one or two ex-miners who work there'.

Here was a town once, and not that many years ago, dominated by the coal industry. And yet, 11 years after the closure of the local colliery, their continued exclusion — voluntary or involuntary — from both the small business sector and the biggest local employer, was striking.

Seventy per cent of those working at the factory were manual workers. Their tasks varied, but mostly they could be summed up as operating machinery, attending machinery, driving machinery. The pattern of machine-minding seen in the small business sector is maintained, on a much larger scale. The trade unionist described it:

> *'There are different machines....you've got your corrugating machines....other machines produce different packets......there is the foam shop, which produces foam inserts for boxes, there are fork lift truck drivers....electrical engineers....mechanical engineers...'*

If you work at the packaging company, you either operate machinery, or you mend it. Your life is spent as a kind of appendage to a machine.

In the small business sector in Featherstone, you would find yourself working 'regular days'. Early mornings; sometimes, if you worked overtime, long days. The typical structure would be to start at 7.30 in the morning, and carry on until the official closing time of 4 in the afternoon, or 6 if you wanted to work overtime. Saturday mornings would also be worked on overtime. Overtime was popular. If it was there, you took it. Few turned it down. It meant extra money, and extra money meant that life was more manageable.

In the packaging company, however, you would work shifts. Shifts which last 12 hours. Some are on permanent 12-hour nights. The majority work a version of what is called 'Continental' shifts. The general pattern here is that a worker would do two 12-hour days, starting at 6 in the morning, and two 12-hour nights. Then there would be a few days off. You are never on the same shift for more than three days, and it is usually two. You never know whether to have breakfast or dinner. The extent to which workers were 'happy' with this pattern of existence was encapsulated in a terse phrase of the trade unionist: 'it gets it out of the way.' You didn't really want to go to work. But you knew you had to in order to survive. You might as well get as much of it done at one stretch as you possibly could.

The real incentive for trying to secure a job at the packaging company was money. It was as much as you were going to make anywhere in Featherstone. The minimum you would earn, on regular days, was £179 per week, before stoppages. On shifts — permanent nights or Continental — you'd earn £300 per week. As the trade unionist said: 'it's quite good money'. Bob thought that the pay was 'very good'. He had previously been a motor mechanic, but that was not good enough when you get domestic responsibilities. 'You get married', he told me with a deadpan delivery that indicated that this was the only possible trajectory of life that he could envisage, 'you go to work at the packaging company. You double your wages'.

It's not bad compared to what those who remained in mining earned. At the Prince of Wales pit, the basic pay for a grade one faceworker — the highest earner among the manual workers — was £40 per shift over 1996/97: £200 a week basic. If geological conditions were good, if the machinery didn't break down, the faceworker might get £40 or £45 bonus per shift.

Bob went on to tell me that the man who owns the packaging company is worth £170 million. He is youngish, younger than Bob, in his early forties. He drives a top-of-the-range BMW, and his modesty is reflected in his choice of number plate. Rather than one which portrayed his own eminence and importance, Bob assured me, he has one which merely represents the initials of one of the company's subsidiaries. Such immense modesty. There is no class warfare evident in Bob's voice. It was a 'good luck to him' attitude. There was no raging revolutionary socialism. The bloke's done well, even if he did inherit it from his father. He's providing jobs. And Bob is keen to impress upon you that the company owner is a 'nice bloke'. This gives the impression that you've met him, even, maybe, that you actually know him. When he comes to the factory, 'he comes up and has a word'. Good of him, that.

Henry is 50, and has worked for the plastics division of Humb Store for 18 years. His father worked in the offices at a nearby pit. His wife's father was a miner. He's the salt of the earth. There's nothing he wouldn't do for you. The first time I met him, he offered to fix my car. You could rely on men like this to save your life. And if you thanked them for it, they would be embarrassed and insist that you stopped.

He started off his career at the factory as a 'packer'. Everyone does. Your job is this: you stand at a table, and you put a whole bunch of polystyrene meat trays into a polythene sleeve. Then you put the sleeve into a cardboard box. You do this all day. And you do it for 12 hours at a stretch. 'This', Henry told me, 'is the lowest of the low'.

Henry has progressed. Now he is a 'fast food setter'. This means that he works on the line that produces the boxes for take-away hamburgers. Anything that needs repairing on this line, he does it. If any new tools need fitting, he does it. When he's not doing that, he operates the line itself.

You ask him if he likes the work. You realise from his answer that nobody would do this if there was any other way of getting money:

'Factory work is different. A factory worker is like a zombie.....[at this point he pulls a face meant to indicate brain death].....you swipe on and swipe off....[he pulls the face again].......it's unbelievable.......

'Factory workers are a good set of people....they will give you a hand.....they won't see you towing....the camaraderie is good...but the management now are trying to push and push, which is making it worse.......there are some good lads....we have a good laugh....you've got to....it's monotonous.....you've got to break it somehow.....

'Our team leader's ok.....but some aren't...they are always trying to get you to do more....they want to get into management.....we call 'em "wannabes"...'

Coal is our Life referred to 'arsecreepers'. These were the workers seen by others to be 'bosses men'. They're still there. They always will be. There's always some.

He doesn't like the shifts, the 12 hours at a stretch, but he puts a brave face on it, like honourable working-class men always did:

'I've just done Friday/Saturday days......I've got today and tomorrow off....you get plenty of time off...we can go to Bridlington when there's nobody there.....we have to go with market demand, so we have to work shifts....'

His wife interjects, 'we work round it'.

Really, he's not happy at all about the shifts. But he realises that there's nothing that can be done about it. He's resigned to the inevitable.

Henry is in the union, like all manual workers are. He was once shop steward. He rushes to tell you, quickly, that he was 'not militant'. He realises that if anyone thought that that was the case it might bring him problems. There was a real fear here. Fear governs so much in Featherstone. It reminded me of McCarthyism in the 1950s and all those actors who had to vehemently deny ever, in their entire lives, having had an even mildly social democratic, never mind communist, thought. However, he went on: 'you must have a union, otherwise management will tread all over you'.

'There has never been a strike, but there have been overtime bans'.

Though, as it happens, only two or three in 18 years. They lasted about two days each. It was a pretty muted class war.

You ask directly: 'is the union strong?' And the answer is similarly direct, brief, accurate: 'No'.

All in all, Henry thought this a good company to work for. 'It's good money and it's on the doorstep'. Working there had allowed Henry to buy an old, red, 3-series BMW. He was very proud of it. Everybody has to be proud of something. In the first three or four sentences we exchange, he mentions it twice.

It's a good company but, unlike Bob, Henry couldn't claim to have met the wealthy young man that owned the business. In fact, the wealthy young man hardly ever turned up:

> *'I've seen him three times in 18 years'.*

But the wealthy young man did ensure that the local management took care of their workers. 'They look after you'. Henry lifted his wrist: 'that's a ten-year gold watch, and after 25 years you get an even better gold watch. They give you a hamper at Christmas and there's a dinner and dance'.

In Featherstone, there aren't many choices. If you get chance of a job at the packaging factory, you take it. You think yourself lucky to receive what you see as decent money, and a gold watch, and to get an invitation to a dinner and dance at Christmas.

If you don't get a job at the packaging factory, you might try the second biggest employer, a haulage company that stands next to the packaging firm. It's on land reclaimed from a slag heap. It's a relative newcomer to Featherstone, locating there in 1984, just as the pit was in its death-throes.

The owner is an 'ordinary bloke' in his mid-fifties who's made a bob or two. There are no airs and graces. He started life in a council house with five brothers and sisters in a mining village near Rotherham. Things have moved on. He's not quite sure how many he employs. It's about 150. He's not quite sure how many trucks he has. About 97. Mere details.

If in many businesses in Featherstone you end up machine minding, there is more to working here than simply doing that. Two-thirds of those employed are drivers and, whilst trucks are machines, at least you get to see a bit of scenery, rather than being stuck inside a steel shed or converted chapel. There are a number of other jobs here: administration; accounts; sales; warehousing; mechanics; fitters.

The appearance is of variety. But the distinct impression is that this is not a very exciting place to work. On the way into the building I met a security guard. He was peremptory and questioning, as security guards are meant to be. When I told him I was going to see the boss there was a transformation to a new-found respect. On my return, I met him in the yard again. By this time, he was defused, more open, more honest. He was a native of Featherstone, in his early or, at the very most, middle thirties. At one time it is a near certainty that he would have worked at the pit, especially given what was probably a lack of formal qualifications. I asked him about the work, and whether he liked it. 'It's a job', he shrugged. He didn't really think much to it, you could tell, but it was the best he was going to do.

In the office, a collection of men sit around computers dressed in the usual dress for administrative-type work, white shirts and ties. They didn't seem to be doing much, except staring at screens. They make the odd telephone call. It is a static atmosphere. The days must drag. You must get there in the morning and, as soon as you've arrived, want to get out again.

If you're not in the office, and you're not doing one of the support jobs to the main operation, you'll be the real thing, a trucker. That, too, according to the owner, 'is a fuckin' 'orrible job'. He's never actually been a trucker. He's always managed to avoid it. It's far better just to own the trucks, and get someone else to drive them.

Trucking is not like being in the packaging company, where people come and stay for life. There is a 25 per cent turnover of workers across the industry, not just in Featherstone, but everywhere. That's because it's a fuckin' 'orrible job, and if you're driving to the Continent, which is 98 per cent of this company's business, you end up spending weeks away from the family, which creates, as it is often put euphemistically, 'domestic pressures'. That means blazing rows with the wife. So, recruitment in this industry can be a problem or, at least, recruitment of a good driver can be a problem:

> '....the best way to find out if he [the potential new recruit] is a good driver is to go to the house.....the wife is the gaffer of the house.....if the wife's all right, it makes a big difference.'

The wife being the 'gaffer' of the house means that she will organise the household: she'll use the trucker's money, but it is her that will actually organise the paying of the bills, the sorting out of any dealings with authorities. It is the same division of labour noted in *Coal is our Life*, a traditional pattern of working-class life that exists still among certain sections of it, scarcely modified as the years pass. The miner would earn, but the woman would 'manage' the household. That included everything from stopping the milk, to food provision and preparation, through to raising the kids. If the woman fails to carry out any of these duties, she is seen to be failing in her job.

But the 'domestic pressures' in the trucker's life sometimes get too much. Women, at whatever level in the social class structure, retain at least some power, at least over certain men:

> '....the drivers leave us at the click of a finger.....it tends to be a woman who's behind it.'

In other words, it is a woman who's told the trucker to pack it in and find something that will keep him at home more often. Or at least that's what the drivers say. They frequently 'pack it in' and can't adjust to the other forms of work that might be available for a trucker without formal educational qualifications. They often try to return:

> 'I could give you a list of thirty blokes I've taken back....I've took 'em back unless I couldn't.....but, if he goes again, that's it'.

There is no shortage of applications for jobs at the trucking company. The problem is getting drivers who are good, and who will stay. That's why, if you find someone who's good, you don't let them go:

> 'We're always getting applications here from all over.....they write letters or physically turn up....only once, four or five years ago, did we advertise for fellas....if we see a quality man, we'll set him on....and I'll find him a job....only two in ten are quality....the problem is, you get desperate for a bloke'.

The nature of trucking means that drivers can be drawn from much further afield than the immediate locality. The drivers 'come from all over the place', but he couldn't recall that any of them actually came from Featherstone itself. He didn't think that they did. Some were from nearby townships, and some of those townships had been associated with mining, but this operation, as a whole, offered little employment to the residents of Featherstone. The security guard was from Featherstone, and two of the men in the office but, apart from that, no one could be identified who was.

The absence of ex-miners, as in so many other businesses in Featherstone, was also a feature here. There was no deliberate attempt to exclude them but, for many of the jobs they were just considered unsuitable. They were not seen as possibilities, for example, in the accounts or sales or other administrative work. They would require extensive re-training, and the employer faced with the prospect of re-training a 40 year old ex-miner or setting on someone at 20 will normally pick the latter. Had the company ever employed ex-miners?

> *'We must have done in the warehouse.....we've employed ex-miners as drivers.....they'd have accidents......the real comparison is forces blokes.....we got tank transporters.....we could get them for a month for nowt.....but they couldn't couple up a trailer...'*

No ex-miners. Few Featherstone people working there. To complete the equation of the modern economy in this post-coal location, no trade unions. In fact, the ordinary bloke hated trade unions. Were any of his workers members of trade unions?

> *'I don't know.....I'm not interested.....if they all got in a union together I'd sell up.....we pay good wages for our drivers.....I try to give 'em the biggest and best cab.....I try to get their expenses as high as they can go'.*

They should be grateful for it. They shouldn't even consider joining a trade union. His hatred stemmed from his experiences in the 1970s in Hull, where he was involved in haulage to South Africa.

Doing business with South Africa was not, at the time, popular with everybody. His own particular problem came about because a forwarding agent he had employed had unloaded some cargo at an unregistered port.

They 'got very militant there......The first year in business, I was blacked off Hull docks'. The only way a truck can earn money he explained, is if it is 'doing mileage'. And at Hull, in those days, trucks were sitting there all day long, not moving. Unions were no good. They had stopped him making money far too many times. It seems inconceivable from the perspective of the late 1990s that something such as this could happen. The 1970s were different times.

If you're an ordinary worker, you could earn more money working for the ordinary bloke as a trucker than you could at the packaging factory. The basic pay, before tax, was £350 per week. On top of that were the tax free expenses payable for nights away while abroad. Other companies, the ordinary bloke said, paid £10 to £12 per night. His company paid £24 per night. Your average trucker could get £200 per week expenses on top of his basic.

And it would be 'his' basic. At this site, as with so many others across Featherstone, the world of work remains largely a man's world. There are no women drivers, and no women mechanics, fitters, warehouse staff. Women can drive cars. It's difficult to see why they can't drive trucks. Yet the old divisions of labour, into 'men's' and 'women's' jobs, remain. Of the 150 employed at the site, only 10 are women, all of whom are confined to office-only work.

Like so many of the other companies, one of the main advantages seen with Featherstone as a site was that it was cheap. It was also close to a number of the company's customers and, apart from that, the company is here because it started off moving loads for the packaging company. That business has long since been transferred to cheaper French drivers. The disadvantage of the place was the extent of vandalism and thieving. Trucks would have their canopies slashed at the side, in order to get at the goods inside. This ceased in the late 1990s because of improved security. When lorries are parked up now, if they are empty, the doors are left open to show that there is 'nowt to nick'. In the yard, there are lights, alarms, fences, and three local men that have been set on as security guards to replace the former 'bent' security firm. There weren't many jobs for Featherstone locals here, but least these three had secured these low-paid positions. After all, ordinary blokes have to look after their wealth. Especially if other ordinary blokes haven't got any.

Across the road from the packaging company is a pop factory. This is the third biggest employer in Featherstone. It is a long-standing local business, having been started in the early part of the 1890s. Its longevity means that it shared a parallel existence with the pit. For much of the twentieth century, while some were going down the pit shaft, others were coming here to clock-in.

The markets this pop factory used to service were local. It provided all the soft drinks for all the working men's clubs in Featherstone. And there were six working men's clubs in a town of 14,000 in the fifties and sixties. Given that some of these 14,000 were too young to go into working men's clubs, and given that quite a good proportion were women who wouldn't and couldn't go in them, it's a pretty high ratio of clubs to people. It sounds almost like a wind-up, but the company won the contract to supply vinegar to Woolworths all over the country. The vinegar used to be taken by tractor to Featherstone station, and then distributed by train. They also won the contract to supply pop to all the Woolworths in Yorkshire.

There was vinegar, and they used to sell pickled eggs and crisps. People would think, as they pack their trolleys in the late 1990s with guacamole and pecan nuts and micro-waveable Indian meals in any one of the out-of-town supermarkets that ring every major settlement in Britain, that all this is some kind of ghastly caricature of the working class. It isn't. We really did eat pickled onions. Malt vinegar — or the ersatz 'non-brewed condiment' — did have a certain ubiquity. Pop and crisps were a cheap and commonly-had treat. For many, they still are.

The pop produced at Featherstone in the late 1990s is for supermarkets' own brands, and comes in those big plastic bottles. This is, in itself, a reflection of how consumer habits have changed. At one time, before everyone started going to supermarkets, men with small lorries used to come round and deliver pop, in glass bottles, to your door-step. Dandelion and burdock was pretty common then. It seems to have fallen from favour now.

The pop factory also produces Virgin cola. Which is a long, long, way from pickled eggs. Your ever-so-cool Virgin cola, drunk by ever-so-cool people, who are always smiling, and have no problems, and have lots of friends and parties to go to every weekend, is made in a collection of ageing, drab, decidedly uncool buildings in down-to-earth, mining, Featherstone. It is a triumph of marketing by Virgin: we're all so very cool; we fly around the world in balloons; we're philanthropic and caring. You'd never know where your cola really comes from.

And while you're flying around in balloons, at the pop factory work is not much fun. Kathleen had worked there since she left school at

16. She's 40 now. She's lived all her life in Featherstone. Her husband works at a sweet factory in a nearby town. He used to be a miner, but was made redundant. Together they can have a real sugar-treat with pop and sweets.

'I hate it. I hate the 12 hour continental shifts, and I have to work weekends as well. But I don't think I could get a job anywhere else'.

The pop factory is owned by a Canadian multi-national. They took over the existing pop factory in 1995. Prior to this company's forays in the cola market in association with big name supermarkets, Pepsi and Coca Cola enjoyed an international duopoly. The pop factory represented the only foreign investment in Featherstone. Yet foreign investment, we were told throughout the 1980s as deindustrialisation savaged large parts of the economy, was going to be the salvation of local economies. Looking at a small town like this gets you away from the platitudes and generalisations of national politicians who wouldn't even know where Featherstone is except when it's needed to provide a rock-solid Labour seat for some anointed rising star. Clearly, foreign inward investment isn't going to happen everywhere. It hasn't happened here. It can only happen when the conditions are right: the site; the infrastructure; the workforce; the 'package' put together by various agencies to lure companies. It has happened nearby, at Normanton, where the Japanese company Pioneer established a plant in 1991. But inward investment by multinationals is not going to happen in Featherstone, at least not on a substantial scale, and everybody knows it. Yet these were the two themes of the 1980s and much of the 1990s: a newly rejuvenated small businesses sector, and inward investment by multinationals, were going to transform the economy. Neither has happened in Featherstone; and neither will.

But the pop factory did provide employment for the local population, a function it had served throughout its existence. You can be a syrup operative, or a syrup supervisor, or a fork-lift truck driver. If you're really lucky you could end up as a 'leading hand', which is something approaching what a foreman used to be, when we all spoke the same language instead of inventing euphemisms to try to disguise what is simply the same old, drab, reality. Immediately next to the factory is a council estate. Most of the workers are drawn from it. Many of the workers are related to each other. That is partly a consequence of a small town economy, and partly the result of a word-of-mouth recruitment policy: you get your brother a job, your sister, and your brother's friend.

Ex-miners get more of a look-in here than elsewhere. They have been employed in the past and still are, though no records are kept of which workers, and how many of them, have been miners before. There is a high percentage of them. The 'human resources assistant' told me that there are no negative feelings towards ex-miners, they are just employed on the same basis as anyone else.

Despite the proximity of the council estate, despite the clamouring for jobs amongst the people of Featherstone, recruiting the 'right' kind of worker has not always been easy.

> 'The labour market is a bit of a problem.....generally, the skills level is low....people who are bright tend to move out of the area.....you can always get someone to mind a machine....but getting people who can do the more skilled jobs is more of a problem'.

Again, the problem of the skills level was raised. The human resources assistant also thought that getting people with a 'quality' focus was a bit of a problem. Ever since I came across the term 'quality' in the management-speak lexicon, ever since I saw the extent of its elevation among the curricula of MBAs, I have become highly suspicious of it. 'Quality' used to be a condition that was qualified by other terms: good, bad, poor, outstanding. Now, in management-speak, 'quality' seems to mean 'good quality', and yet it is used in such a glib sense by people as to render it almost meaningless. An entire discipline has been created, books written, consultants lavishly remunerated, conferences organised, on 'Total Quality Management'. It just means doing a decent job.

The gist of the message from the 'human resources assistant' was that they could get plenty of average workers, but getting hold of good ones was a bit of a problem. I wondered what it was that was being looked for in a 'good worker'.

'A bit of spark, in terms of health and safety, hygiene.....'

Nevertheless, the pop factory did meet the requirement for a particular level of job from a particular kind of worker. To be blunt, it provided jobs for the unskilled. No qualifications are necessary to work at the pop factory.

'We are not looking for that at all, in fact it wouldn't come into it. What we are looking for is some evidence of continuity of employment....and some awareness of quality issues'.

No qualifications are necessary, but 'quality' is. There are a range of jobs within this factory in which you can deploy this 'quality': warehousing; fork-lift truck driving. More likely than not, you'll be a 'production operative'. This means that you are looking after machines. Looking after machines has probably become the most important economic activity in Featherstone.

Unlike the packaging company, where there is an official equal opportunities stance, at the pop factory there is no such policy. In fact, 'equal opportunities is a joke....there are no formal policies....no particular groups are targeted'.

I asked if there were any disabled people employed at the pop factory. Apparently, there was no target to do that, but they might have employed someone inadvertently. They might have employed someone with a limp, for example.

The 'human resources assistant' himself, apart from a shift manager who was not white but was Featherstone born and bred, was the only ethnic minority person in the entire factory. Did that make him feel an outsider? Everyone was an outsider in Featherstone, he said, anybody at all, unless you are born and bred. It summed things up.

The pop factory, like so many other businesses in Featherstone, is a man's world, and it's a manual world. The change in the economy seen in so many other places, characterised by a far greater proportion of women in the labour force and a move from the industrial to the service sector, has not happened here. Ninety per cent of the workers here are manual; more than 80 per cent of them are men. The management team is exclusively male. Women hold some of the lower paid jobs in the office. It conforms to the stereotype prevalent in the 1960s and 1970s. It may now be a Canadian multinational with a chairman who writes up-beat newsletters to the employees. But nothing much has really changed, not much really since the 1970s, the 1960s, even the 1950s.

It's a man's world, and if you get a job there you'll end up working continental shifts. It's a particularly hellish form of 12-hour days and 12-hour nights. The day is divided into two: you either start work at 6 in the morning, or 6 at night. It's a disruptive pattern, and it certainly doesn't add to the fun of being a machine operative in a pop factory. You work two day shifts, then have two days off, work three night shifts and have two days off, then the cycle finishes with another two 12 hour days followed by three days off. There used to be a traditional 8-hour three shift pattern of mornings, afternoons and nights, and this new roster had been in place only since 1996. Some people resisted the change, refusing to work the new shifts until they had worked through the statutory period of change, though the majority accepted the new arrangements without any protest. Those reluctant to accept the new shift patterns were seen as being bolshe. It did their promotion chances no good at all. Not that there really were any. Following the change, the factory now works 24 hours a day, 7 days a week, 52 weeks a year. This is the modern, flexible, economy. We have to do this to be competitive. This is the reality of the modern, flexible, labour market. It is what Prime Minister Blair told the CBI in November 1997 that we have to strive for across the whole of the European Union:

> 'Europe will need to demonstrate a new adaptability and flexibility.
> We will fight hard for a modern and flexible labour market in Europe' [6].

Modernity. Flexibility. It sounds good. Until you have to work in it.

The money at the pop factory is regarded as 'very good' for the area. At £250 basic pay per week, it's not quite as good as the packaging factory but, as with so many other workplaces in Featherstone, there is plenty of overtime. In fact, local households seem to be able to get by because of the overtime: the local economy runs on it. You wonder how they would manage to survive without it. Production at this factory was expanding in the 1996/97 period, and most of the expansion was covered by overtime working. It wasn't clear how long this would last. Production was set to

continue expanding, but new workers might be set on, and this
would reduce the prospects for overtime.

Like the packaging factory, there is trade unionism at the pop
factory, but it is weak trade unionism. Ninety per cent of the
manual workers are in the union, and the union is recognised by
the management for negotiating purposes. The administrative staff
are not unionised and, if any of them are individual union
members, there is no recognition of a union for administrative
workers by the management. There are no industrial disputes.
Privately, the management sees the union as being 'tame' and, like
so many employers here, they like to think that they 'go about
things the right way' so that there isn't really all that much need for
a union.

It was reminiscent of the packaging factory. There, 95 per cent of the
workers are in the union. It is a single union site, and Bob, the 45
year-old shift leader saw that this was 'only because it is easier for
management to negotiate with one union'. Bob thought it was 'not a
militant place'. He had worked there for ten years and couldn't
remember a single strike. Bob said that the union recognised that
'the world had moved on'.

So did the full-time union official who represented the workers at
Humb Store:

> '....there are no winners in industrial disputes, only losers'.

There was some militancy when the pit was here. It's history now.
In the pop factory, there is an authoritarian management style. The
swashbuckling Canadian multinational may have come in, there are
upbeat newsletters and trendy labels on pop bottles, but the
management style hasn't changed for years, probably hardly

changed since the company was established. The pervasive culture was deference: you knew your place. The workers called the trilby-hatted factory manager, who strode the shop floor with his air of superiority and authority, 'Sir'. The trilby was a symbol of his elevated position within the company. It was once a commonplace. Those who had achieved greatness, or aspired to do so, would wear a trilby hat and a light, long, grey nylon coat. I can remember it distinctly as the uniform of the upper working class who thought that they had reached the dizziest of social heights in the engineering factories in South Yorkshire in the 1970s.

You know your place. You'd better not step out of line. There are plenty more where you come from. Weak trade unionism. Deference. It's a modern world, and we all drink Virgin cola. It's so modern that it's not that much different from 50 or 60 years ago.

Though it's a man's world in most of the businesses in Featherstone, women who want to work have to work somewhere. Traditionally, the counterpart to coal for women was clothing and textiles. In Featherstone, long after mining has gone, the major centre for work for women is still a clothing factory. With 130 employees, it is the fourth biggest employer.

Physically, it is the same clothing factory that the authors of *Coal is our Life* mentioned to in 1956. But it's in different ownership, and a different kind of market is catered for.

In the fifties and sixties, 330 worked at this site, the overwhelming majority women. In the late 1990s, there were less than half that, though it was still a substantial employer.

In its previous incarnation, the clothing factory was in the ownership of a small, private concern. In the mid-1960s, in that frenzy of mergers which characterised the British economy then, it was bought out by one of the very big British-owned clothing and textile companies.

The factory closed in 1990. The man who had been the production manager bought the site, and re-opened it with a slimmed-down workforce and a new marketing strategy. In the past, the factory had made fashion items for High Street chains and mail order companies. But increasingly, as the 1970s and 1980s wore on, such concerns began to source their buying more and more abroad. The average British clothing factory worker was never well-paid, but even they could not compete with sweated labour in the 'newly industrialising' countries. So the new company moved away from fashion and found itself a market 'niche': they now produce uniforms for 'business and corporate wear'. Effectively, this means uniforms for building societies, banks, bus companies, railway companies. Railway privatisation in late 1990s was a major boost for them: all the new train companies needed new uniforms.

Like the pop factory, the clothing factory serves a purpose for a town like this. It provides jobs for local women, jobs which require dexterity and an ability to withstand what look, at least to an outsider, to be long periods of boredom. Ninety per cent of the workforce is female. Most of them live close enough to walk to work. There are no ex-mineworkers amongst the small numbers of men. Most of the men are on the cutting and warehousing side; none sit beside the sewing machines which form the main furniture. The men in the cutting room will earn up to twice as much as the women. This is common throughout the industry. It is a long-standing tradition that they do. It still applied in the late 1990s. If they conform to the norm, they will have been cutters all their working lives. Their far higher wages than the women earn are justified on the basis that they are doing a different job, a job which requires more skill or harder work. It is not a job that women are incapable of doing. It is just that they are traditionally excluded. Nor would all agree that, in truth, it is a job which requires any more skill than that being employed by the women. The full-time trade unionist who used to represent the workers here told me that it was simply a long-standing tradition in the industry that men were paid more than women. There was no logical justification for it. It dated back to the days when men were seen as the 'breadwinner' and women, by contrast, were working for 'pin money'. 'Pin money' was money additional to the main, basic income coming into a household. People would often be derogatory about 'pin money': it was seen to be money that could be spent on frivolities, like going out and new clothes. The real serious business, by contrast, was feeding and clothing your family. There was sometimes a resentment about those people earning 'pin money'. They were seen to be enjoying some kind of special advantage in the struggle to get by in life.

'It's on'y pin money, anyway', they would say, dismissively.

Even where the female has become the main breadwinner in the household, evidence from elsewhere — the clothing industry in Nottinghamshire — suggests that 'managers....continue to hold these stereotypical perceptions of women and work' [7].

The owner's view was clear cut. It was good for both this business and the area itself that this factory was located here years ago. Recruiting labour was easy:

> *'It was a mining area and there was nothing for the girls to do'.*

Though the high absenteeism rate amongst miners at the time fed through into absenteeism at the clothing factory:

'...they were wives and daughters of miners....there was certainly an absenteeism rate of 16 to 24 per cent then'.

If the man decided to stay at home, say on what was often called 'collier Monday', 'their lass' [wife or girlfriend] might stay at home as well. In any case, work was seen by the women then, as now, only as a means to make a bit of money. It wasn't part of a grand career plan:

'In Featherstone in particular, the women don't want a career....they want to get married and have kids....they don't have a lot of ambition...women still seem to be the women of 20 or 25 years ago'.

Nor, on this view, have the social attitudes of the men changed all that much:

'....the Featherstone man is the most chauvinistic of all'.

The full-time trade unionist, however, had a more qualified explanation for absenteeism in clothing factories. The job itself was highly repetitive, immensely boring, and gave rise to ill health and injuries. 'The nature of the job didn't encourage people to work five days'.

Times have changed. The nature of the work hasn't. Now, boring and repetitive as the work might be, you daren't take any time off, at least not on a regular basis. On the other hand, if you own one of these places, you daren't sack anybody either: you might not get somebody with the right skills who's prepared to sit there for hours on end every day that God sends for little money. Skill shortages in the clothing textile industry are, throughout the country, endemic in the late 1990s. In a survey of companies in Nottinghamshire, published in 1994, one third of firms examined reported skills shortages [8].

The women who work in this factory range in age from about 20 to about their mid-50s. Some of the older ones were here when the factory was in its earlier incarnation, when there were many more people here, churning out clothes for high street chains. Many of them have known no other kind of paid work. The factory itself is basically a giant hall, with hordes of women sitting in serried rows, each with a table in front of them with a sewing machine on it. There are also a few pressing machines, which entail a woman lifting a small but long platform into the air and bringing it back down again. At a particular time every day, 1 o'clock, the entire factory stops work immediately. The machines go dead all together. For half an hour, all the women move to a part of the factory in the corner with tables and chairs that is designated the 'canteen'. It is not separated from the rest of the factory by walls. It is just a collection of chairs put together at one end. Some women go outside to smoke during this period. And in the owner's office you can see examples of the fruit of their hours of carrying out the same repetitive tasks sitting at sewing machines: crimson blazers for bus drivers and royal blue two piece outfits for women who work in building societies. It looks a nightmarishly boring place to be.

And you don't get compensated all that well. The owner was coy about what they pay, but they adhere to 'minimum levels negotiated by the relevant trade union and the national industrial association body'. In a similar clothing factory in nearby Barnsley, that would amount to £128 per week starting pay and then, after that, rates based on piecework, so earnings can be higher for hard workers. If you are fast, you get more money. But if you're older, and your speed is not quite what it used to be, you won't pull in as much. 'Piecework' means exactly that: you are doing one piece of a bigger job. You might have the same few stitches to perform on a piece of cloth one hundred times an hour, for eight hours. It could drive your soul into the ground.

From the £128 minimum that you have earned, you have to deduct tax, national insurance. There's not much left. But, then again, there aren't that many places to work if you are a woman, and the other possibilities in Featherstone itself — in a shop, or working as a 'care assistant' in a home for older people — are not going to pay much either.

The low pay feeds into problems of recruitment, though it's not just low pay that prevents people from wanting to work in places like this: it's poor conditions; it's because you need to be skilled to get a job here in the first place, and you haven't been trained; it's because of the sheer boredom of it all. The owner said that there had been a vacancy at his factory signposted in the local Job Centre for four weeks. He had not had one indication of interest from anybody. I checked it out with the local Job Centre. Yes, there had been a vacancy advertised for four weeks. The reason there had been no response was that the wage that was quoted was 'negotiable'. No one in employment was going to move for that. Whereas 'negotiable' at the top end of the social scale means that the money is likely to be good — companies, and governments, always 'negotiate' on pay with their prospective incoming chief executives — at the bottom end it means that it is likely to be bad. It's funny how the same word can have such different connotations depending on where you are in the social class hierarchy. Other women who have worked in sewing factories before are not going to tempted to return: working in a sewing factory causes back strain, and neck ache, and repetitive injuries. It isn't fun.

The factory owner, of course, didn't see it in these terms. As far as he was concerned, there were two problems. The first was that the big Japanese investor, Pioneer, a manufacturer of CD players, tuners, and 'mini-systems' — whatever they are — four miles away was able to poach the labour that might otherwise have come to the clothing factory. On this count, at least, the clothing factory owner was probably right. Zenkichi Igarashi, the managing director of Pioneer, discussing the reasons for choosing this site, wrote in one of those one-sheet, glossy promotions produced by local authorities to tell you how wonderful their town is:

> *'.....investigations revealed that there was a large pool of labour in Yorkshire and that the skills available in the textile industry can be quickly applied to the mass production manufacturing process in consumer electronics'.*

Of course, the Japanese would never have been able to poach it if they hadn't have been paying more money. It didn't take that much to beat Featherstone's clothing factory.

And then, of course, there was the problem of single mothers and women getting pregnant. They'd got a hell of a lot to answer for.

> *'.......the amount of financial cushioning from the state means that the incentive for a woman to work is not there.....that's why unemployed women from Featherstone do not come.....they get pregnant on purpose....they want to get the hell out of their family home....the council will give them somewhere to live'.*

The thesis that single motherhood does not make a beneficial contribution to achieving a harmonious, work-orientated, prosperous society was given some academic support, ironically enough, by one of the authors of *Coal is our Life*. The 'problem', as it was perceived by Norman Dennis and his fellow author George Erdos, was not so much single-motherhood as a non-committed, absent, father. It had deleterious effects for society as a whole: the children were more likely to under-achieve, educationally; more likely to suffer ill-health; probably to have a greater proclivity towards crime [9]. Norman Dennis went on to develop the thesis later, connecting crime more strongly with the 'dismembered family'[10]. The blame for legitimising alternative forms of child-rearing to the nuclear family — such as single-motherhood — was placed at the door of the 'intelligentsia': the educated middle-class intellectuals whom Dennis argues think they know what is best for us.

By the time we got to late 1997, the Labour government was attacking the position of lone parents which, for the most part, meant lone mothers. New claimant lone parents were to have their benefits cut, in line with the plans of the previous Conservative government. They would be encouraged to find jobs in the government's 'Welfare to Work' programme. There is, of course, nothing wrong with the idea of helping women who want to work find jobs. It is the element of coercion that is problematic, and the implied assumption that, somehow, if you are a single mother, it's always your fault. You've done it on purpose. To get a council flat. To get benefits. There are instances of this, undoubtedly. But the reality of life is more complicated. The reality of life is that single motherhood is often the result of broken relationships. Relationships which you had hoped would never break. There is also, seemingly, the implied assumption that motherhood, by itself, is somehow not a sufficient contribution to society, to the world.

The logic was compellingly illogical: it was ok for another woman to come in to look after your kids, because she was being paid and therefore had a 'job'. But for the mother herself to look after the kids did not constitute a 'job'. She had to go out and find other work in order to pay the other woman to come in and look after the kids. It was emblematic of the state of British politics in the late 1990s: here was a political party which had for years drawn its support from, and meant to be representative of, ordinary people and here it was, squeezing one of the most vulnerable groups in society. Even beyond this absurdity, the entire proposal was divorced from reality. Just where, in Featherstone, were these lone mothers supposed to find jobs? It already had enough care assistants, and shop assistants, and hairdressers. And you weren't going to get near the concrete producers and little engineering shops, even if you wanted to.

The company that had been on this site running the clothing company previously had been the recipient of all kinds of government financial assistance in the 1960s and 1970s. One grant in the late 1970s was for close to £1 million. According to the owner of the successor company, this was from 'some kind of clothing industry scheme' and was from 'somewhere like the DTI'. It was used to invest in new equipment. They got grants for buildings between 1964 and 1976. Both Labour and Conservatives gave grants.

A vast academic debate raged during the 1980s on the merits or otherwise of what was called at the time 'selective intervention'. People wrote entire books about it. Some got university chairs based on writing the books. In a nutshell, the argument was simple. Did this money coming from the government help to create jobs, or at least maintain them, or was it a waste of effort and resources? Was it, in fact, a form of 'propping up capitalism' as some of the then left in the Labour Party, and the left outside the Labour Party, seemed to think? This clothing factory represented a classic case of selective intervention to help a multi-national company in an area which, then as now, had few opportunities for women workers. Perhaps it did preserve jobs for a while. Given the economic conditions, perhaps that was worthwhile. But the whole exercise also points up some of the futility of what in general terms was called 'industrial policy'. If the conditions within global markets are against you, it is difficult to see how financial assistance, by itself, can really change much.

Of course, like so many other places in Featherstone, there was no trade union here. And, like so many other owners of businesses, the owner of this one could scarcely see the point in having one:

> '.....to be frank, if there are any union members here, I don't know about it....I'm very pleased that they haven't felt the need to join one....there are a very close community'.

There used to be a union. Prior to the management buy-out, all the women were in the union that organised in the clothing factories, the National Union of Tailor and Garment Workers. It was never a particularly strong union, like the men had had in the NUM.. It was a union, nevertheless. It gave the women a voice, and a bit of collective protection against the potential worst excesses of management. It was a voice that they exercised. According to the full-time trade union official:

> 'They did have disputes.....they stopped work several times. If they felt something was wrong and the manager wouldn't move they would stop work and go and sit in the canteen. It was quite traditional in those days'.

These disputes might last as little as half a day, or less, or sometimes a full day. They could be over anything that the workers saw as being unfair.

The trade unionist told me that there had been a couple of attempts to re-establish the union amongst the women, but both had seen 'management pull the shutter down'. If management tells the women not to join a union, the women will be too scared to join one. They might have a legal right to do so but they know that, on the ground, it wouldn't do them any good in Featherstone. There are no disputes now and, as workers, they know that they have little power.

The owner had worked here since the 1960s, but was from the south of England originally. He didn't live in Featherstone. He knew the town well, but he would still rank as an outsider. On the view of an outsider, Featherstone had changed very little from the way it was portrayed as being seen in *Coal is our Life*:

> *'I've got an affection for Featherstone....I think it's a dump personally....but the people are nice....back in the 1960s and 1970s....it looked like a dump then.....but it was a thriving dump'.*

It is no longer thriving.

A few yards up the road, in yet another converted chapel, there used to be another clothing factory where women worked. Funny how the discards of religion become useful to capitalism. It must be some strange twist on the Protestant work ethic. At its height, up to 90 women worked here. It closed in the mid-1980s. It was dirtier than the larger clothing factory, and far more old fashioned. They used to make trousers here but, as with so many other clothing factories, it met its demise after the high street concerns started buying overseas. The women here were in the same union as the women in the bigger factory. It was better to work at the bigger factory: better pay, better conditions, better machinery. You would aspire to move if you could. The chapel, according to the union man, was 'quite a bloody miserable place to go into, which they all were'. It was miserable, but you got by, despite the low pay and the repetitive, boring tasks. You looked forward to the short breaks, and the chit-chat that you could exchange with your co-workers. There were kids to feed. You had to do it. You'd try, if you could, to get to the bigger factory. But, apparently, not all women were 'up to the standards' required in the bigger factory.

The clothing company of 1997 occupied only a part of the former clothing company's premises. The larger part was occupied by another company involved in packaging, labelling and other assorted jobs, which had been trading there since 1996. It was very new. The management styles and employment practices were also something quite new to Featherstone.

This company was owned by a man who saw himself as an energetic entrepreneur. He tells you about his origins in a council house, and about when he worked as a bus driver in Leeds. The implication is that if only others were as hard-working as he is, they would hit the big time too. Undoubtedly, the British economy would be the most competitive in the world. He wastes no time in getting round to telling me that he

> '*drives a beautiful car, has a beautiful house, and a wonderful family, but I've grafted for it'.*

Employment levels at the factory vary. On this particular day in November 1996, there were 65 working there. Only 35 of these are 'permanent'. The rest are brought in for specific jobs, and employed for two or three weeks at a time. Sometimes, if there is a big order on, the employment period can be two or three months. It is the ultimate in casualisation, the very extreme of the 'flexible' workforce. In this company, you do what you are told.

> '*The men went to the pit, the women came here. It went bankrupt in 1990. Within a year the place was like a bomb site. The roof was*

smashed. Every window was smashed. The floor had come up, because of water coming in. Every piece of lead had been stripped out. Graffiti was everywhere. We had to come in with torches. There were rooms which even the estate agent didn't know existed.

'We bought it in September 1995. If it hadn't have been in such a state, we'd have been in before Christmas, employing 50 people'.

The gist of his message was that the whole community had watched the place being smashed up, and no one had 'lifted a finger' to stop it. This, he thought, was bad for the local economy. After all, who would move into a bombed out place? To him, it was common sense not to vandalise a place like this, for fear of deterring a possible inward investor.

The energetic entrepreneur is conscious of the fact that work there is 'mind-bogglingly boring' but, 'they do the work, they have to'. The 'business and corporate wear' clothing company boss had confessed to me that, in the past, he had felt guilty about how boring the jobs were in his factory. Now his guilt was assuaged. He had seen the jobs in this packaging factory, and realised that working at a sewing machine was not 'half as boring'.

The nature of the energetic entrepreneur's business is this. The company gets orders from big concerns, from high street retailers, or internationally-known food companies, or toy manufacturers. As individual tasks, they are all smallish operations. It might be putting cellophane wrapping on to a box of chocolates, or sticking a sachet of after-shave into a magazine, or attaching a small, coloured, decorative bow to a bottle of bubble bath. Doing one or two would be fine. Doing hundreds a day probably induces near paralysis of the mind.

The labour force here, in the classic Marxian sense, is a means to achieve profit, and is brought in as, and when, required. Don't waste the owner's time by talking about 'human resources' or 'training' or 'job security'. They are not concepts that apply to this factory. They are meaningless things talked about by interfering do-gooders. Those who can't get a job have only themselves to blame, and that includes redundant mineworkers.

> *'We haven't employed many ex-miners, probably 20 over the period here. Most of them haven't got a job because they won't get off their arse and get out of Featherstone, so they won't get a job. When they are faced with some of the tasks here, you can visibly see them wince. There is a perception that they are still the bread winners, and there is a sharp intake of breath when they are faced with some of the tasks and when they can see a slip of a lass can do the same as them, and earn the same as them'.*

There is no 'paternalistic' capitalism here. You are told what to do and you do it. It's your fault if you don't like it. And if you don't like it, you can always leave.

> *'Some people don't fit in here. If you don't like the work, you can leave correctly, and it's ok. If you just walk out, you don't get paid for that day. We have a clock and card system. Everyone is a fire hazard'.*

Everyone is a fire hazard. Just as he said it, the words of an old friend of mine who used to be a miner came back into my head. He reminisced about what it was like to work at the pit, about the way that, at one time, they'd try to keep your job no matter what:

> *'Tha'd got to feight to get t'sack'.*

At this factory, if you're asked to work overtime, you work overtime, even if it is on a Sunday, as it often is if there is a deadline to meet. If you refuse — families to be with, perhaps, or just a basic need for a day off 'mind-bogglingly boring' work — your already low wages are reduced still further to £3.40 per hour for the whole week's work. If you're really good, and you do as you're told, you can earn a bit more than this.

As with many other businesses in Featherstone, recruitment is through the Job Centre. Company policy is to talk to every member of the new intake when they arrive. They are recruited in groups so the owner, or one of what he calls the 'awesome foursome' that comprise the management team — his wife, his daughter, his daughter's husband — talks to them collectively. They are told that if they as an individual, or any member of their family, cause any damage to the company premises, then they no longer have a job. If your brother smashes a window, if your cousin sprays graffiti on the wall, you're out of work. The social control of the company extends beyond their own employees and on to members of the employee's family. You may not be able to control your recalcitrant brother or cousin. That's your problem. There's a social hierarchy and, if you want to play the game, you have to recognise it. The management are better than you. They are superior to you.

You are spared continental shifts. It is the day shift only. You can have breaks. Quarter of an hour in the morning. Quarter of an hour in the afternoon. Half an hour for lunch. Don't take a minute longer. Respect is important. That is, respect for the management.

> 'We explain at the induction that we don't stand for anything other
> than respect. If someone's not working hard enough, it's not his job
> that has gone — that's already gone — it's the person's job who's

standing next to him on the line. Someone who is not pulling their weight is stealing off his mates'.

I thought about the employment world we are now in, and I thought about what George, the retired deputy at Ackton Hall, had told me earlier:

'....there was a lot of comradeship, and friendship about the job. There was a willingness to do the job. There was a wonderful spirit'.

Times have obviously changed.

The owner took a dim view of the workforce:

'....linking words together....they can't do it....they can't string a sentence together....you have to speak in words of one syllable....you can't blame the teachers.....but you can blame the parents....getting the right kind of people is difficult.....you have to employ 10 to get two good ones....'

Featherstone has been good for the packaging company. His previous factory had been in a prosperous part of north Yorkshire. No one would come and do this kind of work there. Nobody would do this work, unless they really had to. The owner was 'delighted' with Featherstone. 'The reason we moved was for people'. You can get people in Featherstone. And you can treat them like shit.

Some of the workers took a dim view of him. Debbie, daughter of a miner, is 19. Years ago, by this age, she would be courting a miner, soon to wed. It's a day off from the factory. She's with her friends. One of them works in a similar factory in a nearby town. The other is training to be a hairdresser. The sun is shining. Debbie's making the most of it: ' 'e doesn't like us having a day off'. Working at the packaging factory is 'boring, it's crap. He's a horrible man'.

She's trapped here and she hates it. She's been trapped for two years. But before you can escape from anything, you need a direction. And Debbie had no idea what she really wanted to do, or where she wanted to be. There would have been a time, not long ago, when the choice would have been made for her. In a world of certainties, you have a social position, your life is structured. But Featherstone is no longer a world of certainties.

Men and women work here in varying, but roughly equal, proportions. Most of them are young, mostly between 20 and 40, the majority between 20 and 25. They come from Featherstone, and also from surrounding ex-mining towns. The company was on the site in Featherstone because it was much cheaper than sites elsewhere. The land was cheap; the labour is cheap. In fact, it struck me that, in the battle for economic survival, cheapness is all that Featherstone has to offer.

Don't even think about joining a trade union. Industrial relations issues are black and white. The owner has the power.

> 'We pay above union rates. If there is a gripe....let's sit down and sort it out. You either work or you ain't got a job'.

I remember during the mineworkers' strike of 1984/85, the issue focused on by the government was the 'management's right to manage'. The miners, according to the government and British Coal, were challenging that right. They kept chanting it on television, like a mantra. I sat opposite the friendly, ebullient, opinionated 'entrepreneur', well-dressed in casual clothes, who owned the factory. We were only yards away from the pit site where the 'management's right to manage' had been challenged. Only yards away from where the cars of people trying to enter the pit and go to work had been turned over. We could have been a world away. We could have been in a different dimension.

Problems in the past were caused by structures and by culture. Public sector ownership of industry, for example, was a structure which had disastrous consequences.

'Nationalised industry meant that you didn't have to bloody work'.

Then there was the cultural problem. People were not sufficiently work-orientated. They were too bolshe. Too much into trade unions. They didn't have enough 'respect' for management. They weren't entrepreneurs. Selby, for example, was a quiet, quaint, market town in North Yorkshire. Then, in the mid and late 1970s, it became the epicentre for the biggest coal development in Western Europe.

'When the miners moved into Selby, the culture literally changed overnight'.

It had been all right up until then, Selby had.

In days gone by, when you started at the pit, you could expect to retire at the pit, unless something better came along. Now, the workers who came for jobs at this factory 'commonly have had seven jobs before they're 18'. That is 'seven they can remember and put down on the application form, probably they have had more'. Like most mineworkers, they won't have many formal qualifications. But they have to have something. The owner is quite specific about his requirements:

'If they are stood up, have two hands and two eyes, they're ok'.

Unlike the miners, those 'stood up' [sic] with two arms and legs have no job security whatsoever. This, perhaps, is the price of not challenging the 'management's right to manage'. It's what happens when you don't resist, or your resistance fails.

Of course, the lack of job security, the lack of a job, the inability to get on in the world, is all the worker's fault. The 'entrepreneur' related to me the story of three men who had, at some stage in the past, worked in his factory.

> *They were three big guys, good workers. One was formerly a miner, one formerly a security guard at a car showroom. They were never late. I was going to make them permanent. I thought they were team leader material'.*

At this factory, to be a 'team leader' is something to aspire to. One day, the 'entrepreneur' noticed that one of the workers had not turned in. After a more prolonged period of absence, the 'entrepreneur' took it that this worker had left, but the worker had not even told the him he wouldn't be coming any longer. There was 'not a word'. He would never be allowed to work here again. And it wouldn't do him any good when he was looking for work elsewhere.

Next, the friend of the worker who had left went off sick. After he had been off for 2 or 3 days, the 'entrepreneur' asked the remaining friend when he would be back. 'Oh, Tom's not coming back'. Tom had never said anything to the entrepreneur. Like his friend, Tom had obviously found another job, a better job. Good luck to them, I thought. The entrepreneur was disconcerted. Obviously, it showed a lack of 'respect'.

'I have never seen such a lack of common courtesy. I guarantee he will be out of work in six months'.

One of the most prevalent psychological characteristics of a mining town was pride. You were proud to be a man, you were proud of your strength, you were proud of your culture, you were proud of your village. You were proud of the best clothes you wore when you went out with 'your lass', you were proud of 'your lass'. Whether you were young, or whether you were old, it was the same. As Geoffrey Goodman argued in October 1992, when the Conservative government wanted to close down the largest part of what remained of Britain's coal industry:

'...miners, by and large, were a special breed. Their pride in their work was a pride in their manhood; their pride in their politics was their manifestation of a radical culture based on brotherhood at work' [11].

Now, you get the feeling, as you sit opposite the ebullient 'entrepreneur' in his office, as you stand in the yard where the lorries come and go with the merchandise, with packet-after-packet of cellophane-wrapped tins of chocolate brazil nuts, and bottle-after-bottle of bubble bath adorned with decorative bows, that working here destroys your pride. Your autonomy as a human being, your dignity, your individuality, is crushed beneath the 'management's right to manage', the management's right to hire and fire, the management's right to control your life, the management's right to control the lives of your family. Mining communities fought for generations to break free of this. It's back. It sneaked back in different clothes. The 'modernised' economy, with its 'flexible' labour force, is really the nineteenth century revisited. The past has been crushed, with all the pain to individuals and families that that caused, to make way for people like this. This is the only way we'll compete as an economy.

It was argued in *Coal is our Life* that in the 1950s, 'the prestige of the miner in the working class is higher than it has ever been, and the miner knows this' [12].

In the late 1990s, as the sons and grandsons, daughters and granddaughters of miners turn up, every day, to be told what to do, and how to do it, by the ebullient 'entrepreneur' and the rest of the 'awesome foursome', there is no prestige, and there is no pride. And everybody knows it.

The ebullient, hard-working, entrepreneur's black-and-white view on the world was not shared by everyone in Featherstone. John, the ex-diesel fitter in the pit, had a different black-and-white view. His anger, his wounded pride, was immediately evident when he was asked his views on this factory and its owner:

> *'I'd like to put a bomb under it....he needs a fist down his throat.....I'd like to put my fist down his throat.....he thinks he's doing us a favour by being here......'*

John thought that the ebullient, hard-working, entrepreneur had contempt for local people, and contempt for ex-miners in particular.

> *'At one recruitment meeting he asked all those who were ex-miners to put their hands up. Not one of them got set on'.*

Temporary contracts and casualisation characterise Featherstone and the surrounding towns. Karen, John's co-worker in the security business, married to a one-time miner who had to find work elsewhere, and who thought that the ebullient, hard-working entrepreneur was a 'horid man', explained to me how widespread it was.

'*My husband is on a temporary contract......everybody is....*'

John: '*temporary contracts......the stress that sets up is terrible......Forty years ago, they wouldn't have known what you meant by a temporary contract*'.

Others had little time for the ebullient entrepreneur's 'management style'. Peter, a former administrative worker in a nearby town, 'early retired', like so many others:

'*his attitude is like most employers to employees......he thinks employees are 10 a penny....*'

Apart from the sewing factory, a few jobs at the pop factory, some here at this packaging and wrapping factory, even fewer at the local authority's area housing office, there isn't much work for women in Featherstone. Everywhere you visit is staffed by men. *Coal is our Life* noted the absence of employment opportunities for women, stating that 'in 1944 Featherstone was scheduled as an area which required facilities for female employment' [13]. In Featherstone itself, with a few exceptions, this has not changed significantly. Most women who do work have to travel to other, nearby former mining towns. John:

'It's the women who go out of town to work'. They work in shops, or banks, or for the local authority in roles which might range from administrative work to being home helps and cleaning. The wife of Henry, the Humb Store worker, works three days a week for the local authority, washing old people.

The Union

Casualisation. Temporary work. Insecurity. Low pay. The post-coal economy of Featherstone and every other former mining town is characterised by the same themes. On the site of the former colliery, there isn't a single trade union in evidence. Elsewhere, at the bigger packaging company and the pop factory, there is a form of weak trade unionism. It so weak as to be virtually insignificant. At the most charitable level, unions were probably considered, certainly by management and owners, as being irrelevant in what were relatively small businesses. An anachronism in this post-coal, 'modernised' sector. From another viewpoint, things were more stark: employers didn't want them and workers daren't join them. It is an immense contrast with the past. Here, on this very same, blackened, ground where the colliery once stood, the trade union had once held great sway. To an extent, they had ruled.

The very first day you signed up as an employee at the pit, you became a member of the NUM.. Arthur, the former branch secretary at Ackton Hall, told me:

'You signed on for the NCB, you were in the union. You had no choice, it was compulsory'. The situation hadn't changed up to him leaving, when Ackton Hall closed, in 1985. It was accepted by all: if you were a worker there, you were in the union. The idea that you might choose not to be a member wouldn't even enter your head.

The union's influence was considerable. The branch secretary, whose job it was to deal with day-to-day issues, was allowed quite a bit of time off to attend to these duties, at the company's expense. In truth, once you became branch secretary, that was the last you'd see of manual work for the 'Board', as the NCB and later British Coal was still referred to. Being the branch secretary was a full-time

job. You were a man of influence. It gave you a credibility in the
community. If you were seen in a pub or a working men's club, it
would be pointed out to anyone who didn't know you, in a quiet
tone so that you wouldn't hear it yourself, 'that's Dave, 'e's branch
secretary tha knows'.

The NCB would give the NUM its own office, which usually
amounted to a shed in the pit yard, but it was, nonetheless,
recognition of the importance of the union. And, in any case, all this
was beneficial to British Coal. The branch secretary of the still
operating Prince of Wales colliery nearby told me that 'it works in
their interests' to have him doing this job more or less full-time.
There had been no change to his position since the outfit was
privatised in 1995. Things were all right as it was at the moment. He
did not know what the future might hold, either for his position, or
for the pit itself. They had 'left me alone' but there is 'fuck all
outside of the pit' [in terms of employment].

The union wasn't there simply to deal with grievances and
disputes, though that always remained its major role. It had a series
of other roles, of varying importance. At the mundane level, it
might help to decide who was working when. Arthur said 'they
were allass wanting somebody to work neets'. It wasn't what
everybody wanted. 'It was always a bone of contention'. The union
might be in a position to 'persuade' somebody. It would have
representatives on the health and safety committee. Any change in
conditions, or local pay arrangements, would be something to be
taken up by the union. At the few surviving pits, this changed little
even up to the 1990s. The Prince of Wales colliery, three miles away
from Featherstone, provided an example.

In late 1997, there was a dispute rumbling over changes to terms
and conditions proposed by management. It was all about getting

the men to work 11 hours on Saturday rather than the normal six. The men thought that this would create a precedent. They'd never get back to six hours. While I was there, a delegation of about seven miners came into the NUM's shed-office to complain bitterly about the proposed changes. You got the feeling that, even after all that they had been through in terms of job insecurity and the diminishing power of the workers vis-à-vis the management, they were not men to take things lying down. They would fight, and they expected others to fight on their behalf.

In the past, becoming prominent and active in the NUM might lead to elevation elsewhere. Becoming a school governor was one route into becoming 'important' in local society. Becoming a justice of the peace was another. Working your way up in the local Labour Party was a further, often combined, route to social elevation. You might become the chairman or the secretary or the treasurer of the local party. A particular prize was to be chosen as the Labour Party's candidate for the local council elections. Given the politics of the areas, this meant that you would be elected to the council. To secure the NUM's support carried considerable sway within local Labour Parties. This carried on long, long, after the pits had closed. In March 1998, in Worsbrough, for example, which had seen its own pit close in 1985, the Labour Party's candidate at a local government by-election was the NUM's man. He had, until just a few months before, worked at the Prince of Wales colliery. He took 71 per cent of the vote, beating off the wife of the current National President of the NUM, who came second, taking 17 per cent, standing for the newly-created Socialist Labour Party. What level of importance the local voters attached to this by-election is probably obvious from the level of turnout: 25.5 per cent.

The union was part of the social structure. It was part of your life, day-in, day-out. It would fight on your behalf, through the courts, anywhere they could, for compensation for diseases caused by working in the pit. It would give your widow a small grant on your death. In 1997, it was £50. The men knew that the union was on their side. Again, it boiled down to trust. You might not know quite whom you could trust in the management: but you could always trust the union. Even if they got things wrong occasionally, they would never do so intentionally. Inevitably, and for generations, this had widened the role of the union beyond simply the industrial. As Arthur told me:

> *'.....they'd bring things up to the office.....sometimes they couldn't understand things.....they'd get things wrong.....one bloke was renting a television.....and he thought that, after six years, the tele was his....but it weren't......I used to be involved in the staffing of the faces... a list would be put up.......but they'd come up and say "where am I working?".........they couldn't read.....but I never betrayed 'em....I wouldn't show 'em up...'*

Some were prepared to acknowledge those aspects of the union's influence that might not be universally regarded as positive. Harry, the 66 year-old winder:

> *'There were too many men at the pit without a job.....because of the strength of the union'.*

The NUM's role in the 1970s and 1980s was often castigated, particularly by Conservative politicians and journalists of one sort or another who had little knowledge of what it was like to live in a mining town. But, overall, the NUM was a force for the good. It fought to get industrial diseases recognised, it fought compensation claims for the far too many people killed and injured in the industry, it fought for better wages and conditions on behalf of ordinary men who would not have been able to achieve that on their own. It could be anything: a posthumous claim for 'dust'; a dispute on a claim for concesssionary coal. The role of the union would extend beyond the lives of people currently working at any particular pit. The Prince of Wales colliery, for example, had 400 widows associated with it in 1997 and more than 300 retired employees. Their days at the pit, or their husband's days, were their touchstone of reality. At any time, they might need assistance. They would look to the union to provide it.

The focus of the criticism, obviously, was the strikes and other industrial disputes, especially the national strikes. The mineworkers' union was characterised by some throughout the 1970s as being greedy, irresponsible. It was always far too simplistic an analysis. Disputes exist for a reason.

Largely the important national disputes were out of the local NUM branch's control. Far more important, in terms of trying to understand this underground world, was the high frequency of local disputes.

At Ackton Hall itself 'unofficial disputes were common', according to Arthur. 'There were a lot of relationship problems between the men and the officials'. Ackton Hall 'was a militant pit'. But it wasn't militancy without a reason:

> *'it was simply because there were two seams and one seam was really hot...this was very militant.....the slightest thing, and they'd be going home.....the other seam wasn't as hot, and it wasn't as militant....they worked in the hot seam in a pair of second-hand army shorts....boots and army shorts....that's all they'd wear on the coal face....instead a taking down a flask of water, they'd take down a bloody great dudly'.*

Though the men didn't always secure a 'victory' in a local dispute, 'prior to the '84/85 strike, we'd often go back on our terms.....they wouldn't negotiate while you were out on strike....but once back, it would often be on our terms'.

It was much the same at the Prince of Wales colliery. Dennis, the branch secretary, said:

'....every situation in life is a compromise....if you're going to move forward....it's all a question of balance.....militancy is borne out of the situation that is confronting you.....there's no fuckin' change under privatisation'.

At Prince of Wales,

'yeah.....there were unofficial disputes.....we probably had more than anybody...we had 33 disputes in twelve months'.

And that was after the 1984/85 strike, when the number of disputes had declined. After the strike, at Ackton Hall, Arthur said,

'the disputes quietened down.......the men were flattened ......they were in debt...'

It wasn't as if people wanted militancy. They didn't go into work everyday seeking a rag up. As Dennis said, 'militancy is borne out of a particular situation.....if you treat people heavy handedly, you are going to get a hostile response from the lads....because of the way management treated them...'

The strike of 1984/85, at its end, marked the death of Ackton Hall and the death of the NUM. And its ramifications were even wider. At the Prince of Wales pit, even in this bastion of trade unionism, union membership was down to 70 per cent of the workforce by

1997. Much of this reduction in 'union density', as industrial relations specialists call it, was down to fear. Dennis:

'There has been a large influx of contractors....and these had a reluctance to take up union membership.....they might not get taken on again'.

To be associated with the union, for a temporary contractor dependent upon securing continuing employment through renewal of contracts was too big a risk to take.

Yet, at one time, even the contractors had no choice but to be in the union. Arthur:

'.....they 'ad to be in t'union.....and they were very rare, only brought in for specialist jobs'.

Dennis acknowledged that the environment, the organisation, had changed. But you shouldn't push the workers too far:

'....the workers are a lot more cautious now.....certainly since RJB took over....we know for a fact that it's a business and he's got to make money here, but certain things we will not accept. Certain things will get a bad reaction'.

By the time of the late 1990s, trade unionism in Featherstone, as a social and economic force, was virtually dead. There were no industrial disputes, anywhere in Featherstone, ever. Certainly not at the small employers. Nor at any of the larger ones. In the new economic world, you are cowed and deferential. No longer proud. You can't strike. You daren't.

Private and Public Ownership

All industry, all businesses, in Featherstone in the late 1990s were privately-owned, from the four fish and chip shops through to the haulage and packaging companies that were the town's biggest employers. In the early 1950s, by contrast, and even through the 1960s and 1970s, public ownership had a dominance. The majority of male workers were mineworkers, and all of Britain's large collieries had been nationalised by Attlee's Labour government in 1947.

By the late 1980s and 1990s, 'public ownership' had become so unfashionable an idea that many people no longer even knew its meaning. It had been expunged from the political agenda, expunged from the popular consciousness, expunged from the social lexicon. Even people in positions of responsibility in the public relations departments of privatised companies — people who should have been educated enough to know better — seemed to have no comprehension of its meaning. You question them about how long ago it was that they were in public ownership, nationalised. 'We've been publicly-owned for ten years,' they say. 'No,' you think in response, 'you've been publicly quoted for ten years. You were publicly *owned* before then'. But, of course, you are too polite to say it. And the momentary thought that these people have had hundreds of thousands of pounds of taxpayers' money spent on their education you let quietly pass.

Public ownership, unfashionable as it might have become as we approached the millennium, had never simply meant 'government-ownership' in the coalfields, at least certainly not back in the forties, when it first came in, or even in the fifties. It may never have lived up to its promise, but it had been seen as being about much more than that. It was about power. About moving power from the despised coal barons to the workers. As Geoffrey Goodman argued in 1992, it was 'a dream come true. They believed it was *their* industry' [14].

For a moment in history, it *was* a dream come true. This was the start of something new. A new era. New found security, new found prosperity. It was something the miners' union had fought for since the early part of the century. Nationalisation itself generated enormous optimism among ordinary miners. The past, of accidents caused by mine owners scrimping on money and compromising safety standards, of poverty wages, of traipsing miles on foot to try to find a colliery where you might be able to get a job, was gone. Prior to nationalisation, uncertainty had figured prominently in the miners' life. Piecework wages meant that the miner feared old age or infirmity because he would not be able to work as hard as he once had, and couldn't earn as much money. The very existence of his job was often uncertain: colliery owners would respond to falls in demand for coal by reducing wages, finishing colliers, or closing pits. But nationalisation would end all this. There would now be planned production of an economic resource, and the organisation itself would be owned by the government. As if to emphasise the point, plaques were erected outside each colliery which declared, in heroic, socialist, fashion:

'This colliery is now owned and managed by the people'.

It wasn't just the miners, their union, and the Labour Party that favoured nationalisation. Even the Tories accepted it. Under the Coal Act of 1938, initiated under a coalition 'National' government dominated by the Conservatives, the private ownership of coal royalties came to and end. Ownership of coal deposits in the ground was vested in a Coal Commission set up by the act. Even Winston Churchill, Prime Minister and Conservative leader, and never forgiven for setting troops against miner as Home Secretary in Tonypandy more than 30 years earlier, stated in 1943 that:

> *'The principle of nationalisation is accepted by all, provided proper compensation is paid'* [15].

Funny how times change. You talk to the 'entrepreneurs', whether they are the dynamic, ebullient, aggressively assertive, or whether they are laid-back, ordinary-blokes-made-good who can't remember how many lorries they own or how many people they employ, and you just cannot imagine such a sign, and everything it symbolised, anywhere at all. It is a spirit, a culture, a world, that has passed. It was a fleeting moment in political history; a moment in which it was thought that the collective could achieve more than the individual. It will never happen again. All that is believed in the 1990s, by 'Labour' and by Conservative, is that the successful entrepreneur is the 'key player' in the economy. There's nothing else. There are no grand ideas anymore. Nothing we can strive for, and be proud to call our own.

That is why so many business leaders and 'entrepreneurs' were invited to Downing Street after Labour's general election victory in May 1997, to talk and party with Tony Blair, and Cherie Blair, and Gordon Brown. That is why so many give money to the Labour Party, and hold high positions within it. There used to be a time when you could tell apart the typical high-up in the Labour Party from the typical businessman. You look now, at the parties at Number 10, from tycoon to Labour politician, and from Labour politician to tycoon, and you realise that they are indistinguishable.

Public ownership of industry was also about pride and pride in its most intense form was about heroism. The industry was ours, and we were proud of it. In our way, for short, escapist, periods of time, we were minor heroes.

In the mines and in the coalfields, such heroism was important. It was a social anaesthetiser and a social stimulant at the same time. It calmed us, and it kept us going, even in the difficult times. There was no fat coal baron you were making rich. The heroism of masculinity, provided for by the hardest workers, achieving feats beyond the means of ordinary physical mortals, smashing production record after production record. The heroism of rescue teams, fighting against incomparable danger to save workmates, friends, the loved ones of others, in the bowels of the earth. And, strange as it might seem in the urban lands of the late 1990s, where politically we all believe the same and nobody believes in anything in particular anymore, there was a heroism provided for by public ownership. Public ownership would end all the problems faced by miners and mining communities. It would end the sweat-brow work; the job insecurity; the poverty wages of some workers; the grudge. As the Miners' President, Will Lawther, wrote prior to nationalisation being achieved :

> *'What could be achieved through public ownership? It would win the complete confidence of the miners and their families. Generations of suspicion and hatred would be wiped out, and an entirely new attitude developed towards the coal industry. How can you run an industry efficiently, and get the best out of it, if every miner loathes his industry because of its owners; if every miner's wife swears "her boy will not go down the pit"; if in every miner's home the pit is looked upon as an accursed thing?'* [16].

It never happened. Public ownership was a dream which achieved a presence in name only. Like so many others, it was a dream never realised. It finally came to and end, probably forever, when the

Conservative government privatised the rump of the coal industry in 1994, selling most of what was left to RJB Mining. Well, some said it was selling. Others thought it was more like giving it away. RJB originally offered £914 million. Then it managed to negotiate a reduction of nearly £100 million to bring the price down to £815 million. Then there was the small matter of the debts that were written off by the government: a mere £1.6 billion (17). What RJB got for £815 million was an industry which had had literally hundreds of millions of pounds of taxpayers' investment in the years prior to the sell-off. Maltby colliery, near Rotherham — to take just one pit — had had £200 million in the few years prior to privatisation. For more than three years, the industry had a guaranteed market for its product. Any 'entrepreneur' who couldn't make a go of this had some serious deficiencies.

Come New Year's Day 1995, the industry was back in private hands for the first time since 1946. We'd had our dream. It was back to reality. Then again, there was always Labour. We could always rely on Labour. It was our party. During the course of the privatisation bill in 1994, Labour's then energy spokesman, Martin O'Neill, had made clear his position. There were no ifs, there were no buts. He told the Commons:

> *'The Labour Party is not simply opposed to the bill. It is committed to the re-introduction of public ownership of the coal industry.*

> *'We believe that the coal industry can be safe only when it is in the people's hands and only when miners are employed as public servants'.*

Within six months, Labour had jettisoned these views. In November 1994, the same Mr O'Neill told a coal industry meeting in London:

'While we envisage a national role for coal in our energy strategy, we do not intend to nationalise the industry.'

Labour went on to jettison many more before it eventually won power in 1997. By this time, much of the core Labour values and principles — equality of opportunity, redistribution of wealth from rich to poor — had been diminished or simply abandoned. The prize of power was worth any concession, any twist, any principle. And the working class voters, the voters in the old mining towns, had nowhere else to go. Labour knew that. It could always count on them to provide a bedrock of support, to turn out of their council houses, dutifully, and put the cross in the right place, as they had done for years, and years, and years. You could always win Featherstone. And you could always win Barnsley. They were in the bag.

Politics, in its broadest sense, can be seen to emanate from the economic and social worlds people inhabit and experience. Political attitudes and values emerge from a synthesis of this reality and the way the world is presented to them: by the media, by leading figures in political parties, perhaps by leading figures in a trade union or a company that you work for.

Mining areas were no exception to this general rule. Work was hard, and conditions frequently appalling. Job insecurity had been an integral part of working life at least until nationalisation in 1947, some would argue for longer. Depending on where you were in the country, you might frequently have to move jobs. You might have to uproot your entire family and move them from Scotland, or from the Durham coalfield, and hole them up in some pit village in Yorkshire or Nottinghamshire.

It is almost a law of nature that this kind of economic and social world would lead to the creation of a particular kind of psychological and political world. There were a number of key factors to this, and almost all of them were connected to the concept of 'loyalty'.

First of all, it was crucial that you were loyal, and seen to be loyal, to your family. It followed from this that you must be the 'provider'. The wife would do the domestic work, but the wife and kids must be fed, and that was your responsibility. It stemmed from the same psychological root that infidelity was frowned upon. You were cheating. You were being disloyal. It was this generally accepted psychological outlook that maintained the institution of marriage. As *Coal is our Life* noted: 'marriages in Featherstone do hang together; disintegrations are rare' [18].

I was with a retired miner one evening in the early 1980s in a pub in Barnsley. He was in his late seventies and, after spending 50 years on a coal cutting machine, he was pretty deaf. In the corner, he saw a man with a woman, kissing her. When you're deaf, you shout. He turned to me in what was meant to be a quiet aside. 'That's not 'is wife, yu knu'. He might as well have addressed the entire pub. Not that it mattered to him. He was only telling the truth. The man was cheating.

After loyalty to your family, it was also considered to be of crucial importance that you were loyal to the union. This was central. As a fitter at the pit said, when asked his views on those returning to work before the end of the strike in 1985:

'I don't agree with everything the union does but you don't desert it' [19].

And, whatever your level of involvement in politics — even if it was simply as a voter in periodic local and general elections — it was important to be loyal to the Labour Party. To not vote Labour was seen, at best, as being the product of eccentricity. At worst, it was seen as a betrayal of the community, the actions of someone guilty of disloyalty.

Mining towns returned MPs to parliament with the largest of Labour majorities. There used to be a joke that there wouldn't be a count of Labour votes: they'd simply weigh them.

Labour changed dramatically after Tony Blair became leader in 1994. The voters in the former coalfields remained loyal to Labour, but not everyone within the miners' union, and not everyone within the wider trade union movement, were happy with the reforms. As John, the ex-diesel fitter in the pit, and also a Labour parish councillor, told me:

> *'I detest New Labour....I'm a hypocrite because I'll stand under the Labour banner....we're getting no help from the Labour Party here at local level....the party was put there to redress the balance between rich and poor....it has no intention of doing that....'*

Dennis, the branch secretary of the Prince of Wales colliery:

> *'Look at it from the fucking Labour perspective.....they've done nowt for me....they've done nowt for us......I've got a letter from [John] Battle saying nowt about doing owt for coal....'*

Battle had ministerial responsibility for coal. Labour had, in fact, done something, or at least started to do something. December 1998 saw the announcement of the Coalfields Regeneration Trust and the Coalfields Enterprise fund. The former was set up as an independent charity, backed by government money, aiming to bring about some kind of regeneration in 'pit villages'. The latter was targeted at stimulating the small business sector. All in all, there would be a further £354 million of government money to spend over three years. But by this time, it was too late to save the coal industry itself. And from the perspective of the canteen at Prince of Wales colliery, it is easy to see why it felt like 'nowt'.

If the issue was that there was nowhere else for the working class voter to go, there was an attempt to provide them with an alternative home, and the attempt was started in the coalfields. The 'Socialist Labour Party' was launched, officially, on 1 May, 1996, by the mineworkers' president, Arthur Scargill. Some others from the miners' union followed him. Frank Cave, Yorkshire NUM Chairman and National NUM Vice-President, was one; Ken Capstick, who had been Vice-Chairman of the Yorkshire NUM, another. It was to be a party of uncompromising socialism. It was in favour of equality, and public ownership, and it would encourage 'industrial action' in defiance of 'unjust laws'. It would 'require a simple socialist constitution and a structure designed to fight our class enemies' [20].

Scargill had, of course, for years been a member of the Labour Party. But when Scargill was a member, the Labour Party had room for those who were openly committed to socialism. Scargill was, and made no secret of it. Alongside Tony Benn, he was, for many years, seen as a leader of the left within the Party. After Tony Blair's elevation to the leadership, Labour ceased to have any truck at all with anything that remotely resembled socialism. Mrs Thatcher, when Prime Minister in the 1980s, used to state that one of her main political aims was 'killing socialism'. For a Conservative, that seems entirely laudable. Mr Blair sought to kill it within the Labour Party.

'New' Labour was a complete re-definition of the party: what it shared in common with its predecessor was confined to its name.

Disloyalty to the Labour Party might traditionally have been seen within mining communities as being bad. But now, the claim that was being presented was that the far greater crime was Labour's: they had betrayed their own community, betrayed the cause of socialism. The greatest apostasy, on this viewpoint, was Labour's abandonment of its constitutional commitment to common ownership, Clause IV, at the April 1995 special conference. According to Scargill, the Socialist Labour Party was:

> *'....born in response to New Labour's betrayal of the commitment to common ownership, abandonment of socialism and open support for the "free market" and capitalism'* [21].

Yet Scargill's belief in the need for a new party has not found a great deal of accord within the former mining towns, or indeed in many other places, if electoral results are be taken as the test of popularity. Featherstone itself formed one part of a parliamentary constituency where there was a by-election in February 1996. It should have been promising territory for Socialist Labour: it had, until recently, been a mining area, with one of the heaviest concentrations of mining in western Europe; its candidate had been a prominent member of the Women Against Pit Closures pressure group; Scargill's own connection to mining was obvious and, in theory at least, as president of the NUM, he should have been able to command some loyalty from former miners and their families, and from those still at work in the industry.

But they didn't win; and they didn't come anywhere near to winning. Socialist Labour won 1,193 votes, or 5.4 per cent of those cast, coming fourth behind the Liberal Democrats, who secured

1,516, or 6.8 per cent. Whether or not this represents any kind of success is a matter of debate. Securing more than 5 per cent meant that they saved their deposit, and Scargill himself made great play of this. Moreover, when compared with how 'far left' parties have fared electorally in other places, the vote gained was highly respectable. It doesn't really matter where you look for comparisons, but if the 1992 general election is taken as an example, a Revolutionary Communist Party candidate standing in Birmingham Selly Oak gained a grand total of 84 votes, or two per cent of the total votes cast; in the same election, a Communist League candidate standing in Sheffield Central succeeded in securing 92 votes, or 0.3 per cent of those cast [22].

It is not clear, however, that these are the right kind of comparisons to make. The Revolutionary Communist Party, the Communist League, the Socialist Workers' Party, and all the rest of the permutations never stood any chance anywhere. Scargill had far greater pretensions for the Socialist Labour Party. They wanted to replace Labour in these areas, and they didn't. And yet, somehow, as he had done with the strike of 1984/85, Scargill managed to contrive a victory out of the situation:

> 'To nearly equal the Liberal Democrats when we did [sic] not launch the party until May is remarkable. Five per cent is excellent. We did not lose our deposit. A century ago Keir Hardy lost his deposit and went on to form a mass party and the rest is history' [23].

There was another by-election in an adjacent seat, another formerly heavily-mined constituency, in December 1996. It was the same story. Again, there should have been some potential for Socialist Labour. Their candidate was well-known within the mining industry, having been vice-chairman of the Yorkshire NUM. Large parts of the constituency were in poverty. But it didn't break the inertia of the Labour vote, not that that many people bothered to turn out. Socialist Labour took just over 5 per cent of the vote, managing to get 949 people to put the cross in the requisite place. Less than 34 per cent bothered to go down to the polling booth. Might as well watch telly.

Others took a view different from that of Scargill on the new direction of the Labour Party. George, the former deputy at Ackton Hall, and Labour parish councillor, reflecting on the creation of 'New' Labour told me that:

> *'summat had to be done to win power. There's no other way to get in. All we want is to get into power'.*

By the time of the Paisley South by-election, in November 1997, Socialist Labour's vote had dropped to 153. They beat the Natural Law Party, but were pushed behind 'Scottish Independent Labour — Justified and Ancient', 'Scottish Socialist Alliance — Fighting Corruption', and the Pro-Life Alliance. 153 was the level of that normally gained by the Revolutionary Communist Party, the Communist League, the Socialist Worker Party....

The 'new' world has displaced the old in mining areas. Scargill's Socialist Labour Party was, at least in part, an attempt to rebuild the old. But it didn't work, and it probably couldn't work, because there were so many social, political and economic forces against it.

You can summarise the 'new' world in Featherstone. You won't be in a union. You'll be on low pay. You'll do what the factory manager says. You'll mind machinery. If you work and you're a woman, it will be out of town. You'll vote Labour, because you can't bring yourself to vote for anybody else. You'll pray to God, every day, that you win the lottery.

NOTES

1. Paul Thompson with Tony Waylay and Trevor Lumps, 1983 *Living the Fishing*. History Workshop Series. Routledge and Kegan Paul.

2. Coalfield Communities Campaign, 1986 'The written evidence of the Coalfield Communities Campaign. Presented to the House of Commons Energy Committee during their investigation into the coal industry in February 1986. Prepared by the Secretariat of the Coalfield Communities Campaign,' in *Working Papers*, Volume 4, Coalfield Communities Campaign, Barnsley.

3. For an overview, see R.Turner, 1993 *Regenerating the Coalfields*. Policy and Politics in the 1980s and early 1990s. Avebury. Aldershot.

4. Gareth Rees and Marilyn Thomas, 1991 'From Coalminers to Entrepreneurs? A case study in re-industrialisation', in Malcolm Cross and Geoff Payne (eds) *Work and the Enterprise Culture*. Falmer, London.

5. *Coal is our Life*. Page76.

6. *The Daily Telegraph*, 12 November 1997.

7. A.Wigfield, 1997 *Post-Fordism, Gender and Work: Restructuring in the Nottinghamshire Clothing Industry*. Unpublished PhD thesis. Nottingham Trent University.

8. Nottinghamshire European Textiles and Clothing Observatory, 1994 *The Nottinghamshire Textile and Clothing Sector*. A State of the Industry Report. An Initiative in support of the Nottinghamshire Apparel Industry. December.

9. Norman Dennis and George Erdos, 1992 *Families without Fatherhood*. Institute of Economic Affairs Health and Welfare Unit, London.

10. Norman Dennis, 1993 *Rising Crime and the Dismembered Family*. How Conformist Intellectuals Have Campaigned Against Common Sense. Institute of Economic Affairs Health and Welfare Unit, London.

11. Geoffrey Goodman, 'A proud history, on the slag heap', *The Independent*, 15 October 1992.

12. *Coal is our Life*. Page 90.

13. *Coal is our Life*. Page 76.

14. Goodman, 'A proud history, on the slag heap'.

15. *House of Commons*, Official Report, Vol 392, col. 921, 13 October 1943.

16. Quoted in Margot Heinemann, 1944 *Britain's Coal*. A study of the mining crisis. Victor Gollancz, London, pp 11-12.

17. *The Guardian*, 31 March 1995.

19. *Pontefract and Castleford Express*, 14 February 1985.

20. Arthur Scargill, 'An open invitation', *Red Pepper*, No. 20, January 1996.

21. Arthur Scargill, 'Why Socialist Labour', *Socialist News*, Paper of Socialist Labour. September 1996.

22. R.Turner, 1995 '"New Labour" and whatever happened to the British left?' *Contemporary Review*, Volume 267, Number 1555, August.

23. *The Guardian*, 3 February 1996.

PLAY

Leisure pursuits have seen both change and continuity in the four decades since *Coal is our Life* was published. There is still a bingo hall, there is still a rugby club. Most of the same pubs and clubs still exist. Beer is still the main social lubricant, though other substances which induce physical and mood changes, never used at all in the Featherstone of 1956, are now not uncommon.

Leisure in the 1950s, like so much else in life in Featherstone, was governed by the constraints imposed by, and the requirements of, the coal industry. Coal was not simply an industry, not simply a job. Coal was a way of life.

In the 1950s, when *Coal is our Life* was published, you would have started work at 15 in the pit. Prior to 1947, a 'lad' would have started at 14. This ordered life and instilled a compulsory form of social discipline. You were a callow youth, but you were in a man's world. It was likely that you worked close to your father, your brother, your cousin, the boys you went to school with. Your father probably got you the job. There wasn't the opportunity to step out of line, to transgress the norms of the community. You'd soon be brought to heel. As a former faceworker at one of the local collieries who went on, ironically, to work as an undercover drugs agent for the police, said to me:

> *'You'd leave school, start at the pit, there'd be peer pressure to make you act sensibly. You don't have that now. They just drift. If you were seen to be acting anti-socially in the past, you'd soon get it in the neck. When I started at the pit, my father worked there as well. If I did something wrong, my dad would soon find out. You were stuck in a confined space with older blokes. You haven't got that now'.*

Orwell noted in *The Road to Wigan Pier* that people from the middle class such as him might see being forced to start work so young as cruel, but that it was not seen by the working class in these terms.

> *'It seemed to me dreadful that the doom of a "job" should descend upon anyone at fourteen. Of course I know now that there is not one working-class boy in a thousand who does not pine for the day when he leaves school. He wants to be doing real work, not wasting his time on ridiculous rubbish like history and geography. To the working class, the notion of staying at school till you are nearly grown-up seems merely contemptible and unmanly'* [1].

And so it did. The tradition in northern mining communities, throughout the 1950s, 1960s, 1970s and 1980s, was that you left school as early as possible and, if you were destined for it, started at the pit as soon as you could. You wanted the money.

The undercover policeman's pit was one of the last to close in the area, surviving until November 1993. Whilst pits all around had been closing for years, the closure of Frickley-South Elmsall had not been expected. It was one of British Coal's most productive collieries. It had been described by them as late as August 1990 as 'a big-hitting colliery....it will last well into the next century' [2]. That it was closed so peremptorily, and after long term promises had been made, further dashed the hope and the morale of people in the locality. If Frickley could close, nothing would surprise anybody any more. Nothing was safe. British Coal's promises obviously weren't worth the paper they were written on. It was the same as with Ackton Hall: hopes raised, only to be dashed.

The Welfare

Apart from the pit head winding towers which disappeared in the mid-1980s, the most dominant building in Featherstone up until the early 1990s was the massive miners' welfare building. Most mining villages in Britain, from Fife to Kent, had 'welfares', though their size and function varied considerably. In some places, they were often little more than sports changing rooms with communal halls. Great Houghton's looks like an old chapel. It dates from the early part of the century and is basically just a hall, which could and still can be used for meetings or dances. There is no alcohol on sale there and never has been. Elsewhere, however, welfares were veritable cathedrals of the proletariat, architecturally distinctive outside, and inside, selling beer, displaying photographs of moustachioed and sometimes bearded working class heroes, and other potent working class symbols: trade union leaders, mine rescue teams, local NUM branch banners.

Miners' welfare clubs were truly communal facilities. Some started off as cinemas and libraries. In many cases, they were often the only real focal point in the village. When they were first established there was little or no public transport, and no private transport, except for bikes. You couldn't get very far, and had to look to your own village for everything. This was particularly important given that many mining localities were somewhat isolated geographically though, as the authors of *Coal is our Life* noted, this was never a problem for Featherstone even if it remained, in some ways, socially isolated. The importance of welfares should not be overlooked. In 1955, the same time as the research for the first book on Featherstone was being carried out, the miners' welfare clubs were the fifth biggest distributor of films in the country.

Many industrial workers have had, still do have, 'clubs' of some sort: bus drivers, railway workers, steel workers. But none of these places became the focus of social activity that miners' welfares became. Generally, the largest institutes were in South Wales. There the institute would often have a library, cinema and function room. It was the cultural, social hub of the community. It was physically the biggest building in the village. And it was much more than simply a workers' drinking club. Even as late as the 1984/85 miners' strike, welfares were often the epicentre of strike organisation and of the 'alternative' welfare state that developed at the local level. Some became soup kitchens, more reminiscent of 1930s depression-hit Britain than the late twentieth century. If you drove through a mining town such as Barnsley at particular times of day, you would see long queues of men with their children waiting to see what food had arrived at the welfare, either in collections from the local community, or in donations from sympathetic trade unions.

Coal is our Life describes how the miners' welfare institute was 'by far the biggest building in Featherstone'. It provided a focus for a wide range of social and cultural activities there: a venue for amateur dramatics; occasional concerts; a dance for young people where you might find yourself a girlfriend or a boyfriend; a boys' club and a boxing club; billiards; a meeting place for the local Labour Party. As Harry, the former winder, told me: 'it had a dance hall, and people came from all over. Lots of places had dances on Saturday nights — Hemsworth, Pontefract — they were always full of young people'. Pitt, writing about the Kent coalfield, noted that it was the same there [3].

In South Wales in particular, but also in some other coalfields, there was a strong link with education. Adult literacy classes would be run at the welfare. Welfares were infused with the spirit of progress: if we worked together, if we supported each other, we could make it into a better world. And if we couldn't, our children would. There would be no public library in the village, so one would be set up at

the welfare. Reading rooms would be established: many otherwise
would never have read a newspaper. Many could not afford to buy
one. Indeed, in Featherstone, the old library established by the
defunct West Riding County Council was built adjacent to the
former welfare. Prior to that, there was a reading room on the
ground floor of the welfare itself. If you go to the former mining
village of Pilley, just south of Barnsley, the working men's club there
still incorporates 'reading room' into its title on the sign outside.

Now in South Wales the link is not so much with adult education as
with drugs. In the heart of what was the coalfield, by 1996 two
welfares — Markham and Crumlin — housed drug and alcohol
counselling teams. The clients range from 16 upwards. The team
was funded by the government for three years, but then they had to
turn to Comic Relief for money. If it wasn't so bloody tragic, it
would be comic. Next, they were turning to the Lottery. Life is a
lottery. Don't be born in a pit village in South Wales. Don't be born
in Featherstone.

Joan, the co-ordinator of the counselling service, explained how, in
the last 15 years, the problem had 'increased dramatically'. What,
did she think, were the reasons?

*'A lot of them have personal problems. Where else would you expect
kids with no work to keep quiet?'*

Featherstone's welfare, Harry said, had a 'unique front': an entrance
with a double staircase. On the ground floor of the imposing
miners' welfare institute was a billiards room with seven or eight
tables. There was a reading room on the ground floor. Subscriptions
would be collected from miners for an accident fund, emphasising
the ever-present threat of personal or collective disaster. It is not so

many years ago that such collections were being made regularly. Yet, it seems a world away from the lives of so many people now who never have need to stop for a minute to consider that going to work on a particular day might irreparably physically damage them, or even kill them. Coal was a way of life. Danger was a way of life. It was there every day. If you heard loud alarms ringing at an unusual time at the pit, your first thought was that there'd probably been an accident. And your second was that it might be someone you cared for. Someone you loved.

On the first floor of Featherstone's welfare was a dance hall with a hard wood floor. There was also a stage. In this centre for working class culture, there were even dressing rooms on the top floor for aspiring local thespians. We didn't skimp. It was important to demonstrate to the outside world that we were as good as anybody. It was a matter of pride.

But it didn't last long. In retrospect, we should have known it wouldn't have. Mining communities were always fiercely proud. It was a trademark characteristic. There was a collectivity which instilled a culture of pride based on traditions of hard work, 'providing' for the family, and sharing and dealing with problems within the community. It was a culture fostered on a dream that tomorrow would be ours. There was a strong sense of realisation that yes, we were pretty close to the bottom of the social heap. And yet, I can remember so vividly the way that this was dealt with, the way that community pride provided the solution that stopped the problem dead. It was simple and, like so much else in mining towns, it was blunt. To anyone from another social class, from another social background: 'Tha no better than me.'

And, of course, in the old scheme of things, nobody was, at least in the perception of the miners and their families. I remember 1972 so vividly, the year of strike victory. This was the apogee. This, we thought, was the start of the realisation of the dream. All of a sudden, we were the kings. Nobody could touch us. We were proud, we were happy. We were needed. The country needed the coal and, all of a sudden, the country needed us.

Returning to Featherstone in the late 1990s, the welfare building has gone, gutted by fire earlier in the decade. It closed as a miners' welfare in the late 1960s. You stand outside and reflect on the new world in Featherstone. It is as if the spirit of collectivism which it symbolised has gone with it too. It has given way to a more modern, less grandiose building of smaller proportions, which housed five small businesses: a taxi company, a motor repairs company, an industrial and commercial decorators, an industrial and commercial electrical business, and a gym. Three of the five businesses are in the ownership of the same family, which also owns the building itself. The old library still stands, and that too is in the same family ownership. It was occupied in the late 1990s by a man in the construction trade who sprayed polyurethane on to roof tiles to stop them slipping.

The first person I met as I entered the building was Paul. Paul was 32. He used to repair machinery, initially at one of the local pits and then later at Selby. He was forced to take redundancy from his job because, in an early prelude to complete privatisation, the work he was doing was taken over by a firm of contractors. As the ultimate symbol of the transition to post-industrialism, he now looked after the gym, alongside another male instructor. It was from work to play, where the play had become the work. He had always 'worked out' as a hobby. He asked me if I ever 'worked out'. I offered an evasive answer. To have been honest, to have told him that it had never even entered my head, might have demoralised still further an already demoralised man. Demoralised, but tall and strong. Strength had been a useful attribute at the pit, and was useful here.

He'd come into this work by chance, through his contacts in the
physical fitness 'industry'. If he hadn't have ended up here, he'd no
idea what he might be do.

His life story, in many respects, seemed to reflect in microcosm the
new uncertainty that gripped mining areas in the 1980s and 1990s.
He was earning 'less than a third' of what he had previously earned
at the pit. He was, he said, 'lucky to earn £150 a week'. It was, just,
enough to keep body together. But his soul was being torn apart by
a rapidly disintegrating marriage. He wanted to tell me all about it.
About how he needed a social life, but his wife wouldn't let him
have one. About how his wife didn't want children, but how he did.
And about how he had to find some woman who did want children
before it was 'too late'. His mind was in turmoil. 'I'm telling this to
a total stranger', he said, repeatedly and with desperation, 'but I've
got to tell someone'.

I was someone, but I was not anyone in particular. I reflected back,
to the time when the welfare was still standing, still buzzing with
waistcoated miners coming and going in-between their day and
night shifts, and I thought back about the shared camaraderie
amongst the men. Paul needed to talk to a man. For this particular
purpose, on this particular day, a woman simply would not do.
There would have been many a man willing to lend an ear, in those
days, as they leant over billiard tables, pretending to be more
interested in potting the ball than listening, yet their serious, fixed,
lined faces would betray the fact that what they were really
thinking about was their own quiet, personal lives, their own
dilemmas and anxieties and, perhaps, sharing those problems with
Paul. The billiards were fun. But on days like this, you were
thinking of things other than potting the ball. In the 1990s, the
camaraderie that had been such a therapeutic strength, such a force
for good, had gone forever. Now, it was replaced by a few
decorators, loading up their van and going off to do a painting job

somewhere. Around the corner, yet another car would have yet another exhaust fitted. Women would come for their weekly aerobics and step classes at night, overweight thighs clad in tight purple lycra. Huge hulks of men, thick necks with veins bulging out of them, would heave their muscles against the constraints of some steel and rubber body-wrenching machine, convinced in their own minds that this had some purpose. What remained on the site of the old welfare — the decorators, the electricians, the motor repairers — no longer provided the old socialising, anaesthetizing, and collectivising function. There were no longer any symbols of social progression and community pride. It was simply a receptacle for minor forms of economic activity. It could have been any old building.

Paul explained too that not enough people were coming to the gym to make it viable. His insecurity was compounded by this. At the pit, at least until the 1980s, you'd known that your job was fairly safe. And, even if it was taken away from you, you'd get redundancy money. 'Featherstone is a bigger drinking place than an exercise place', he said, by way of explanation as to the lack of customers. Some things never change.

Beer itself, however, was never sold at the welfare. But you could easily get beer. There were two working men's clubs within one minute's walk, and a pub the same distance away.

The end of the welfare itself seems to have been brought about by a parochialism so excessive that it led to self-destruction. Miners' welfare clubs were run by committees, nominated by the management of the then NCB, NACODS and the NUM. Some of those on the committee at the time were involved with other clubs, in particular with the social club of the local rugby team. To get rid of the welfare would reduce the competition facing the other clubs. George, the former deputy, told me:

> 'They sold it. They got £27,000. There was a lot of intrigue in them days. But it knocked the bottom out of our social life. There was nowhere to go. We lost it for dramatics, dancing. Featherstone used to be buzzing'.

The money that was received was used to build a big pavilion on a recreation ground some distance from the town centre. Or, as George put it, less charitably:

> 'Instead of having another welfare hall, they spent it on a big pavilion. A bloody useless thing'.

There was another explanation — other than rivalry and parochialism — of why the welfare met its end. Harry believed that 'the welfare went into decline because no one was using it'. Its demise was probably a combination of lack of customers and parochialism.

In any case, parochialism in mining communities was endemic. To make such a statement is not to castigate or criticise, but social reality cannot be ignored. In fact, in some ways, parochialism was a source of community strength and a totem of community pride. As Pitt stated in his 1970s study of Kent miners:

> 'The pit and the village isolated the miners from their fellow industrial workers and turned them inwards, away from the outside world and towards their workmates, wives and families' [4].

Parochialism was reflected in the lack of willingness to leave a locality and in the inward-looking nature of the community, which looked to its own to socialise, to help when assistance was needed, to procreate. Sometimes its intensity was such that it might be difficult for outsiders to understand. Barbara, the ex-miner's wife in her sixties, hadn't been on holiday for 15 years when I spoke to her in 1998 in Great Houghton. She wasn't rich, but it wasn't a lack of money that stopped her going. Rather, she couldn't bear to leave this village of 2,300 souls. She might miss something.

She wasn't alone. Tony represented the next village, also a mining area, on the council. He was in his late fifties. He'd been a 'skilled machinist' at one of the British Coal workshops there used to be dotted about to mend equipment from the pits. He'd been exposed to the world: involved in the cut and thrust of local politics, meeting national political figures. He'd been abroad on trade missions, going with other council representatives to Chicago, for instance. But for him, like so many others, there was a comfort and security in the pit village, where you knew everybody. And you can understand it. You can see it as negative, because it's parochial and inward looking, or you can see it as a sanctuary: you know everybody, and everybody knows you. He told me, 'I don't like being away from home.....I miss it'. Not married, he lived next to his sister in this former pit village of 8,000 people on the east side of Barnsley.

John, the ex-diesel fitter, who had worked in a pit in a village a couple of miles away from Featherstone, provided another example as he described attitudes there:

> 'It's like another world......they don't like anyone coming into the pit from another pit, or from another village....they are all related...'

Yet another reflection of it was that you didn't expect to travel far to work. Your work and your friends and your family, ideally, should be on your doorstep. Dick had been a deputy in the smaller of the two pits at Little Houghton. We met at Great Houghton miners' welfare hall in 1998. He volunteered the information about his lifestyle and summed up how life might have to change in Great Houghton:

> '....I was made redundant.....I couldn't handle not going to work.....I missed my friends.....we were brought up not to travel far...we used to walk to work......younger people are going to have to get used to travelling....we might think 10 miles is a long way.....we got to get used to that...'

Parochialism was limiting, but parochialism also meant strength, because parochialism meant information. You knew who you could trust. You knew whether your daughter should marry someone's son from the next street, because you knew the family, the lineage, whether or not someone had come from 'good stock'. There was none of the turbulence and transience that characterised inner city populations from the 1970s onwards. You knew where you stood.

The welfare was an arena of close co-operation between coal industry management and the miners' union. The dominant image of miners throughout the 1970s and 1980s was of militancy. There was substance behind the image. But in the hidden world, co-operation at the welfare remained intact. There could be bitter industrial struggles taking place outside, such as in 1972, 1974 or 1984, but at the welfare the committees of union men and management men still met. Co-operation, in normal times, took several forms. A worker would often be seconded to be the groundsman and handy man at the welfare, for example. He would be paid the same as when he worked in the pit. He would cut the grass, roll the cricket pitch, lay down the white lines for football. He would be regarded as a 'lucky bastard' to have secured such salubrious work. In the pub, they'd call him that with mock derision. 'Charlie, you fuckin' lucky bastard, get pints in'. Charlie would laugh. They'd all laugh.

Whatever materials were needed by the welfare would be provided from the pit if possible. If the wiring needed fixing, the electrician from the pit would come to do it, in British Coal time. Often, it would be a British Coal accountant that would do the books for the charitable trust that ran the welfare. These activities all imposed financial costs on the industry, but this was considered more than worthwhile in the maintenance of goodwill.

Contrast it with now. Goodwill? Between workers and management? It's a rare commodity. You go to Featherstone in the 1990s, and you talk to the ebullient entrepreneur, and he tells you that he'll set workers on for three weeks at a time, to do 'mind bogglingly boring' tasks, and he tells you that 'they do the work, they have to'. At least when the coal was there, goodwill was important. An anecdotal tale from the Yorkshire coalfield has it that, in the move to 'macho-management' which characterised the early 1980s and onwards, management at national level wanted to stop this support to welfare institutions in order to cut costs. The director of the Yorkshire coalfield is said to have refused to comply, insisting that the disharmony that would be provoked would cost far more in reducing goodwill between management and workers. And of course he was right.

Sport

Traditionally, inextricably linked to the welfares was an emphasis on sport. Sport was often seen as being crucially important by sections of the community, and the welfares provided places where it could be organised and played. An outsider would scarcely

believe the extent of provision in some of the small pit villages. If
you go to Dodworth, just to the west of Barnsley, you will see a bit
of a welfare building, but not notice anything very special about it.
If you delve further in, behind it are acres devoted to sport: football
pitch after football pitch, bowls, five-a-side football on tarmaced
ground, cricket pitches, changing rooms, even a bit of a grandstand.
Whichever pit village you were in, there were always rumours that
some scout from one of the big clubs had spotted the footballing
talents of one of the local lads, and were poised to change his life
forever, get him out of the pit, offer big money for him. I can't
remember it ever actually happening.

Soccer and cricket were particularly important. If you could excel at
both, you would become particularly admired. All the welfares had
soccer and cricket teams, and many of the players would work at
the pit. The playing facilities were often lavish and extensive. There
was often more than one football pitch, in later years there might be
floodlights. There might be cricket pitches and bowling greens. In
the Yorkshire coalfield, in particular, there was a great emphasis on
outdoor recreation. Rossington welfare, near Doncaster, for
example, had 20 acres of land for sports; Brodsworth, Thorne, and
Bentley, also all near Doncaster, had 20 and 20 acres respectively.
Sport was an important part of life. And you need not ever give it
up. You could progress from a fit soccer player in your youth to the
more relaxed pastime of bowls later on.

One of the differences between sport in Featherstone and sport in
some other mining villages was the emphasis on rugby league.
Rugby league is, of course, important in some other towns
associated in the past with mining, but often these were much
bigger commercial centres, such as Wigan and St Helens.
Featherstone is small and yet managed for many years to sustain a
famous and, at least at times, successful rugby club. And rugby isn't
just played at that level. There are several other, amateur, rugby

clubs, some of them associated with pubs. Ziggy used to play rugby, and once had trials for the national side. But his 10-year gaol sentence put paid to both his sporting and career ambitions. He didn't tell me what his 10-year gaol sentence was for. And I really didn't want to ask.

In *Coal is our Life*, the authors focus on the importance of rugby to Featherstone, citing how it was a central topic of conversation in the pubs, clubs and down the pit. Others argued subsequently that they over-played this, catching the town when it was in a mood of euphoria. Featherstone's team had, after all, reached a turning point in 1952, making it to Wembley to the Challenge Cup final. They lost at Wembley, but it was an outstanding achievement for a small club.

Rugby is still important in the late 1990s, but it is no longer so dominant. The teams are still there, and it is still an outlet for a fair number of people that way inclined. When preparations were being made for the new Super League, and a proposal was made to merge Featherstone Rovers with two nearby clubs in order to gain entry, many fans felt sufficiently angered to invade the pitch, and block the main street through Featherstone with traffic. But I never came across anybody in a pub or a club talking about Featherstone Rovers. For many, it was no longer important at all. George, the former deputy at Ackton Hall, told me that:

> 'The interest has gone. When we were down the pit, Featherstone Rovers were the conversation from Monday to Friday. You **had** to be a Rovers man'.

The local side failed to make it into Rupert Murdoch's 'Super League', created in 1996. To qualify, you had to finish in the first 10 of the former first division. Featherstone finished eleventh. As with so many other things, Featherstone didn't quite make it. And of course, in not making it, they missed out on the big money that went to the Super League clubs.

Coal had reached into the world of rugby, just as it had reached into everything else. In the glory days of Featherstone Rovers — the late 1950s and early 1960s; 1967, when they won the Challenge Cup; the early 1970s, when they won it again — many of the players were 'local lads'. Many of them had worked, or still did work, at the pit. These were the days prior to the huge commercialisation of rugby and soccer and cricket and everything else, the days prior to Rupert Murdoch's gladiatorial triumphalism over sport, politics, society, television. You'd play rugby for the Rovers, and keep your job at the pit. You had to in order to make ends meet. They'd let you out of the pit for the training though, and they'd make sure you got paid, somehow.

The extent of the connection between rugby and coal was even stronger than this. Prior to the 1984/85 strike, for example, a lot of mineworkers would be members of the club, and if they bought season tickets, they would have an amount deducted each week from their pay. They wouldn't notice it and often, even after they had stopped going to matches, they wouldn't do anything to have the deductions stopped. Since the pits closed, this source of income for the club dried up.

The coal industry has gone from Featherstone, but there is at least a remnant of its connection to rugby. RJB Mining, Britain's biggest deep mine company which took over British Coal's pits on privatisation, was the main sponsor of Featherstone's rugby team in 1997.

But interest in rugby is no longer what it was. Crowds at the ground are seldom more than 2,000, though in a town of 14,000, proportionately, that is still a high turnout. Perhaps half of them are from Featherstone itself. Some disagreed, arguing that rugby was still important. Bob, the 45 year-old packaging factory shift leader, said to me:

> *'Rugby is still a big passion for the town. You've got to get it into proportion. There are only 14,000 live in Featherstone, but you get 2,000 at the matches. There are 10 million live in Greater Manchester, but only 50,000 are at Old Trafford'.*

But that's because you can only get 50,000 into Old Trafford. If you could get more in, more would come. Featherstone Rovers' ground can hold 6,500. Back in the 1950s and 1960s, its attendance was 4,500 to 5,000 regularly.

The chief executive of Featherstone Rovers put the waning enthusiasm down to changes in the times:

> *'Within the town, there are changing social habits. Men started going shopping with their wives in cars — this was unheard of in the 1950s'.*

In the fifties, men didn't go shopping. Not in Featherstone, anyway.

The emphasis on sport was, at least partly, a reflection of the fact that mineworkers liked being outside. You couldn't blame them. It was good to be outside if you'd been cooped up in an underground hole for hours on end, day after day, where the only light was artificial light. That they kept ferrets, whippets and pigeons is something of a social caricature, but not all caricatures are completely untrue. Keeping whippets and pigeons got you outside,

177

into the fresh air. It was a bit of social escapism, too. Your dog, your pigeon, might actually win the race, you might actually collect the prize money, you might, just might, hit the big time. Being outside, similarly, was part of the motivation for gardening or, if you hadn't got a garden, keeping an allotment. Amongst the older miners, the gardening and allotment tradition survived, even after the pits had gone. You can't give up everything. I asked Betty, the cleaner at Great Houghton miners' welfare hall, what her husband did now that the pit had gone:

'He works on the allotment....I never have to buy any veg or flowers'.

Whippets and pigeons were not as prevalent in the 1980s and 1990s, but they continued to be popular with many. In Barnsley, one man decided to put his house up for sale in 1998. But first he had a few conversions to do. For years, the entire house was a pigeon loft. No humans lived there. He wanted the best for his pigeons.

In one of the former mining areas where I used to live, I took a walk in a 'rec' sometime in the late 1990s. 'Rec' is short for recreation ground. This one was no more than a muddy grass field with some rusting goal posts. Most of them were no more than that. On this particular day I bumped into a friend in his mid 40s. He used to work at the local pit until it closed in 1985. He was exercising two whippets, a black one and a smaller whitish-grey one. I asked him what he was doing now that he'd finished at the pit.

'Nowt, except a bit a dog racing'.

The dogs were obviously important to him, so I asked him about them. His face lit up with pride when he talked about the black one. He'd been 'all o'er' — all over the country — with it. He didn't use these words, but this was a dog underestimated in the whippet world:

'They niver fuckin' expect it to win. But it fuckin' does, lad'.

If you are a man, you often get referred to as 'lad', even if you're 80.

Here was another proud man. Proud of the black dog, proud of winning when others thought it impossible.

I noticed how he hadn't said anything about the whitish-grey one, so I asked him about that. He took the dog's head with both hands and twisted it. He turned his own head on to one side, and contorted his moustachioed face, pulling his lips back to bear his teeth.

'That's nowt', he said with disdain.

'Tha can get a mediocre bitch like that for 'undred quid'.

'She's just here to keep 'im 'appy', he added with evident contempt.

Funny, I thought to myself later, how the division of worlds between men and women extends into a dog-bitch division in the whippet world.

Being good at sport could also get you a job or, at the very least, influence where you worked, and get you some perks. Sometimes, when a pit manager moved from one colliery to another, he would take perhaps six workers with him: not necessarily because they were good workers, more likely than that was that they were in the football team. All this has disappeared. In Featherstone in the late

1990s, work is scarce but, if you can get it, work is work, and sport is sport. There is no inter-connection between the two. And, for most people, the sport that they will see will be beamed in via satellite to a screen in a pub. You won't find anybody changing out of their pit 'rags', as they used to call them, into the Featherstone Rovers strip.

George, the former deputy, recalled the story of his early years in the industry. The pit he had been working at, a few miles away from Featherstone itself, closed down just after the Second World War because of a serious fire. As a young man, he needed another job. As a 'brilliant sportsman', he had little trouble in finding work in the coal industry. On hearing he needed work, someone from the management of Ackton Hall visited the man's father. Clearly, the young man himself could not be entrusted with a decision on where he should work. This was a decision for older men, grown-up men, wiser men. It was agreed between this man and the young man's father that a job would be found at Ackton Hall. The real motivation was that the colliery representative wanted George to play cricket for the local welfare club. At the pit, he was given the job of underground timekeeper, and he got £1 extra — a substantial sum in those days — for playing cricket. They'd make it look as if the £1 was for something else. But, really, it was for playing cricket. Money for playing cricket. You look at the world of the late 1990s where, at least as workers, we've all got to be more 'competitive' and we've got to 'cut-our-costs' and we've got to 'accept pay increases below the rate of inflation', and you ask yourself which was the better world, which was the more comfortable, in which was there the most goodwill?

Pubs and Clubs

There are three pubs on, or just off, the high street that runs through Featherstone. They were there in 1956, and they were there in 1998.

The most popular is nicknamed the 'top 'ouse'. This, too, is a tradition in mining towns. Where it was geographically appropriate, there was often a pub which would be called the 'top 'ouse'. And its counterpart at the other extremity of the street or the hill would often be the 'bottom 'ouse'. Their real names would never get used. It was like this in Featherstone, it was like it in Worsbrough, it was like it all over the place in the mining villages.

In the late 1990s, the 'top 'ouse' in Featherstone is still one of the most socially-important pubs, if it is not too pretentious to call a pub 'socially-important'. It is the most popular pub, it's the pub that is officially named after the town itself, it's the biggest pub, and it's the pub where Featherstone's only identifiable semi-famous man, a local historian who occasionally appears on television, drinks.

It is divided into two rooms: the 'best' side, with its draylon seats and slightly superior decor; and what had undoubtedly in the past been the 'tap oil' (tap 'hole', or room). 'Tap oils' were those rooms in pubs which were slightly less well furnished, would very often not be carpeted, and which would often have a dart board, sometimes a pool or snooker table. It was where older men would play dominoes. And it was nearly always only men who would inhabit unrefurbished tap oils. They would drink steadily, and smoke almost continuously. They still do. There are fewer of them in there but every afternoon, in Featherstone or Great Houghton, you'll find some. They wonder who you are when you walk in. They're not used to strangers.

This tap oil had been spruced up a bit in an attempt to appeal to what was always referred to as 'the younger end'. You never actually questioned phrases like this, because they were in constant usage. And yet, when you think about it, you wonder how these phrases get established. Another one is 'sluffoned'. It's not in the dictionary, but it's still used, especially by the 'older end'. It means sad, despondent, distraught. It was quite a big tap oil, and had a pool table, a 'fruit' machine which collected money from those who voluntarily pushed it into a slot on its front, and occasionally paid some out in return, just to make the punters sufficiently happy to keep returning to push in further coins.

On Friday nights, there is a disco in the best room of 'top 'ouse'. Most times there are between 15 and 20 people there, of both sexes, who range in age from their late twenties to their mid-forties. The music, largely pop 'classics' from the 1970s, 1980s and 1990s, is so loud that conversation is virtually impossible. Excessive decibels is usually associated with youth, but few here would merit that complimentary description. Many here are married couples, or other couples 'going steady'. They've made an effort to dress up a bit. That was also something that stood out in the mining towns: you'd been in rags all day long, all week, so you wanted to dress up when you went out. Especially if you were with your lass. The middle classes didn't seem to care as much. There wasn't so much of a contrast. You might have been dressed up all day, after all.

In the past, if you were an older man, it was often particularly important to pay attention to your hair. A preparation called 'Vitalis' was popular: it was a sort of oil that would keep your hair slicked back. Hair had to be neat, and preferably fairly short. If it was too long, this might be seen as an indication that you were a 'jessie' or a 'nancy boy'. I always thought that Vitalis must have stained the pillows 'summat rotten', as they used to say.

The disc jockey tonight in the 'top 'ouse' is a man in his early forties who stands behind his deck near the door. The poor man has a neck so stiff that, in order to bend his head to look at something, he has to move his entire body in the same direction. But he seems happy. He laughs a lot. His jokes mainly relate to picking on someone in the small band of sedate revellers here and pointing some mild ridicule at them, based upon the state of their appearance, or their alleged laziness at work, or their alleged sexual prowess. The important thing is to make public the perceived private weakness, shortcoming, failure or achievement. The DJ with the stiff neck shouts the ridicule into the microphone so that everyone can hear, even over the deafening sound of Fleetwood Mac or the Eagles. It goes down very well. Ridicule is good fun. Crucially, also, it is important to be able to take it. You have a serious social failing if you can't cope with having the piss taken out of you. It was the same at the pit. Those who behaved too seriously, those who wouldn't, or couldn't, join in with the banter, were subjected to the most acute and prolonged piss-taking. They deserved it. They had to learn to be able to take the piss.

So, even here in a pub on Friday night, while men shovel down pints of bitter, and women imbibe halves of lager more slowly, there are social tests to pass, based upon an ability to deal effectively with ridicule. It has an impact on how you are seen by the rest of the community.

There are limits as to who the social tests will be imposed upon. On another night in the 'top 'ouse', there was a party of men and women with learning disabilities. It was their yearly outing from a communal home that they had a few miles away. Again, there was a disco, but this time there was also karoke. One man, in his late twenties and about five foot tall, was wearing an Elvis suit. He had bought the suit from a shop in a nearby town which sold second-hand fancy dress. He was a big Elvis fan. The suit, white, with red flared insets in the bottom end of the trousers, was tatty and ridiculous. But the suit was his pride and joy. He would volunteer, to anyone who would listen, information on how much it cost, and how long it had taken him to save up for it.

Eventually, as he meandered across the pub floor which had been turned into a makeshift dance-floor, he was passed the microphone.

'Weee......ca....n't....go on too.....gether', he faltered, out of tune, out of timing, out of key, out of rhythm, 'wiith suspicio....us minds'.

But nobody would take the piss out of Elvis. Before the piss is taken out of you, a quick assessment has to be made as to whether the sarcasm is below the belt, as to whether or not you were liable to go too far. Any physical or mental shortcoming would never be pointed to as an object of humour. Nobody would have retorted to the piss being thrown at them by the DJ by calling him a stiff-necked bastard.

If the music is too loud for you on a Friday night in the best room of the top 'ouse, you can always escape to the tap oil. On this Friday night, there were another 15 people in the tap oil. Most of them were much younger, in their twenties. Because this place had been spruced up, there were both men and women customers. Ironically, it was quieter where the younger people were. Cannabis was being smoked openly. Perhaps it is better if it is quieter when cannabis is being smoked. Perhaps the cannabis takes the place of the noise. The cannabis smoking was mainly initiated by a man in his mid-twenties, who looked as if he did this every night that he came into this, or any other, pub, as if it was part of the normal social currency. The smell was all-pervasive, and must have been obvious to the bar staff, but there was no attempt to do anything about it. One of the men involved was at least 50 and, for him too, cannabis smoking was obviously second nature. There was none of the fumbling or inquisitiveness associated with the novice.

As strangers in the top 'ouse, we aroused the curiosity of a tall, thick-necked, big shouldered man in his early thirties who had shaved off what remained of his hair. His bare forearms were covered in tattoos. You could tell that he wondered why we were there and who we were. But he didn't speak. Instead, he just came very close to the table that we were sitting at and stared, for what seemed like several minutes. He just stood there, motionless, fixed, immutable, solid like a rock. It was a menacing stare, a bit like that from a dog guarding its territory from intruders, but without the hissing and the barking that might accompany the stare of a dog. We were intruders. And we were duly warned, lest we do something which might antagonise or patronise.

On Thursday nights, there is a pub quiz in the 'top 'ouse'. This is one of the most popular nights of all, and the pub might get 30 or 40 customers. Towards the end of the night, sandwiches and other food, such as sausage rolls, are brought round. Thursday night was traditionally pay day here, in the days when most industrial workers were paid by the week. So Thursday always had the status of a night when you were relatively 'flush' and could afford a drink. The tradition of Thursday as pay day has largely gone, but the night retains its special status as a night for going out, and the quiz is an added entertainment bonus. The drinking doesn't stop when it is legally supposed to stop. Like some other drinking places in Featherstone, after hours consumption is the norm. You can tell that such bending of the rules is not new. It has been going on for years.

The next pub on the high street also has a quiz on the same night, and again food is brought round as the evening wears on. In this pub Thursday night is unquestionably the most popular night of the week. Quizzes bring people in. There is a chance of winning a gallon of beer.

The third of the three pubs on Featherstone's high street, which is the pub occasionally frequented by Ziggy, and where you will sometimes see three or four slightly overweight women in their late forties in the 'ladies' darts' team, has a 'turn' on a Thursday night. Again, this is the most popular night of the week. Sunday through to Wednesday is dead. Just a handful of people would normally go in, mainly men, sitting there sedately, drinking pint after pint fairly steadily. George, the retired former deputy, explained to me how this pub's fortunes had changed:

> *'Ten years ago, it was one of the best places in Featherstone. There were a lot of houses down there then [small terraced houses, where mineworkers and their families would live]. A lot of pit men used to go in. The houses are knocked down now'.*

'Turns' are popular, not just at this pub, but across the working men's clubs in Featherstone and, indeed, across the north of England. A 'turn' is basically a minor entertainer. It might be a singer or a band, or a comedian. Securing the right 'turn' was a very important issue for the committee. 'Committee men' take their duties very seriously. You have a contribution to make to the local community if you are a committee man, and matters such as making sure the entertainment is up to scratch, deciding on disciplinary action on members who had stepped out of line, are significant issues. Discipline is taken very seriously. Being abusive through drink to other members is probably the most common 'offence'. The committee will often meet on a Sunday morning, and the miscreant will be hauled in front of them to explain his actions. If he apologises, puts it down to the drink and a few 'domestic' problems, and promises it will never happen again, he'll get let off with a stern warning. Little has changed in this respect, despite the massive changes in the economy outside of the door of the working men's club. It's been like this for as long as I can remember. You suspect it always will be.

But the committee is taken very seriously, and takes itself very seriously. A friend of mine once pointed out to me that the stereotypical committee man always had a disposable ball-point pen in the outside top pocket of his jacket. You never knew when you might have to take note of something. Really important committee men would have several disposable ball-point pens, sometimes with different coloured ink, with the tops clearly visible. We used to call them 'pen top' men.

Not many years ago in mining areas, if a 'turn' was not considered to be sufficiently good enough, there would be shouts from the audience to 'pay 'im up'. Where these calls were felt to represent majority opinion within the audience, the act would, indeed, be 'paid up'. This meant that the 'turn' would be paid the money that he or she had been promised, but asked to stop performing. He or she would never be invited back. To be 'paid up' was judged to be a considerable humiliation.

There are three traditional-style working men's clubs on or just off the main high street in Featherstone. All of them have turns on some nights during the week. All of them have roughly the same kind of decor and ambience: the lighting is bright; the seating is basic; the bar is functional, wooden, unadorned; near the stage there is always some element of glitz, usually provided for by brightly-coloured, sometimes sequinned, curtains; the customers are similar types of people because all the clubs have overlapping membership. You escape here for a few hours. You're in the same world, but a different world at the same time. It's different because there's music, different decor, conversation, it gets you out of the house, but it's the same world because you know everybody: all your friends, and your neighbours, and your relatives, are here. It's safe. It's not cosmopolitan. Nothing unexpected will happen. It will still be here tomorrow night, and it will still be the same.

The most popular club remains the one which was most popular in the town in the 'fifties, Red Lane. On a Thursday, it would average 40 people, a few more than the numbers at the 'Top 'ouse'. Mainly, the clientele is male. On this particular night in 1997, amongst the 40 people, there were only 4 women. The ages of the people in there varied. The majority were in their fifties and sixties, but there were some younger ones in their late twenties and early and mid-thirties, a few in their forties. Like voting Labour, like 'providing' for the family, here was another institution where 'loyalty' was seen to be important. If you live in Featherstone and you are not a member, you're not allowed in. If you live outside Featherstone and you're not a member, you can go in. The idea is that if you live in Featherstone, you should be a member as a matter of course. Non-membership is a clear sign of disloyalty to the community itself, as this is the main working men's club in the town. Tom, the former electrician at Ackton Hall, and 'pioneer' at Selby, told me:

> *'They have some owd codger on the door who knows everybody. If someone comes in who's not a member, he'll say "tha's not a member 'ere"'.*

The committee members at this particular club obviously took their obligations towards the local leisure industry very seriously. The club had just spent £180,000 refurbishing its concert room. And the steward, Jim, was particularly well-pleased with himself. Jim, who prior to going into this business had worked as a development worker down the pit, had been nominated for the national award of 'steward of the year'. His move into clubland had been rationally calculated, and he was of the opinion that, with hindsight, he had made the right move. He had been wanting to take redundancy from the pit for a while after the 1984/85 strike had finished, and had tried three times unsuccessfully. On the fourth attempt, he succeeded. Part of his reason for wanting to go was that the atmosphere had changed, very much for the worse, after the strike.

The management were very much more authoritarian and, 'they wouldn't let us work'. He relayed the story of when one manager had told him to go and get something from the stores so that work could begin on developing a new face. When he got to the stores, the workmen at the stores had been told by another manager that nothing must be supplied for this particular pit. 'The atmosphere after the strike was terrible', he said, in that studied way in which people talk when they want to add emphasis. In taking redundancy from the pit early, before it closed, part of his reasoning was that if he didn't get out then and get another job, he'd be competing with another 800 others looking for the same thing.

There is entertainment, in the shape of a turn, three nights a week at this club. On other nights, there is bingo. Posters tell of forthcoming turns, and bill them as 'fabulous boy-girl duo', 'top vocalist', 'knockout duo', 'star trio'.

In the 'Corra', at the other end of the high street, Friday night means bingo. There is bingo most nights of the week. In fact, it's there every night but one. The club's official name, the name on the sign outside, is not 'Corra', or Coronation Club, for which Corra is short, at all. It has a more formal name, after the street it is situated on. So, if you went looking for a place called 'Corra', you would never find it. But, years ago, this place must have been called 'Corra', so 'Corra' stuck. They have the same system of filtering who comes in, making sure only members gain entry. As you walk in, there is a man sitting behind a small, openable, glass window. He is late sixties, or perhaps seventy years old, smoking a pipe, clad in a pale blue zip-up cardigan, with various designs in darker shades of blue towards the top.

This Friday, there are about 70 people in the 'concert room'. Mostly, they are of the older 'end' but there are some here, mainly women, in their twenties and thirties. Some of the older women drink pints. Secondary smoking is compulsory. The air is thick in a blue, lingering, tobacco fug. While the numbers for the bingo itself are being called, you hardly have time to take the cigarette out of your mouth. Tar congeals with saliva, and this keeps it stuck to your lips. A long cylinder of ash forms, and falls into places it is not meant to.

Tonight, on bingo night, there are very formal, ritualistic, rules to adhere to. Bingo is very important and, as with everything else that is important, there have to be rules. Rules provide the structure. Rules signify importance. That is why committees in working men's clubs were and are so important: they implement rules. There were strict procedural rules for Labour Party meetings also, for example, which at one time at least, were important. There were standing orders, and questions through the chair. You could get anything debated, or prevented from being debated, if you knew which sub-clause of which rule to invoke. There were very strict rules for health and safety in the pit. And health and safety in the pit was very important.

At a kind of podium in one corner of the large room sit two men. They obviously have some kind of official position within the club. They probably sit on the 'committee'. At the start of the bingo session, one of the men creates a large banging sound by hitting a microphone with the palm of his hand. This both tests that the microphone is working and, at the same time, calls the players to attention.

The game starts. It is accompanied by a sudden, deafening, hush. This is a serious business. The financial rewards at stake are too important to chance the distraction of a conversation, and you can't risk the seconds it would take to remove the cigarette periodically from the mouth: you might mis-hear a number. After a while, someone shouts 'house' and the silence, and the tension that accompanies it, is suddenly, quickly, broken. There is perceptible relief. People can briefly talk again, let out a little laughter, a little banter, take the cigarette out of their mouth, rock a little in their chairs, cross, or uncross, their legs, move their position. The bingo card is checked. It has been a correct call. It's a full house. Ten pounds goes to the lucky winner. Quickly, silence descends again for another game. It's eyes down. Another tenner is at stake.

Bingo is at one and the same time a strange mixture of the deadly serious and the outrageously hilarious. Yes, it is legs 11, and 2 fat ladies, but while the game is going on the faces here are masks of serious demeanour. As a man once said to me a couple of nights after a near win in another mining town to the south of Featherstone:

> *'A wah sweatin' twice fo't chicken on Setdi neet' [I twice nearly won the chicken on Saturday night].*

Bingo is a ritual, and also a serious game. Like other forms of gambling, it enables you to escape, for a while. And yet it is also symbolic of a kind of entrapment: you're there, every other night, in the same place, with the same people, and every other night you're trapped. Trapped, as you sit there, with the same limited life chances. I asked Peter, the former administrative worker in his late fifties, whether he thought people should seek to leave Featherstone to find employment or, perhaps, broaden their horizons. It was one of the few instances of a local thinking that people should leave. And he immediately brought up the Corra:

> *'Go for the pot of gold, but don't forget where you come from......I was in the Corra last night.....that's it for the rest of their lives, even the youngsters!......unless they win the lottery...'*

Bingo also takes place elsewhere. What was Featherstone's cinema is now a bingo hall. Bingo used to be popular in the converted cinema, especially among middle-aged and older women, though the attendance declined in the late 1990s. George, the former deputy, elaborated on the falling numbers of bingo-players, and the reasons for it:

> *'At one time, you could guarantee a full turn out. Now, they're having to turn the heating off half-way through....On Tuesday and Thursday, there's lucky to be a dozen in. Bingo used to be full. There'd be 500 in.*

> *'There's no money in the economy. There's no money. They've got no money to spend. What they've got, they spend on bingo, or in the clubs. There's nowt else in Featherstone'.*

It was the same with the pubs and working men's clubs. Both during the day and in the evening, there are few customers in unless there is a quiz night or some other attraction. Tom, the former electrician at Ackton Hall, told me:

> *'All the pubs and clubs used to be much busier. Now, if you go into the pubs in the afternoons, you will see the same few people sitting there. The clubs used to be packed on Friday, Saturday, Sunday. They no longer are'.*

It was different in the past. As Tom said:

> *'You had your miner who went out every night. They were all day down the mine, and the rest of the time in the pub'.*

It was the same in Great Houghton. Along the one main street there stood six pubs or working men's clubs. Going in them all in early

1998, none of them had very many customers any more. And drinking, like fish and chips, was a 'cultural norm' in mining villages. The fish and chip shop itself was for sale.

The Night Club

If you are young in Featherstone and you want to find yourself a girlfriend or a boyfriend you go to a night-club at nearby Pontefract named after a state of social and political paradise. The idea of a 'night-club' is relatively new. They were not an aspect of life in Featherstone in the 1950s. They didn't emerge at all in the smaller, northern working class towns until the early and mid-sixties and even then, by and large, they were devoted to cabaret. They hadn't transmogrified at that stage into the darkened halls for thumping music and illegal drugs that they later became. Instead, in the fifties you might visit a dance hall with a live band. In those days, the polite man seeking to gain the attention, and eventually the affection, of a young woman would begin by asking her to dance. Social rituals have since been somewhat modified.

Inside the social and political paradise, it is loud, hot and tacky. But it serves its purpose. All northern towns have a loud, hot and tacky night-club to serve the same end. All of them claim to be the 'most beautiful discotheque in the world' or 'voted the best discotheque in the north' or...... In all of them, music which is indistinguishable from the last and next piece of music is played continuously, and played so loud that no one can verbally communicate with each other. Modified versions of verbal communication take over. You have to get your mouth as close as you possibly can to the ear of the person that you wish to pass a message to, and shout at the top of your voice. You have to repeat this effort two or three times. Even then, it is mostly misheard. Eventually, you give up and slightly raise both arms together while, at the same time, putting your head slightly to one side and tightening the muscles underneath your

bottom lip. This means that you will pass the message on at another
time when it's more easy.

Sometimes, a machine squirts foam onto the dance-floor.
Sometimes, they have young male and female dancers on podiums.
The dancers take themselves very seriously. They never smile. It is
not cool to smile. Young men with short hair and their shirts
hanging out drink directly from small bottles of hugely expensive
lager which tastes exactly like any other lager. Sexual
communication is provided for, at least among the females, by the
wearing of revealing clothing.

The night-clubs change ownership frequently, from one set of
'entrepreneurs' who started life as painters and decorators and
progressed on into letting out property, to another set. They drive
Mitsubishi Shoguns or, if times are really good, Ferraris. Sometimes
the varying owners are friends, and sometimes they feud. But they
are united by one over-riding objective: they are absolutely
determined to make money. Money is more important than
anything. You have to have it. Money is a god.

The last time I went to the social and political paradise was in 1976.
It wasn't a social and political paradise then. It was a tropical
paradise. It had plastic palm trees and fish tanks built into the
walls. The predominant colour, I remember, was a garish purple.
But, then again, this was the 1970s. And Pontefract was a different
world. It had eleven coal mines within a five-mile radius,
employing nearly 11,000. It had full employment. Labour was in
government with at least a semblance of an ideology, instead of the
managerialism that provided the totality of its focus in 1997 and
1998. Fish tanks were tacky, purple was tacky, and moustachioed
men trying to impress women drove tacky sports cars that they had
parked outside, but we didn't mind being tacky in those days. We

were only playing at it anyway. We had other parts to our lives. This was simply a night-time diversion.

The only real difference, returning now, is that there aren't as many customers. Friday and Saturday nights are the only times there are any substantial numbers in but, even then, there aren't as many as there used to be. Thursday nights used to be popular in the seventies, but they're dead now.

Many young men and women 'going steady' in Featherstone in the 1990s initially formed their unions at the social and political paradise. Earlier generations in Featherstone met their partners through family, through school, just through knowing people because this was such a small place. By the time we got to the 1990s, people had started to venture a bit further-a-field in their social lives: nearby towns and cities came within reach for a night out. In this, there was some continuity between the mechanism of introductions and meeting people that served the youth of the late 1990s and the generation immediately before, their parents. A woman caretaker at a youth club in Featherstone described her 19 year old daughter's social life:

> *'She goes to the night-club in Pontefract, or sometimes Cassanova's in Wakefield. Only around Christmas time would she go 'round Featherstone, because there are no buses then. Her boyfriend, who she is going to marry, comes from a few miles outside Featherstone. She met him at the night-club in Pontefract'.*

And she herself recalled how she had first met her husband to be in what was, at the time, Bailey's night-club in Sheffield. It is called Corporation in the late 1990s.

All northern ex-mining towns — Pontefract, Castleford, Barnsley, Mansfield — have night-clubs, and disco pubs which act as feeders to the clubs, that are pretty much the same.

Near to the social and political paradise, there is another night club which caters for the 'older end'. Anything above 25 is the older end. Above the one bar in the place is an illuminated orange strip-light with 'The Scene to Be Seen' emblazoned upon it. Very often, there is an effort in night-clubs to recruit glamorous, female, bar staff. Not here. Most of them are middle aged, and certainly not glamorous. While there are some amongst the crowd in their thirties and forties, nobody on the dance floor is over thirty, but most would pass for ten years older than that. Another, deserted bar within the club is called the 'Can-Can' bar. A tacky picture of two women dancers in can-can pose adorns one of the walls. People, both men and women, dance strange dances, or rather contort their bodies as if to dance, yet to the outside world it would not be recognised as a dance. At the door, three or four men stand together. They are dressed identically, in synthetic, shiny, dark overcoats which rest at their knees, black fake-bill shoes. Their hair is short, and some of them don't have any at all. Their faces are big, and clean shaved. From their ears to their mouths are stretched black plastic devices which connect them to a communication system within the club. At any sign of trouble, they will go into action. They are tough, and there is a credibility associated with it. This is the job to have. This is the place to be.

Heroin

Once, the nearest a miner would get to drugs was chewing tobacco. It was one of the social rituals of mining, something the novice had to be initiated into if he was to be fully a part of his new underground social world. It kept the mouth closed, so it kept out the ever-present coal dust. Some said it quenched the thirst. To those who hadn't acquired a taste for it, it was bitter and foul, and if even a tiny bit of it trickled down your throat, it would make you retch. But if you persevered with the bitter and foul stuff, if you really kept at it, you'd eventually get used to it. It was a part of the miner's world. It was a drug, but it was a legal drug. Many things in the miner's life might not have done him much good — working in the pit, for one thing, smoking, drinking — though most aspects of his life were within the law. And it was a social ritual that you had to incorporate into your life. Malcolm Pitt, in his graphic study of Kent miners in the 1970s, described the ritualistic process:

> *'The chewer bites, or cuts off, about an inch from a half ounce of tobacco leaf rolled into a rope-like strip. He proceeds to champ away at the chew like a cow chewing the cud, until he has extracted all the juice, and spits out a soggy, bleached-brown ball'* [5].

Pitt notes how chewing tobacco was generally condemned as a 'filthy habit'. Yes, it was filthy. It stained your teeth, and your tongue, and your fingers. But it was legal.

Then, there was snuff. You couldn't smoke down the pit. If you did you would risk an explosion by igniting methane ('fire-damp', as the miners called it). It was instant dismissal for anyone found with smoking materials. Nobody would have any sympathy with you if you were caught. You were risking everyone's life. So, like chewing tobacco, snuff was a way of imbibing nicotine without smoking. Some people thought that this, too, was unsavoury. It was habit-forming. It might leave brown stains on your hands. God knows what it did to your nostrils. But it was legal.

And, then, of course, there was beer. Beer drinking was always important. You'd had enough of work, so you'd sink a few. It was a release. For some, what was important was the achievement of a particular level of inebriation. As a man in his mid-fifties said to me as the night was moving towards its end in the urinals of a popular working men's club in what, in mining areas, were the relatively prosperous 1970s:

> ' *t'beer in 'ere is fuckin' rotten. Ass bi glad when av ed enough'. [I shall be glad when I have had enough]*.

But beer, too, despite the extent of health problems its excessive use might promote, despite the number of lost days the economy might suffer through its abuse, beer, too, was legal.

If you visited any former mining settlement in West or South Yorkshire in the late 1990s, you would find that the children and grandchildren of mineworkers have graduated on to something far more powerful, far more addictive, far more threatening to lifestyle, than chewing tobacco, or snorting snuff, ever was. The old mining settlements, where a strict moral working class code of ethics had held sway for generations, governing behaviour and ensuring that the illegal was rarely dabbled with, had become engulfed with heroin by the late 1990s. Featherstone was no exception. Whoever you spoke to who had any contact with youth — police, social workers, youth workers, housing officers, councillors — who had any contact with life outside of that of the cosy, carpeted houses where people sat glued to their tv sets night after night, acknowledged that this was the worst social problem they had ever faced.

PC Somer, a local policemen involved in working with youth and drugs, told me that 'in 1975, if we arrested somebody for drugs, it was a novelty....you might have one a year. Now, it's one a day'.

Vanessa is a part-time youth worker at the local youth club. We talk about the kind of work she does, trying to keep up the interest of the kids: ice skating; building dens in the woods. And then she volunteers the information, without me even asking: 'there is a very big drugs problem in Featherstone'.

John, the former diesel fitter in the pit, on being asked the differences in Featherstone between the time *Coal is our Life* was published and the 1990s, volunteered the following view without any prompting:

> *'The biggest difference between when that book was written and now is drugs. They came to the mining towns from the south.'*

I took a walk on Featherstone's high street, one very ordinary Thursday in Spring 1998. During the space of five minutes, I encountered two separate groups of men smoking cannabis. One was a group of three young men, perhaps 18 or 20 years old. They were reasonably well-dressed and clean cut. One had a mobile 'phone. Another two men, elsewhere on the high street, were a bit older — perhaps 28 — and looked much rougher. They were both covered in tattoos: their faces, their necks, their hands and arms. They wore baseball caps the wrong way round. But both groups were smoking. It's something you would see occasionally in part of a run-down inner city. It's not something you would ever have seen in a small mining town. You wouldn't have got away with it. But now, so many are doing it, you realise that it's a way of life.

I asked John why it was the mining villages to the south of Featherstone that had the drugs problems earlier. John was unequivocal. There was a straight link between economic deprivation and drug misuse.

'They were the most deprived part of the district....they bore the early brunt of the pit closures'.

Featherstone, in his view, had had a drugs problem only since about 1993.

'It's been worse in the last two years. Heroin is one of the biggest problems'.

A precursor to heroin, and then running alongside it, was solvent abuse by kids: sniffing lighter fuel, glue, butane. This was another commonplace. Somebody has to sell this stuff to kids before they can get it. In 1991, recognising that they did, the local Chamber of Commerce decided to 'declare war' on the supplying shopkeepers. Though even 'declaring war' didn't seem to stop the kids getting it from somewhere.

The official age that kids are allowed into the one youth club in Featherstone is 13, but they start to come much earlier, as early as 10. Youth officials, who technically should turn them away, instead turn a blind eye towards their age, aware that there is nothing else for these kids to do in Featherstone. If they were to turn them away, as they were supposed to do, they might end up in an even worse plight than they were already. This might bring trouble for them and for others. Because there's no such thing as trouble affecting only one person. Trouble for one man or woman is always trouble for somebody else.

There are 30 regular attendees, of whom 10 are serious drug abusers. It is not just 'weed'. Weed is commonplace, weed is like tea or tobacco; weed is part of the regular social currency. Now, it is anything: heroin, Ecstasy, speed, 'trips'.

What is so tragic is the age of some of the users. The police claim to know of 2 boys in Featherstone, 8 years old, who are on heroin. Drug counselling agencies in the area claim that they have come across 10-year-olds demonstrating to them how to 'shoot up', and a 13 year old girl funding her habit by turning to prostitution.

One of the volunteer workers at the youth club lived in a far more middle class settlement, closer to Wakefield. She also worked at the youth club there, and described the difference between Featherstone's youth club attendees and those in her home village:

> *'The difference is unbelievable. The 10 year old in Featherstone is as streetwise as the 13 year old in Crofton. In Featherstone, they definitely know about drugs....they know about everything.'*

Taking heroin is not just about a chemical addiction. Like chewing tobacco, this is a drug which is socially-ritualistic. Only the ritual is intensified, elevated, aggravated, it takes the place of all other things. This is a drug which involves the construction, for each person involved with it, of an alternative economic and social world, a hidden world. Fulfilling your role in that world becomes an equivalent to fulfilling the role you might have performed in an earlier, work-orientated, but long-gone, society.

Everyday, there are tasks to be performed, issues to deal with. The first revolves around where to get the next fix from. The second relates to how to pay for it. The third is actually scoring. The fourth is the most ritualistic of all. It involves collecting your friends, if you have any and if you do it with friends, burning the 'brown', as it is referred to, and then 'chasing the dragon' (smoking) or injecting. Then comes the return to the high, the form of 'normality' that you are used to. The hit. And then the process starts again.

Marie Jahoda, writing on employment and unemployment, argued that there are various social-psychological conditions that attend being jobless [6]. The first is an absence of a rigorous time structure. There is nowhere that you have to be, nowhere that you have to get to, at any particular time, except, perhaps, to sign on once a fortnight at the DSS office, or attend an interview to explain why you haven't yet found yourself a job. A second is the reduction of social contacts. A third is 'a lack of participation in collective purposes'. A fourth is the 'absence of an acceptable status', which has damaging consequences for 'personal identity'. And a fifth is the lack of 'regular activity'.

In each case, heroin provides a replacement. It creates a time structure, of sorts, based around organising getting money for the drug, and organising getting hold of the drug itself. Social contacts are made, though your 'friends' are all in the same, drug-infested, long-term unemployment, no hope world that you are in. There is a new 'participation in collective purposes': everybody you know is engaged in the same endeavour, securing the money for, and the next supply of, drugs. 'Acceptable status', too, is gained amongst your peer group: you 'belong'; you are cocooned within the norms of a sub-culture. You have a new personal identity within a 'secret society'. Moreover, you have 'regular activity.' And, if you deal, you are never short of visitors. But they rarely stop long.

There was a 'secret society' remarked upon by the authors of *Coal is our Life*. But it was a different kind: 'The majority of men....take their part in the "secret society" through the medium of the small groups of friends and workmates' [7].

The men were all workers, all trying their best to provide for the family, and they liked to have a drink together in the pub or club. By and large, heroin addicts don't go to the pub. Heroin is not really a social drug. You take it in houses and flats, where you can hide from the world.

And, like the world of work, the world of heroin has its hierarchy. To reach the top of this hierarchy, you have to possess certain attributes. There is room at the very top for only a few. In Featherstone and the surrounding similar ex-mining towns, the police know that it is certain local businessmen who finance the bringing in of large quantities of heroin. They know who they are, and they know where they live. But they lack sufficient evidence to do anything about it. These 'clean' and respectable businessmen would never go near the stuff themselves. None would ever be found on their property. The risks are all taken by others a little way below them in this hierarchy. Those at this level would do the fetching and carrying. The trips to Liverpool and Manchester and Leeds, from the run-down inner city estates which have now exported their social problems to communities where they once had no purchase. Below them are the dealers. The lowest of the low are the 'Joeys'. The dealers themselves rarely hold on to their 'gear'. They pass it on to Joeys who will hold the stuff, and therefore take all the risks, for a bit of free supply.

In the former mining areas of West and South Yorkshire, there is now a heroin dealer on every council estate. The estates I remember from my youth. They were never rich. Many were content with their fairly modest aspirations. But they were proud, they were tidy, they were ordered. The privet hedges were always neatly cut. Anybody breaking the norms of this social orderliness would be disapproved of and talked about. Burning rubber in the back garden, letting your kids run wild, being too frequent a borrower of sugar or milk, were sufficient misdemeanours to incur disapproval.

Years have passed. The estates have slipped into a different dimension. Borrowing a cup of sugar, becoming pregnant out of wedlock, are insignificant compared to reality now, where the estates are engulfed with heroin. There used to be a view in mining areas that it was 'unmanly' for a miner, or any other person who had a claim to be a man, to cry. But if you look now at what has happened to these estates, even the hardest macho man from years ago, the hewer, the faceworker, would be moved close to tears.

Mining towns were totally unprepared for the epidemic of drug abuse that was to hit them. There was nobody in place to turn to who could help with this new problem. Many major cities, especially ports, had been exposed to drugs for generations. It was never like this in mining villages.

Less than 15 miles away from Featherstone as the crow flies lies Mexborough. Mexborough, with a population of just over 15,000, is at the heart of South Yorkshire's Dearne Valley, which is a collection of small townships straddling the boundaries of Barnsley, Rotherham and Doncaster, still connected by the River Dearne and once connected by a common industrial past of coal mining. June, the mother of two heroin addict sons in their twenties, explained to me how she had had to establish her own support group for the relatives of users, because there was nothing else in place. In the past, there was no need for anything to be in place.

> 'We discovered that, when we needed it, there was nobody around to provide drugs counselling services. We tried everyone — the hospitals and everyone'.

Heroin was totally new to Mexborough. Prior to 1994, there was none there. But since then it has been 'flooding the streets'.

The mother told me how, 20 years ago, anybody who used drugs would be such an oddity that they would be pointed out in the streets. And then she described how heroin had affected Mexborough in the late 1990s, and about the 'new' social aspirations within the drug sub-culture:

> *'My next door neighbour's son is affected by drugs. My neighbour on the other side of the street is doing 3 years for drug related offences. The neighbour next to him has 2 sons on heroin. On the other side is a dealer. Across the road is a user. Across the road from there is another dealer. Out of 15 houses, at least 10 are affected.'*

> *'Every user is a potential dealer. That is what they aspire to be'.*

At least 10 out of 15 of those identical, semi-detached, red brick council houses where yes, of course, over the years there had been problems. Not enough money, domestic arguments, illness, the occasional personal disappointment. But there had never been problems like this.

It struck me, talking to users, and those who had worked with users, that self-destruction is pride turned in on itself. There is nothing left to be proud about. There is no great industry, no great dreams, no great vision. There is no aspiration towards socialism, or prosperity, there is no aspiration towards anything. There is simply a social void. And, within that void, there is the individualisation of catastrophe, a self-blame, perhaps even a self-hatred, about heroin abuse.

Conisbrough is the next village to Mexborough. Cadeby colliery used to be here. It was closed in 1986. In a 76 page report, the 'independent' colliery review procedure established by the government after the 1984/85 strike stated that British Coal had a 'moral obligation' to keep the pit open. It was acknowledged that Cadeby would never make money, but Conisbrough's problems were so bad that it ought not to be closed down. It was a waste of 76 pages. British Coal ignored the report.

In mid-1998, posters started to appear across the town centre, naming the man said to be the biggest dealer in the town. 'It's time to get the scum off the streets'. Another one asked parents if their children had been 'steeling [sic] to fund their addiction and pay this evil dealer. Your first thought is that this is a return to type: one more example of self-policing. But, according to those in the know, the posters were put up by rival dealers. They wanted a bigger share of the cake. The named man left town swiftly.

On a sunny day, Conisbrough looks quite quaint. It has old stone buildings in the centre, a church, a Norman castle, refurbished canals which tourists take little trips down. Just out of the centre, one of the main council estates is comprised of flats built in the 1960s. It is not quaint. Collarless dogs roam from one dilapidated flat to another. Hardly anybody works. All the accommodation is above ground level. At the bottom are what the local residents call the 'sheds', where the bins are kept. This is where the smack heads come to burn, and smoke, and shoot-up, and collapse. They drag in mattresses and leave needles and silver-foil around for kids to pick up later.

Again, the real tragedy is what is happening to the youth. The health worker told me she had come across kids of 7 smoking cannabis. She had come across others — 8,9,10 years old — on heroin. They were on it because their parents were on it.

Everybody I spoke to in Conisbrough believed that the drug
problem was there forever. They would never get rid of it. The best
they could do was contain it.

Eric used to work at Cadeby. He is tough, resilient. In his mid-
fifties, but as strong as an ox. 'Young 'ens' wouldn't mess with him.
That's why he can stand up to the dealers, and lead the fight against
smack. But there was a despondency in his voice, a sadness that
reflected the enormity of the problem, when he told me that 'unless
we do something we are going to lose our youth forever'.

It was no different in Maltby. Maltby still has a pit. It was once ear
marked to be turned into one of Britain's 'super-pits'. Millions of
pounds in investment was poured in in the late 1980s and early
1990s. It's a shadow of its former self now. Only 38 men living in
Maltby still work there. Just over 600 in total work at the pit,
travelling in from outside the village. 400 of them are contractors,
lacking any job security at all. Sean represents Maltby on
Rotherham council. He told me in 1998:

> *The drug problem in Maltby has been really serious for 4 years. The
> main drug is amphetamine. The problem drug is heroin'.*

In *Coal is our Life*, leisure pursuits were seen to be governed by the
insecurity faced by the miner and, by extension, his family. The
insecurity was fuelled by the constant fear of serious accident, or
even death. Quite literally, everybody knew someone who had been
affected in this way, usually within their own family. Excessive
drinking, excessive betting, allowed the miner to escape from this
insecurity in a brief episode of intoxication.

Some might argue that insecurity is still a contributory factor
behind the new forms of 'leisure' activity, such as heroin abuse. If it

is, the nature and intensity of that insecurity has changed. It would be tempting to argue, as the 'rational' social scientist might, that in the 1990s, there is an insecurity about the economic future, indeed about the economic present. What kind of job might be available? How long will it last? Will *any* job be available?

If you go to the site of the former colliery in Featherstone, and visit the training company, this is clearly exemplified. Talk to any of the young men about how many jobs they have had, or how many training schemes they have been on. Some of them can't remember how many. At 18, to have been on 6 or 7 is not be unusual. It is a complete contrast to when you started at the pit, or the steelworks, or many other places, in the 1950s, the 1960s, even the 1970s, where you might reasonably have expected to be there for the biggest part of your working life. Now you might be in a job for two months, or even two weeks.

But 'economic insecurity' is not a sufficient explanation. Once in a state of complete dislocation from the rest of society, from those who would have been his peers, the heroin addict, or indeed the amphetamine addict, is beyond this 'economic insecurity' phase. The drug is more important. The drug becomes everything. The drug is your life.

'What am I supposed to fucking do? Get a job?'

This was a former fitter at a pit in Barnsley, approaching 40 years old, and now with a chronic speed addiction. Life now was about where you got the money to buy speed. I can remember when he used to go to the pit, day-in, day-out, and dress up smartly whenever he went out. He couldn't care how he looks now. The only time he goes out is to get speed.

Getting a job was the last thing he wanted, the last thing on his mind. And it was the last thing on the minds of all those other sad users who frequently called at his house for 5, or if they were being really polite, 10 minute periods to collect their drugs. From part of the working class that had once been in regular employment, as this man had, and from that part of it which had never worked, but whose fathers had, there has been spawned an underclass where work is not even a consideration. For that part of it that has succumbed to the use of illegal drugs — and that is a large part — the major individual industry is how you can keep avoiding pressure from the authorities to find work or go on a training scheme.

The growth of heroin abuse in former mining towns has been phenomenal. A few miles away from Featherstone lies Hemsworth. Just over 9,000 people live in Hemsworth. Like Featherstone, it was solidly a mining community, a free-standing settlement surrounded by a belt of farm land and countryside. There were mines all around, and mining overwhelmingly provided the single biggest occupation for men. All the pits have gone, the last ones in the early 1990s. Ron, the head of a voluntary help/counselling drugs service, which had been established in 1986 after the death in the community of a 14 year old boy from solvent abuse, explained to me that, when the service started, solvent abuse was all they had to deal with. It was youngsters sniffing glue and butane. Which is bad enough, but there was no heroin. Heroin was new:

> *'Three years back we had one heroin user. Now we have close to one hundred. We are buried in heroin. We are seeing 7 to 10 new cases a week'.*

Buried with heroin. Flooded with heroin. These were the terms used by everyone I talked to — police, drugs counsellors, ordinary

people just trying to come to terms with the problem — all across
what was the South and West Yorkshire coalfield: Featherstone,
Grimethorpe, Hemsworth, Mexborough, and on and on.

Wherever you look, the story is the same. The town of Doncaster
had many mining 'villages' within its boundaries. In 1997, it still
had two operating collieries, Hatfield and Rossington, though their
workforces were much reduced from days gone-by. June, a social
worker trying to help heroin addicts, told me how heroin abuse had
seen a rapid escalation in Doncaster:

> *'There are a 100 clients waiting to be assessed. Five years ago there
> were none. The waiting list only started in February/March 1996. If
> someone now came in with a heroin problem, we could see them in
> about 10 months'.*

She went on to list the worst hit areas in Doncaster. Armthorpe,
Rossington, Mexborough, Askern......it was like a roll-call of ex-
mining towns.

There is a new sub-culture that embroils Featherstone youth and the
youth of other former mining towns and villages in West and South
Yorkshire, from as early as 10 years onwards. Collectivism — the
collectivism of the union, the welfare, the club trip to Blackpool —
has been succeeded by a kind of enforced individualism. You have
to look after yourself first, take what you can, even if it means
stealing from family, friends, neighbours, in order to secure money
for your drugs, your alcohol, even your cigs.

In the past, there was a clan, but now local society is more atomistic,
more divisive. There is a connection between getting pissed and
getting out of your head on heroin, but there is also a great
difference. If you get pissed, you might end up with a hangover the

next day. You might not be able to get out of bed as early as you really should. You might wish, for a couple of hours in the morning, that you hadn't drunk quite so much. But you wouldn't end up looking like a skeleton which had had a tight, leathery, thin yellow skin stretched over it.

Jane, the mother from Mexborough explained to me how young mineworkers would spend their weekends in the past:

> *'On Friday night they got legless. The lads were fairly clannish. They'd gone to school together, they'd gone to the pit together. It's the same now, but there's a clan of heroin users, a clan of cannabis users, a clan of drinkers'.*

Amongst those who live and work with this new generation of drug users, there is no universal agreement on the causes of the new epidemic. Some believe it is the hopelessness of the economic situation. Jane said of her town:

> *'It's depressing. There is no work. Heroin keeps them in a dream-like state'.*

She went on to describe the breakdown in the community's social discipline, a social discipline that was a shared feature of all mining areas:

> *'There is now a total lack of employment, there is boredom, apathy. The Dearne Valley is termed 'Death Valley'. It was once governed by the miners' union. You daren't do stuff or your dad would have his belt off. These were big miners with big muscles, with belts made from machinery in the pit. Everything has broken down. They wouldn't think twice about clipping a kid round the ear. The village bobby would do the same'.*

June, the social worker from Doncaster expressed a similar
sentiment:

> *'You are looking at communities where there's nowt else to do. Heroin
> is quite good for boredom. When you're not out of your head, you're
> running around trying to find the next lot. If you carry on, what do
> you stand to lose? Nothing. There's no job to lose'.*

Others close to the rot thought that, while a lot of it boiled down to
the state of the local economy, there was more to it than that. Ron,
the drugs counsellor from Hemsworth argued that:

> *'When you ask the kids "what do you see ahead for you?" the answer
> is "nothing". When you look at a bairn at 16 and he thinks "where am
> I going to get a job?" There isn't a job. They are turning to things to
> take things off their minds. Pinching. Drugs. Until someone comes
> and gives these kids hope, they'll never shift it'.*

> *'It's not just because the pits have shut or that there's deprivation, we
> are now into a drug culture situation'.*

PC Evans is close to the ground. For 20 years, he was on the beat in
Hemsworth. It has, he says, a 'serious drug problem'. The state of
the local economy has contributed to it:

> *'Economics has definitely got to be part of it. There is no employment.
> No money. Sheer boredom. I've spent hours talking to these kids who
> sit on gates. With anybody 25 years old or above, they've got conflict.
> In 1996, there were 7 suppliers in Hemsworth. In 1997 there are 39.
> Now, when they get their heroin, they give them crack as well, so that
> eventually they'll come back for more'.*

Crime

The majority of heroin users are young and unemployed. Support groups, social workers, police, estimate that their individual habits range in cost from £20 to £80 per day. That's difficult to find on income support or dole or job seeker's allowance or whatever it's called these days. So people have to resort to other means.

Everyone who has had anything to do with 'streetlife' in Featherstone and the surrounding ex-mining towns has no doubt whatsoever about the direct link between drugs and crime. The kids at the youth club, when asked how their user friends finance their habits, looked astonished that anyone should be so naive as to even pose the question: 'Nick things'.

And, of course, you have to nick quite a bit. One of the 'local senior police sources' who spoke to me told me that to get £70 or £80 in cash, you would need to steal property worth £400 to £500. He also told me that heroin was now 'the biggest problem we've got'.

The seriousness with which the police take the problem underlines its scale:

> 'We have a pro-active police team, a mixture of experienced and less experienced officers, who operate in plain clothes, and work on the basis of intelligence. They can be directed at a moment's notice'.

PC Evans, somewhat further down the hierarchy, explained in similarly direct terms how unemployed heroin addicts paid for their supplies:

*'Thieving, robbing, stealing, borrowing, prostitution....not on the
streets, they keep it within their own fraternity....there is a gang
culture here.....you let me have some of that, and I'll let you.....'*

June, the social worker helping users from the Doncaster former
mining towns explained how the drug bills are paid:

*'Mothers quite often bail out their kids, if the family is able to do that.
For kids living on their own, they get into crime. Burglaries, car
thefts. Most people you know have been burgled or had their car
stolen. Ten years ago in Doncaster it wouldn't have been like that.
Punters can get stuff 'laid on'. They can build up massive debts this
way. They can end up with thousands of pounds-worth of debts. Then
the dealer can go and have someone beaten up for it. It's a very heavy
culture. Sometimes the dealer will say to someone in debt "you go and
flog it. Flog it, and get your deal in." They do, and that's how dealers
get pushers involved. A 17 year old lad becomes a big fish in a small
pond'.*

Crime takes place for other reasons too, of course. Collapsing
economic conditions provide a breeding ground for it. And all
across the coalfields of West and South Yorkshire, pit after pit has
been closed in places that were little more than villages, which had
virtually no other form of economic sustenance.

But it wasn't just economics. The huge increase in rates of recorded
crime in mining areas in the 1990s cannot be divorced from the
massive escalation in drug abuse. The construction of the new drug
culture involved a deconstruction of the old local social order. And
the combination of economic collapse and a burgeoning drug
problem is fatal. Complete social dislocation, rather than mere
'economic insecurity', is a close approximation of the truth.

Harry, the 66 year-old winder, told me

'A lot of the crime in Featherstone is fuelled by the need to get money for drugs.....pensioners often suffer as victims of crime'.

Crime soared in many mining areas after the huge numbers of pit closures in the early 1990s. 'Economic crimes' — burglary, car theft, theft from vehicles — saw the greatest increases. Across England and Wales as a whole, burglaries recorded by police increased by 53 per cent between 1984 and 1993. But go to one, small, mining community, and see what has happened there. Go to Grimethorpe, in South Yorkshire. In just two years, 1992 to 1994, recorded burglary escalated by over 300 per cent. For South Yorkshire as a whole, the figure was 22 per cent over the same period. Recorded car thefts in Grimethorpe increased by 355 per cent over the same two years. To compare this with South Yorkshire as a whole, car thefts over the same period increased by 22 per cent [8].

In fact, in Featherstone, things deteriorated so rapidly that the parish council, for the first time ever in its history, began to employ a security company to patrol parts of the town. George, the former deputy, explained to me:

'We used to have an open door attitude. What a difference now. We've had to employ security guards, because old folk couldn't get on the buses without being harassed. The town hall, the community centre — there are hoodlums there every night. We've had to employ security staff to supervise these places for us. Our bowling green has been broken into twice. The cricket ground has been broken into. There are still a hell of a lot of break-ins. The old people will tell you that they feel safer now that the security guards are on'.

He thought about the past, and he thought about the present. And he summed it up. 'It's a different world Featherstone, now'.

Vandalism is a commonplace. The Northern Area Manager who was a kill-for-the-ladies described to me his experiences since the company he worked for had been located in Featherstone:

> '....*it is beset by crime and nicking. Generally, there is a very poor work ethic. They will nick anything. We now have bars and shutters on the windows and doors. We have coiled barbed wire on the top of the fence. It would do justice to a concentration camp. The last time they came with pick-axe handles. In this area, conventional work is secondary employment. Primarily, you rely on other things: nicking, dealing, benefits'.*

And Henry, the factory worker at Humb Store, told me that they had to be careful about putting the washing out:

> '*You daren't leave washing on the line. It gets pinched, especially the designer sports stuff. You can't put clothes on an insurance policy 'round here'.*

Grimethorpe is similar to Featherstone, though smaller and facing even more serious economic problems. Its gloomy name was never likely, particularly in the individualistic, go-getting 1980s, to create for it the right image to bring economic success. We didn't want to know about grime, and hard work that made you dirty. We wanted powerful motorcycles that could whiz suited men through traffic jams in the City. We wanted mobile 'phones. We wanted exotic fruit from tropical climes. But we didn't want grime. And we didn't want dirt. And we didn't want to be reminded of it.

Grimethorpe lies eight miles from Featherstone. Its population of less than 5,000 was almost solely dependent on coal. Even as late as 1992, 926 were employed at the colliery alone [9]. In a place as small as Grimethorpe, that amounted to a massive employer. But it wasn't the only manifestation of coal. Grimethorpe had a large colliery complex, one of the biggest coal washery plants in Western Europe, British Coal administrative offices, a coking plant, and two small power stations. All of these have gone. The power stations closed in 1991. The offices have long ceased to exist. The colliery itself finally closed, after years of retrenchment, in 1993.

You have to be reminded of Grimethorpe, otherwise you would never know of its existence. It is hidden in an awkward corner of South Yorkshire. The isolation compounds its problems. You have to make a special effort to get there. You traverse unmaintained, winding B-roads, lined at either side by farm land, which belies the true nature of the local economy. For a while you could imagine you were in an English rural idyll. You realise you are not in a by-gone agricultural era when you travel a bit further. Reality hits you with the sight of row after row of council houses standing empty, windows and doors clad in metal shutters to deter potential burglars from salvaging pipes and radiators for scrap. Reality hits you in the face on the gloomy, run-down high street. At one side, the field that extends into the distance is no longer green. It is black and strewn with rubble. Bits of what were once red-brick buildings are half fallen down. It is all that is left of Grimethorpe colliery.

Grimethorpe is not on the road to anywhere, either geographically or economically. You have to have a special reason to go to there. It was created, as a population settlement, like so many other mining villages were, simply to serve the coal industry. It had no other reason to exist. And now that the coal industry has ceased to exist, Grimethorpe itself, abandoned in no-man's land, feels strangely betrayed by the late twentieth century. The late twentieth century has no need of it.

And the crime wave that hit Grimethorpe was replicated across the rest of the defunct South Yorkshire coalfield. Goldthorpe is another former pit township in 'Death Valley'. Like so many others, it is based around one main high street, flanked on either side by rows of terrace houses. At one time, the high street was a hive of commercial activity. There was no need to travel to the nearest big town, Barnsley, to get your shopping in, or visit the bank or the building society. Pubs and clubs on the main street catered for your social life. You could do it all on Goldthorpe's main street.

Goldthorpe was proud of its pit. It broke production record after production record, it stayed profitable long after others had been condemned as 'uneconomic'. In the seven years to 1994 Goldthorpe pit made a profit of £100 million. Its workers were known as the 'Midas Miners'. It was South Yorkshire's most consistently successful colliery.

The pub across the road from the old colliery site, the Miner's Arms, once thriving as miners came and went, stood derelict for quite some time after the pit closed in early 1994. There had been a brief attempt to drum up trade by putting on female striptease acts, but this had failed to pull it round economically. It was finally pulled down and a few houses were built there. If you go to Goldthorpe now, the high street is mainly discount and charity shops, and ex-catalogue shops, catering for people in poverty. The pubs that remain, for most of the week, are empty.

After the pit closed, Goldthorpe succumbed, like so many other mining towns, to the crushing grip of economic collapse. The pride, the pride that had been the lifeblood of the place, the pride that had infused the local community and kept the social order, the pride with which the Midas Miners had smashed production record after production record, was squeezed out. And the transformation from pride to angst was reflected in a new form of social disrespect. No longer was it taboo to steal from your neighbours and those who thought they were your friends. Many of them, undoubtedly, would be distant relatives. Recorded burglaries increased by 92 per cent between 1992 and 1994. Recorded car thefts went up 221 per cent.

Dalton, near to Rotherham, provides another example. Burglaries here increased by 232 per cent between 1992 and 1994. And in a productivity record which much have matched anything ever achieved at the local colliery, Silverwood, which closed in 1994 and which, again, had been one of the most profitable in Britain, car thefts rose by 666 per cent over the same period.

Nearer to Featherstone, Hemsworth, in West Yorkshire, saw burglary reach a low during the miners' strike year of 1985, but it escalated between then and 1994 by 468 per cent [10]. To put this into perspective, burglaries across West Yorkshire as a whole rose by just over 90 per cent during the same period. Hemsworth was a classic mining town. With a population of just over 20,000, as late as 1985 the parliamentary constituency of Hemsworth could still boast 6 pits. The 'local senior police source' told me that there had been 'a huge increase in burglaries in close-knit communities like South Kirkby, South Elmsall. Hemsworth is the worst'.

South Kirkby and South Elmsall, also former pit towns, border Hemsworth.

There is no suggestion that it was former mineworkers themselves that were the perpetrators of the crime. A female police

superintendent in Grimethorpe was adamant that the trouble
causers there, for instance, were not former mineworkers:

*'The criminals are not miners, never have been miners, and for the
most part are too idle to work'.*

What is important is the contrast with the past. For generations
economic stability had provided for social stability. Admittedly, it
was an economic stability that had made no one rich; and, with the
exception of a few miners' trade union leaders, and a few football
managers from mining stock over the years at Manchester United,
Liverpool and Celtic, had made nobody famous, but it was an
economic stability nevertheless. Mining towns and villages were not
like inner cities with their very often transient populations, poor
housing, and turbulent local economies. The population was settled.
The housing was far from luxurious, but, for the most part,
throughout the 1950s, 1960s and 1970s, it was decent. There were
free standing houses with gardens, very little multi-storey or deck-
access type accommodation that you would find in inner cities. Real
housing problems emerged only from the mid- and late 1970s when
NCB-provided housing, often 'jerry built' as the locals used to say
to indicate shoddy workmanship and materials, started to crumble.
There is virtually no dispute that the NCB and its successor were
poor landlords, investing little in maintaining their properties.
Despite the best efforts of the latter to persuade them to do
otherwise, sons very often followed fathers down the pit. You knew
where you stood. You lacked cosmopolitanism, you might have
lacked aspiration, you might have lacked a sense of individual
destiny, but you had stability. In a mining community, it was quite
literally true that everyone knew everyone else. All these aspects of
life fused to form a particular, and peculiar, form of social culture.
And it was from that social culture that the norms of the
community were forged.

The Moral Code

Crime was frowned upon. Crime against one's kith and kin was regarded the lowest of the low. Often, the community had its own ways of dealing with the odd social miscreant who stepped out of line. Sometimes, this was subtle. And sometimes it was brutal. To start with, if anyone did step out of line, everybody knew. Everyone, therefore, was prepared in advance for what an encounter with this person might entail. As with so many other situations in life, to have information conveys power. The social miscreant in an inner city, with its transient population in and out of bed-sits might, for far longer, be able to conceal his nefarious nature. The inner city can provide a cloak of anonymity. There was no such anonymity in a mining village.

In a mining area, a transgression of a social norm became public knowledge, whether the miscreant was a burglar or a peeping tom. And, in the maintenance of social discipline, ostracism, too, would play its part. Anyone who broke the trust of the community norms might find that the community did not want to know him. More severe cases of breaking community trust might be dealt with in a more physical way by strong men at the back of the working men's club. Or even inside it. In Grimethorpe, Boxing Day is for drinking all day long. I had a woman friend who had a boyfriend from Grimethorpe, so one Boxing Day she ended up on an all-day session at a working men's club. It would be the late 1980s. Towards the end of the day, as people were well-inebriated, she saw a collection of young, strong men begin to attack a much older man. Nobody lifted a finger to help the older man. She couldn't believe the lack of assistance forthcoming to an older man who had been, it seemed, beset upon by young thugs. She moved across to try to intervene. A hand grabbed the back of her collar, and pulled her away. She was told to keep out of it, and provided with the brief explanation that the man under attack was a 'molester'. It was summary justice, but no one was going to object. The man had done wrong. The man was being punished. Except in the most severe and unusual of circumstances, the police would not be involved in the administration of law and order to those that had transgressed community norms.

In general, in the fifties, sixties, and even early seventies, crime was never a serious problem in mining villages. There would be drunken fights, usually over women, but then again, all men fight over women, whether they are miners or university professors, and whether or not they use their fists. There would be conflicts, sometimes violent, between father and recalcitrant son, usually after far too much best bitter. But crime itself never got out of hand. As a Labour councillor who had been a mineworker until his colliery closed in 1985, and who represented Goldthorpe on Barnsley council, said to me:

> *They were very law abiding citizens in coal mining communities. People were dependent on others at work in often dangerous conditions....they had their own sort of moral code...you were living with people that you worked with'.*

And you didn't steal from people that you lived and worked with. Even if you didn't like somebody, you didn't steal from them. You might not speak. And you might not look. But you did not steal.

Explanations for the crime wave varied. The councillor representing Goldthorpe thought that economic circumstances had at least contributed to the social breakdown:

> *If you have people in a fairly hopeless situation, who can't see a future, it tends to breed a culture which is less than law abiding'.*

But his firm belief was that the explanation for crime could be laid at the door of a few degenerate individuals:

'There is a minority of people who offend and re-offend. The greater majority of people in mining communities are law abiding'.

Some completely dismissed the 'economic' explanation for crime, as others had done in relation to drugs. The female superintendent in Grimethorpe believed that:

'It is nothing to do with whether there is or isn't a mine'.

Instead, she believed, it was far more to do with disturbing and changing the structure of the population, a population which had been stable, and in which, over the generations, families had come to know each other. 'Outsiders', who had been moved in by housing associations which otherwise would never secure tenants for their houses in these less than fashionable areas, were to blame. Outsiders were not bound by the same moral code. Outsiders did not share the same moral code as insiders. Outsiders did not care.

This was a view shared by Ron, one of the counsellors fighting the losing battle against drug abuse. It was, he believed, outsiders who were a catalyst to the problem and were exacerbating it:

'One of the problems is that they are shipping in people from all over the place, housing associations in particular. A lot of these people aren't local people. When you start bringing people in, you are going to end up with trouble'.

Harry, the 66 year-old winder, explaining to me how Featherstone had changed, took a pretty similar view:

'People knew everybody......it's changing, even that's changing....we're getting people moving into council housing from outside.....they don't have the same feeling for Featherstone...'

Stories abound of people who had houses in Grimethorpe and other small mining towns, but also flats in Toxteth in Liverpool or Chapeltown in Leeds. Clearly, outsiders are to blame. They are the ones who rob and cheat and thieve and vandalise. It couldn't possibly be any other way. It couldn't possibly be us.

The Sex Industry

'How do they pay for it?' I asked Jane, the mother from Mexborough.

'The men? Robberies. The lasses? Well, what would a lassie do?'

A frequent accompaniment to the onset of economic decline is a growth in the sex industry. You can see it wherever you go where there has been economic collapse. Liverpool, which has probably suffered more economic problems than any other major city in England since the late 1960s, is full of prostitutes. They start work early in the morning. If you have an early shift, at 5 or 6, you will see them hanging about, on streets lined with once grand Victorian houses. They nod and beckon. Sometimes, it's mother and daughter together. They open their coats and flash their suspenders and lacy bras to you as you drive past late at night. They scurry down back alleys at any sign of the law.

Featherstone and the surrounding mining townships, at least on the surface, have escaped such sex industry escalation. There have been no reports, for example, of soliciting in Featherstone, though prostitution is not normally associated with small towns anyway.

Too many people would know. In a mining village, if you did it too close to home, everybody would know that you were on the game.

Yet a growth in prostitution is evident elsewhere in ex-mining towns. June, the social worker in Doncaster who, when asked where the worst drug problems were had reeled off a collection of former mining townships, had no doubts at all about where the money came from:

> *'Women tend to go into prostitution and the sex industry. There used to be one massage parlour in Doncaster, but there are quite a few now. Massage parlours and escort agencies are flourishing'.*

In Featherstone and the surrounding similar small ex-mining towns, it is well-known amongst those close to streetlife that sexual favours are used to pay for drugs. If this is 'prostitution', however, it is far less explicit than the streetwalking in the sad red-light districts in the crumbling parts of Britain's inner cities, and the customers are not strangers. Ron, the drugs counsellor in Hemsworth explained:

> *'Most of the women involved are between 18 and 25. They tend to be a partner of a drug user. There aren't many on their own. They cotton on to a dealer so as to able to afford the drug. He'll supply her if she supplies him with sex. There are some disturbing stories. It wouldn't have existed here three years back. It's not prostitution. It's more like a deal'.*

But another drugs counsellor at the same agency thought that the problem was worse than this:

> *'It's not just with dealers. There are stories of lasses getting in cars for sex. They actually congregate. We've had confirmation of this from a lot of small villages within a five or six mile radius of here'.*

Sex and drugs go together in all the other ex-mining towns and villages as well. In Maltby, Sean told me:

> 'To pay, men thieve, steal from shops, break into houses. A minority of the girls go on the game. They do it from the house. People get to know through word of mouth. Six Months ago, there were 3 girls that I know of in Maltby on the game through drugs. One year ago, the biggest dealer in Maltby was taking a couple of 14 year-old girls to Sheffield for prostitution. He's behind bars now'.

Conisbrough is no different. Eric, the former miner, now leading the fight against heroin, told me how the women paid for their smack:

> 'They go on the game. Not in Conisbrough, but in Doncaster'.

If what prostitution there has been has, for the most part, been hidden and informal, rather than the soliciting on the streets kind, many nearby towns have seen extensive examples of the sex industry in its milder forms — topless barmaids and striptease. Pontefract and Castleford, in particular, have played host to a lot of this form of entertainment. The social and political paradise in Pontefract ran a lap-top naked dancing and erotic dancers night for years. And 'one for the boys', as female striptease sessions were often advertised, was a common event in Grimethorpe, South Kirkby, Castleford, and other nearby mining towns. Later, male striptease became more popular. If you look at the local press for 1990, you would find 7 drinking establishments within a 4 mile radius of Featherstone offering female striptease, or topless mudwrestling ('beautiful girls', 'volunteers welcome'), or 'Miss Wet T-Shirt', for entertainment, and 6 establishments offering male striptease.

Stripping by redundant workers, of course, became a big thing within the fashionably 'social concerned' sector of the media in the late 1990s. There was The Full Monty, about redundant Sheffield steel workers taking off their clothes for money, which became the most successful British film of all time. There were television documentaries about others, ex-miners in particular, who would dance and strip. It was everywhere.

The stories were good, but they were sanitised and the dancing carefully choreographed. In reality, in the dingy little pubs and working men's clubs, stripping is, straightforwardly, a live sex show. It's about somebody's tits in your face. Primarily, it's about power. This woman is dancing for you. The more clothes come off, the more powerless she is. Here she is, in a pub full of clothed, leering, grasping men. And she is naked. There is even more power if she is a 'blue' stripper, the kind who pushes plastic dildos into herself. Yet more power if she gets a man from the audience to do it for her.

It's usually women who submit themselves to this kind of thing, or actually like doing it, or think they like doing it, depending on which is more appropriate. But occasionally it's men. There was a former miner in the late 1990s from a pit village near Barnsley who decided to engage in a similar kind of erotic titillation for self-employment. He advertised his services. He would come and dust the house for women who fancied getting someone else to do it. He would wear a little pinny. And nothing else.

Friday night in a large pub in Castleford is one of the venues for topless barmaids. Friday night is traditionally the night for 'piss ups' in mining and other industrial areas. A 'piss up' is where you drink as much beer in one session as you possibly can. Unlike with other social groups, where drinking often takes place within a 'context' — wine with a meal, drinks after the theatre, a glass of beer or wine for guests — here, it is drinking itself that is the central objective. People are here to socialise, of course, but drinking itself is the lubricant of social intercourse. Inviting people round to your house so that they can chat politely about their jobs and their lives, and inquire gently about yours, while at the same time eating some Thai or Chinese meal and drinking semi-expensive wine, is not the normal course of events. The consumption of food, to the northern working classes, is a separate activity from the consumption of drink. It has always been like this. You eat. And then you drink. That's why eating was always early, usually as soon as you got home from work. 'Dinner', later in the evening, was something that the middle classes did. To fuse the two activities of eating and drinking was largely a middle class invention, although the educated sons and daughters of the working classes eventually graduated to it too.

If there are meetings to take place, they take place at the pub or the club. Most social meetings take place there, and the much rarer, and less well-attended, political meetings sometimes do too; as with local branches of the NUM meeting in pubs once the welfare had closed, and as with the anti-drugs groups that have sprung up in the mining villages. What a state of affairs: from union meetings to discussions on how to combat drugs. In looking for continuities between past and present, the pub meeting is certainly one. The only reason that is considered valid for not coming out on a 'piss up' is if you are 'skint': in other words, you have no money. There can be no other legitimate reason. Not coming out on a piss up because your wife or girlfriend has prevented you is considered to be a sign of a particularly weak man. In this sense, again, social culture has changed little since the days of *Coal is our Life* . In discussing exclusively male activities, which included drinking with mates, the book noted that 'a man who gives way to his fiancee or his wife is a weakling' [11]. Beer is part of the religion. Beer has to be drunk. Combining a piss up with a topless barmaid serving the beer is a particularly 'good neet art' [good night out].

The pub in Castleford on this Friday night was large, as pubs in mining areas often were and still are. They were large to fit in all the customers who wanted to drink beer. Here, the pub was divided into two rooms. One room, the public bar, or tap oil, was virtually empty, apart from two leather-jacketed men in their mid-thirties playing pool. The other room, where a 'mobile' DJ was playing loud popular music, gradually filled up as the night wore on. To start with, there were only a few men propped up against the bar. As the night wore on, a steady steam, mostly of men, but amongst them some women, came through the door. After a while, and after the alcohol had reached a particular level, people began to dance. There was much cavorting and jocularity. By the time the topless barmaid arrived, the place was packed, and the men were full of eager anticipation. 'Troy' emerged from a group of drinkers, as if she had been within the crowd, talking to someone. She was dressed in an unbuttoned leather waistcoat and no bra, lacy black briefs, and 'cowboy' style leather leggings. She looked about 19. As she reached the bar, she took off her waistcoat and began to serve the salivating men. Her sun-tanned breasts were firm and large. Her face was cute and girlish. There were other, male, boring, staff who were also behind the bar serving beer, but the punters weren't interested in them. The punters were sweating. Eager. Anxious. They raised their glasses repeatedly to try to catch her eye before the next man did. This activity became especially frenetic at that point where she was about to complete a sale by giving some man his change. If you were served by Jack or Fred it was a bloody terrible disappointment.

The barmaid smiled frequently, and acted no differently to the way you imagine she acted when fully clothed. That a horde of men were starring at her near naked body did not seem to worry her in the slightest.

Troy looked like a sexual goddess. It made you wonder why such an attractive woman had decided to earn her living through taking her clothes off in public and sexually stimulating men who were complete strangers to her. You could imagine how quickly so many men would have snapped her up, married her, provided some kind of stable home life. But perhaps that was not what she wanted. Perhaps that was too boring.

Another Friday night, same pub, another topless barmaid. This one was very different from Troy. This one was not a sexual goddess. Fewer men would have snapped her up, married her, provided some kind of stable home life. But many would have had sexual intercourse with her, given half a chance. In fact, in truth, as they thrust forward their empty pint glasses to her, asking for 'a pint of John's luv', that, really, is all they were thinking about.

Yet most leisure time, these days, isn't spent in the pub or the club. Most of it is spent at home. *Coal is our Life* noted that, for miners, 'staying at home bores them'. Staying at home probably still bores them or, at least, bores the sons and grandsons of miners. But to go out often means spending money, and the money often isn't around.

As it has everywhere, the passive culture of the video and of television has taken over. It is a phenomena that has cut across all social classes. If the classless society were able to seek its totem, it would be the television set. It unifies us all as we stare at it. We point remotes, push small buttons, stare at moving images, confuse soap opera characters with real people. When I talked to Henry, the factory worker at Humb Store, it was a beautiful day. The sun was blazing. It was too hot to wear a jacket. Henry's son, Michael, a man in his early twenties who had secured what was very definitely seen as a 'good job' in the financial services industry in the nearest big city, was watching videos upstairs. It was a rare day off for him. The weather was glorious. The sun was shining. But he chose to stare at a screen. I couldn't understand it.

In the past, leisure here would have had a more pro-active and a more inter-active element. Visiting the miners' welfare to play billiards enforced communication with others outside the family. You wouldn't get a game unless you spoke to someone. Even reading a newspaper involved a conscious decision to actually do something, rather than act as the passive recipient of whatever is portrayed on the television screen. As Tom, the former electrician at Ackton Hall, said, 'It's too easy to just go and get a video. Others just watch telly'.

Some take heroin. Others just watch telly. Some are unemployed. Some in low paid jobs. A few have escaped socially, occasionally physically. It's forty years since the late 1950s. But it's a world apart.

NOTES

1. George Orwell, 1937 *The Road to Wigan Pier*. Martin Secker and Warburg, London. (1969 Reprint). Page 117.

2. British Coal, 1990 Written communication to author.

3. Malcolm Pitt, 1979 *The World On Our Backs*. The Kent Miners and the 1972 Miners' Strike. Lawrence and Wishart, London.

4. Pitt. As above. Page 23.

5. Pitt. As above. Page 62.

6. Marie Jahoda, 1982 *Employment and Unemployment. A Social-Psychological Analysis.* Cambridge University Press, Cambridge. page 39.

7. *Coal is our Life*, page 225.

8. All the crime figures come from South Yorkshire Police.

9. 'Job axe still hangs over Grimethorpe Colliery,' *Barnsley Chronicle*, 24 April 1992.

10. All the crime figures here come from West Yorkshire Police.

11. *Coal is our Life*, page 225.

FUTURE

The past, of mining, of the ordered, settled world, is over.
Everything has changed or, at the very least, is changing. All the
customs and behavioural patterns that held together society in
Featherstone, and every other mining town, are breaking down. If
you work, the job you do will be different from the job your
forbears did. But you might not work. The roles of men and
women, once so clearly defined and separate are, in comparison
with the past, confused and disordered. The substances used by
some of the youth to induce mood changes are very different in
their effect from the beer regularly drank by their granddads. The
nuclear family itself no longer has the social dominance it once had.
John, the ex-diesel fitter:

> *'There's some schools with kids with 3 different dads.....that's different*
> *from 40 years ago....and none of these will be in a marriage... It's the*
> *men here that are not responsible.....the women are more promiscuous*
> *than they were.....at one time, their mothers and fathers would have*
> *made them get married....it doesn't happen now...'*

It is the same everywhere in the coalfields. Don is 65. He lives in an
ex-mining village 4 miles to the east of Barnsley. He's worked on
haulage and on the face at the pit, but he's most proud of the fact
that he was the first dust control officer in Yorkshire. Now, his coal
days behind him, as they are behind everyone else, he represents
his village on the council: 'if we have five houses to let every week,
four of them will go to single mothers'.

Going back 40 years, what was evident in *Coal is our Life* was the
strict 'division of labour' between men and women. The man went
to work. He was the provider. The women did the domestic work.
Men did manual work, gardening, mending things, watching

football, building. Women cooked, and cleaned, and cal'ed, put
plasters on kids' knees, looked after older people. You don't have to
go back 40 years. It was like that in the 1970s and 1980s. Barbara,
from Great Houghton, told me about her husband's working life. It
neatly summed up so much about this world and the ideas that
governed it. Her husband had worked in the pit from being 15. He
finished when he was 50. He worked underground, except for the
last three years. He then worked on the 'top', because he'd had an
accident on the face and after that had 'lost his nerve'. He was
reluctant to work on the top because he thought it was 'a nancy's
job'.

The old divisions as to what men and women should, and should
not, do faced a bit of a challenge in the 1990s, as the old social
structures collapsed. Herbert, a 66 year-old former face worker, who
had been moved from Scotland to Great Houghton, told me about
the difficulties some of his younger friends were having looking for
work:

> 'some men have said to me that they can't get a job that's manly
> enough....so 3 men I know have gone into caring, one at an old
> people's home, one at Barnados...'

It's not something they would have done a few years ago. 'Caring'
was a job for women.

Jobs used to be divided into what women did and what men did.
Even this is changing now. 'Economic restructuring', as it is politely
put, has a direct impact on the way society is organised.

Karen, the wife of a former miner in Featherstone, told me how this
had affected her own family. Her sister, she said, worked at a
nearby chemical factory. 'It's a man's job....like a man's job...' Her

husband stayed at home and looked after the kids. He couldn't find a job that would pay him as much as she gets. Forty years ago, there were not many men who would have come home and started cooking a meal. 'Now they all do'.

What really matters to Featherstone is what the future holds for the local economy and for the youth. Featherstone will either find a new economic base on which to build some prosperity, or it will end up a half-forgotten town, home to those who can secure one of the limited number of jobs available, home to commuters, and home to those left behind by society.

Over the length of a school day in 1997, I spoke to twenty five 14 and 15 year olds at the comprehensive. In one year's time, this cohort would leave the school so familiar to them and enter an entirely new social world. What they thought, what they believed, what they would do with their lives, would create Featherstone's future.

I hadn't realised it to start with, but the headmaster had consciously selected which pupils I got to talk to, and which were kept away from me. I couldn't blame him. He had been guilty merely of wanting to present his school in the best possible light. It was not surprising. These were times of inspectors and Ofsted and stern warnings from both major parties of government about the dire consequences for schools which showed any signs of 'failure'. At its merest inkling, task forces would be sent in, staff sacked and pupils shamed, schools closed down. By the time we had reached September 1997, a hotline to the Department of Education and Employment had been established, so that parents could report schools that had failed to implement policies aimed at 'raising standards'. Schools in the 1990s were existing in a culture of government-induced paranoia, itself induced by an obsessive belief

that unless everyone improved their educational performance the
entire country's economy would fall further behind those of other
advanced nations. Like all obsessive beliefs, it was probably
irrational. But obsessive beliefs are difficult to dislodge, for
governments and individuals. I remain unconvinced that you really
need to be certificated to the hilt to stack shelves at Safeway, or
engage in tele-sales operations, though it is jobs such as these that
were the growth area of the 1990s. Nobody wants to do them.
Somebody has to. And whether you've got a certificate to pin to
your wall makes no difference at all. Nevertheless, in such a climate
of fear, you have to guard your back. So, instead of a representative
group, I met the 'school council'. To get on to this school council
you had to be in one of the 'top sets', or you had to have a good
'attitude' or, at the very least, you had to be 'trying hard'. I would
never have made it. Seriously, I wouldn't.

If Featherstone had an elite, this was as close as you would get to it.
It wasn't an elite to the outside world. It had no social privileges
and no social graces. But within the confines of this society, these
were the kids most likely to achieve *some* degree of success. There
were 154 in total in the school year, and the 'elite' comprised the top
16 per cent. For entirely understandable reasons, the rogues and the
no-hopers had been deliberately kept from me.

The rogues and the no-hopers were clearly evident elsewhere,
anyway. In the park, and the churchyard, sniffing glue and smoking
'weed'. Sitting on walls in the back alleys of Featherstone, where
they drink their alcopops and pass cigarettes around. Hanging
outside the supermarket late at night. Shoplifting. Swearing.
Smoking. There was no need to seek them out.

As I talked to the pupils, as I listened as they told me that 'nobody
dare take their kids down to the park', as I thought about the

community and the place, what struck me was the extent to which fear was all around. The head, so scared of a bad reputation for his school, so keen to present an acceptable face, so assiduously trying to massage reality. Not that there was anything to hide: his school was probably no better and no worse than so many others in West and South Yorkshire. Scared even, I imagine, about what I might say, to whom I might talk. And the parents, fearing to take their kids to the park. Fear itself has become a socio-psychological pathology, and one which has taken root so strongly amongst so many different groups. Of all God-damn places, in the 1960s and 1970s, in the mining towns you never feared taking your kids to the park. Karen was emphatic:

'My kids are not allowed in the park, full stop'.

Tom, the former electrician at Ackton Hall and 'pioneer' at Selby, also thought 'it's a very bad place, all in all'. And Peter, the early retired administrative worker, said 'there's a lot of drinking there as well as drugs.....not all the Pakis, but a lot of Pakis, sell drink to the kids...'

There wasn't, as it happened, a big Asian presence in Featherstone, or in any of the surrounding former mining communities. But some of the corner shops were owned by Asians. Like other people, they had their survival strategies. Economically, self-employment might sometimes be the only option.

But here, today, we were away from the joy-riders, the truants, the overtly socially-excluded, and with a group that was clearly trying to build a future. Many of them sported on their ties and lapels little badges on which the words 'form captain' or 'house captain' were written. All were smartly dressed in their uniforms. They were good people. You could sense it. Honest, open, courteous. Giggling but polite. Giggling, for a 14 or 15 year old, is simply a way of managing an unusual situation, defusing an encounter in which otherwise there might be tension. Giggling is OK. But we were still, nevertheless, with something of a social elite, at least within the context of an ex-mining community.

An encounter with an elite, even if it is a minor one, can nevertheless reveal a lot about a community, a place, and its future prospects. If elites stay, and elites prosper, there is a chance that a place may survive and maybe do reasonably well, despite a massive change in the local economy. This is far from arguing in favour of the 'trickle down' effect so beloved of the Thatcher government in the 1980s. Nothing much 'trickled down' then: most redistribution of wealth was a 'trickle up', as an established rich became even richer, and social casualties at the lower end of the working class — who, at one time, would have been sheltered by a more robustly paternalistic capitalism, a stronger welfare state and, in some cases, a strong extended family network — transmogrified into an underclass devoid of hope. Featherstone's minor elite was not from the established rich, nor were they outsiders to the community. They were from within the community itself, part of it. If they could manage to gain some measure of prosperity, then those around them, their family and friends, their future children, might also thrive. Yet there has to be something to keep elites in a locality, even minor elites. That has to be an economic or, in the absence of that, an emotional reason: a tie to family, to friends, to a place. The latter, however, is not always strong enough to prevent a flight. That is why the Irish, love their country as they might, die for their country as many of them have done and still do, are scattered across the globe. And if the skilled, the young, the fit, leave — as they fled Britain's inner cities in the 1970s and 1980s — what is left is a kind of economic and social detritus, peopled by those who cannot leave, even if should they wish to: the elderly, the infirm, the unskilled, and those who might not survive unless they are embraced by their home community. Everybody knows that a thriving economy cannot be built on that.

This elite was in no doubt that I would get different answers from the ones I was getting from them if I spoke to some of the pupils that were not represented on the school council:

> *'A lot of them are not really bothered. A lot don't want to go to college — that's the majority. For many, it's too hard to go to college'.*

And, in any case, PC Somer — who visits schools to counsel against drugs and crime — had already told me:

> *'I try to work in areas where there are the worst offenders....one of the problems I've had is Featherstone....Featherstone High School has a very bad record....but we're not invited in....it's the only school we're not invited in. We keep a record of bad offenders...and this was the worst.*

> *'The ones that are ambitious in Featherstone are in the minority....most accept that they are not going to get a job....most of them are unemployable....their parents are out of work...they get to the stage where they say "me dad's niver worked....he's survived....I can survive"....they learn how to dodge'.*

'College', a term subject to various interpretations, meant further education college, where you might study A-levels, or GNVQ, or take a vocational course in health care, tourism, hairdressing. Such a college did not exist in Featherstone. It was too small. The school did not have a sixth form. But there was a choice of colleges at towns nearby.

Even in talking to adolescents who were perhaps only 2 or 3 years old when the pit closed, the legacy of mining was evident. The fathers of 11 of the 25 pupils had been mineworkers. Two of the 11 still were. One commuted to Selby. The other remaining coal industry employee was an opencast mineworker. Out of the 9 that had worked in the pits but had now left the industry, 3 had serious health problems, almost without doubt brought about by work. When Dave was asked what his father did for a living, he replied, barely stopping to think about it: 'he's got his ill health from the pit'. In other words, he didn't work. There was no stigma that might otherwise arise if laziness was deemed to be the cause of economic inactivity. The blame was apportioned unequivocally. Ill health was an unstoppable corollary of working at the pit. Dave knew that at some stage you got it. It wasn't a question of whether you would become ill. It was only a question of when, and what form illness would take.

Dave elaborated. His father had been a deputy. When ill health hit, about a year before we spoke, he was pensioned off with a lump sum and an allowance of £100 per week. Dave's father was all of 49.

And yet, despite the ill health, there was a certain nostalgia Dave's dad held for mining:

> 'he thinks it was his best working life, at the pit. He was happier there than anywhere else, but he wants me to have a clean job, and well-paid'.

A lump sum, and £100 per week, is better than he would have got elsewhere. It is far more than he would have received in the 1950s or 1960s. It is certainly better than he would have received pre-war. But it is still the end. Dave's father is unlikely ever to work again.

And because he is unlikely ever to work again, he is unlikely ever to have any real measure of prosperity. He'll have fun in his own way, there is no doubt. He'll put the odd bet on; he'll nip down to the club; he'll watch a bit of telly, the odd video. But there won't be much more. He won't get far from Featherstone very often. In other businesses, other jobs, he would probably have had 15 more working years left. Fifteen more years to earn, progress, socialise. Not in coal. Even if the pit had survived, Dave's father would not be able to work in it any longer. The great tragedy is just how common this is. You see it everywhere. If you go to the men's toilets in the top 'ouse, for example, you will regularly hear older men, in their fifties and onwards, coughing their guts up. As a matter of pride, they will suppress these giant, deathly coughs until they are out of sight and out of hearing of others in the pub. But in the toilets, great deep coughs go on continuously for several minutes at a time. It sounds, always, as if they are embarking upon one last, deep, cough; one last determined effort to expel whatever noxious substance their body is so keen to get rid of. But the substance is never properly expelled. It lingers, for years, where it ought not to linger. It festers and develops into conditions nobody dare speak the name of, conditions that everybody hopes will never happen to them. And the next time they go to the toilet, the determined efforts to expel it start all over again.

Mark's father had also left the pit on health grounds. His hearing had been impaired because of the constant loud noise of heavy machinery. If respiratory problems didn't get you, like they got Dave's father, and if 'vibration white finger' — which saps all feelings from the hand and which stops the blood getting to the fingers — didn't get you, you might end up deaf. Something would get you. You'd be lucky to get away unscathed.

Arthur, the former branch secretary of Ackton Hall told me about his father, for example, who had also been a miner:

> '*He ended up with 100 per cent pneumoconiosis....he couldn't walk across the room....he was propped up in bed with six pillows...he had inhalers....things up his backside....he finished work altogether at 59...*'

Yet, for years, there was a refusal even to recognise that some of these illnesses were associated with the industry at all. Vibration White Finger is a classic example. Throughout the 1960s and 1970s, British Coal — to quote the lawyers acting on behalf of victims — whilst acknowledging that the problem existed in other industries 'maintained that the risk did not arise in the coal mining industry. They took no effective steps to either investigate the prevalence of the condition in their workforce or to reduce the risk' [1]. Sufferers of Vibration White Finger won a legal battle in January 1996, when a ruling was made that British Coal should have been aware from January 1973 of the risks associated with it. The ruling found that, from 1975, a 'system of preventative steps including warnings and routine examinations' should have been in place. But, of course, they never were.

Once you've got Vibration White Finger beyond a certain stage, there's nothing you can do about it. The lawyers summed it up: 'The condition is permanent and there is no cure'.

British Coal's decision to ignore Vibration White Finger had a long pedigree. Back in 1952 the Medical Research Council asked the then NCB to take part in a study of the condition. The invitation was not taken up.

It was the same with so many other conditions. Thousands of men ended up deaf, but they never had any compensation. Nobody got any until the mid-1980s, when deafness was first recognised under the Industrial Injuries Scheme as affecting people involved in certain occupations in coal mining. Nor were chronic bronchitis and emphysema officially regarded as 'industrial diseases'. The miners' union had been fighting since the 1940s to have them recognised. They had to battle for 50 years. Not until September 1993 did they achieve official recognition. Thousands of men had died from chronic bronchitis and emphysema. And for years, the official line was that it was nothing to do with their work. Older miners have told me that there were times when they could not see a hand lifted before their face, because of the dust. But ill health was nothing to do with that. It was not until January 1998 that the High Court ruled that the NCB had failed to implement reasonable steps to minimise the 'creation and dispersion' of coal dust. This opened the way for compensation claims. For many it was too late.

Apart from being a bit deaf, in all other ways, Mark's father looked quite fit. He wasn't malnourished. He filled his grey suit well. He had benefited materially from compensation for ill health. I would rather have my hearing, and I'm sure that he would, but his 'deaf claim' from the pit had bought him a white Land Rover Discovery. And white Land Rover Discoveries are well beyond the norm for most ordinary miners. He was agile. He could jump down out of the Discovery like a gambolling spring lamb. Life was good.

The toll of life had left its mark on another ex-miner amongst the kids' parents. Diana's father was long term sick suffering from 'anxiety'. The pit had gone and he had failed to find a new role. Diana's mother had to give up her job, as a hairdresser, in order to look after her husband. The family was left without a breadwinner.

We are not talking about elderly men. We are talking of men in their forties only, and men who had, at one time, been physically strong. In fact, whether you were or not, you had to be seen as being physically strong. People had to think you were. If they didn't, you might be seen as effete. You might even be seen as a homosexual.

One might equate to the other. Whatever, you would be a 'Jessie'. Even in later years, you had to keep up the appearance of being strong. Preferably, you had to demonstrate that you were — still — as strong, if not stronger, than younger men. Any way would do. If a young man couldn't get the top off a bottle of pop, an older man was likely to say 'giz it 'ere' and demonstrate just how easy it was for someone of superior strength to divest the bottle of its cap. Then there was fighting. You could avoid it if you wanted, but there was always someone ready to have a go. Especially after a few too many beers.

Talking to the school kids about their social position, I was struck by the mismatch between self-perception and reality. All the pupils claimed to know the meaning of the terms 'working class', 'middle class' and 'upper class' — dated and imprecise as they might be as social categorisations. Yet pupils whose mothers worked as school cleaners, whose fathers worked repairing machines, whose brothers and sisters worked in factories or in lowly positions in supermarkets, saw themselves as 'middle class'. Dave, for example, son of the former deputy who had now got his 'ill health' and lived on £100 per week, whose mother worked as a cleaner at a school, saw himself unequivocally as being 'middle class'.

Similarly, Mark, son of the now unemployed mineworker who had had his hearing impaired, viewed himself as 'lower middle class'. They owned their own house and a white Land Rover Discovery, so perhaps they were. Another boy, whose father worked as a postman, and whose sister worked as an assistant in a supermarket, also believed himself to be in the same category. Yet another boy, whose father had been long term sick for a year, and prior to that had worked as a manual labourer, categorised himself as 'lower middle class'. Only a small proportion of the pupils saw themselves automatically as 'working class'. Yet, in the broad sense of the term, there is no way that virtually every one of them could possibly be seen as anything other than that.

Probably everyone aspires to a higher social status than that which they are. But these were not merely aspirations. They were definite reflections of self-belief. So I asked them what they thought you had to be, or had to do, to qualify as 'middle class'. You had to be 'comfortable with money', 'own your own house', 'have a decent job', 'afford to have what you want'. Whether or not you were middle class depended on 'whereabouts you were living, type of house, what type of job you do. What you do in your spare time. Play golf. Go to shops and spend money'. Diana wasn't really sure what social class her family belonged to, but she thought she was probably middle class because 'we have always had our own house. Always had proper tellies and everything. Had holidays abroad'.

Your class position was, quite straightforwardly, a reflection of your wealth, or lack of it. Being middle class wasn't about having real money. It was about having *some* money coming in and, mostly, about having a job. It had nothing to do with whether or not you once lived in a council house, your family background, whether your father was a manual worker, whether your mother was a school cleaner. Vicky's parents were divorced. She didn't know what her father did for a living despite seeing him every weekend. She was, she thought, 'probably working class, because my parents are divorced'. Being divorced stretches the finances. Therefore it makes you working class. Vicky's mother worked as a secretary. Had she not been divorced, she would have been seen as 'middle class'.

You can probably put all this down to an innocuous, youthful naiveté, rather than a diminution in some long-held traditional class consciousness. There are some social scientists who like to pretend that large elements of the working classes, especially the northern working classes, are 'politicised', or on the verge of 'politicisation', and overtly conscious of their subordination in society. In truth, this is largely bullshit. You talk to people, and you know it's bullshit. You talk to people who pack blue polystyrene meat trays into polythene sleeves and then into boxes for 12 hours at a bloody stretch, and you talk to people wearing green nylon jackets, walking from machine to machine, pulling a lever and turning a knob, and you know it's bullshit. Yet such imagery frequently fuelled a revolutionary fantasy world being constructed either from some university seminar room, or the side room of some pub at 7 o'clock in the evening. It's early. The seats are slashed. I've heard them plotting revolution. Revolutionaries always meet early. It gives them longer to discuss, in their indefatigable way, mechanisms for the promotion of class consciousness and social revolution. And then they meet again. And again. They have guest speakers with little round glasses who come and talk about a dockers' dispute or hospital workers 'in struggle'. And they meet again. The seats still haven't been repaired. And still the revolution does not come.

The working classes, really, just wanted things to make their lives happier and easier. Revolutionaries believed that the way to this was through an uprising leading to socialism. They would 'agitate' in their anoraks, and sell newspapers at pit gates. If they agitated enough; if they sold enough newspapers; if they talked to enough workers as they started their shift and presented their case to them, there would be politicisation and eventually proletarian rebellion. But the reality is that the working classes — or at least the working class people that I knew, went to school with, grew up with, drank beer with, occasionally fought with — wanted a better life without necessarily desiring to fundamentally alter the prevailing social ideology. This is over-generalising, it is granted but, apart from the odd one or two who had joined the Young Socialists of the Labour Party — when the Party had at least some attachment to socialism

— or the Communist Party of Great Britain, it is largely true. A nice house, money left after you'd paid the bills, good schools for the kids, an ability to afford a decent holiday, not having to work continental shifts. These were the things that really mattered. Orwell knew in the 1930s:

> 'To the ordinary working man, the sort you would meet in any pub on Saturday night, Socialism does not mean much more than better wages and shorter hours and nobody bossing you about.....I have yet to meet a **working** miner, steel-worker, cotton-weaver, docker, navvy or whatnot who was "ideologically" sound'[2].

It was like that in the thirties, and it was like that in the sixties, seventies, eighties and nineties.

The weakness of the far left-wing socialists, idealising, as they did, some semi-mythical 'proletariat', was that they were engaging in what was really simply an extreme form of self-delusion: delusions can become obsessive addictions; for far-left revolutionaries they became addictions that they seemed unable ever to break. Why else would men and women stand in the concrete shopping centres of Britain on Saturday mornings, for sometimes 20 years and more, haranguing passers-by to buy their assorted, and sometimes less than stimulating, socialist rags? Why else would they stand there, year after year, wearing anoraks that had seen much better days and small, wire-rimmed spectacles, red-in-the-face with bellowing 'build socialism now' at people who are completely ignoring them? And why, I wondered for years, until I ceased to care completely, was 'socialism' always pronounced 'sew-shall-ism'?

Many reasons could be found, of course, as to why revolutions hadn't occurred, as to why the salt-of-the-earth hadn't yet risen up to seize control of society and expel the bourgeoisie exploiters, the multinationals and the domestic, 'fat cat' capitalists. That is what happens with self-delusion, whether it is over politics, or some great talent that you desperately believe that you have but which no one else can see, or over a romantic infatuation. You search and search; you rack your brains. You scour your very soul for a reason, an excuse, an answer, as to why the proletariat had not become revolutionary, as to why the publisher had refused your manuscripts, as to why the woman of your desires had spurned your advances. You can always find an excuse, an answer, if you think deep and hard enough, if you think for long enough, if you allow your thoughts to consume your every waking minute. Perhaps another socialist revolutionary group had been providing the proletariat with the wrong messages. The workers had become confused, unsure as they paced across the pit yard as to whether the Soviet Union was a true socialist democracy or merely a degenerative capitalist entity propped up by the state. Perhaps the leadership of the Labour Party had betrayed the working classes, seducing them with their pale social democracy and thus delivering them to the feet of the bourgeoisie enemy. Perhaps the woman of your dreams had simply not yet properly understood just how much better you would be for her than any other man, how much more intellectual, how much more compassionate, how much stronger for her you would have been in bed, holding her close. Perhaps she was engaging in self-delusion. But she would come to realise, in the end. Of course she would. You knew she would. Just as the working classes would eventually come to realise that 'sew-shall-ism' was the only possible way forward.

As I related the story of the working-class-who-think-they-are-middle-class to a young-woman-with-middle-aged-attitudes from another mining community not far from Featherstone, she responded by arguing, quite assertively, that none of this really mattered. What difference did it make? And, of course, the pupils' views on their position in the social hierarchy might indeed be totally unimportant, were it not for what they say about the world they inhabit. For it is clear that misperceptions on social class are another reflection of parochialism, a reflection of a lack of social experience. You don't really know what it is like to be middle class, because you've never mixed with the real middle class.

Miners' wives preparing food in the 1984/85 strike.
Used by kind permission of Yorkshire Newspaper Group.

And you've certainly never seen real wealth. You've seen colour televisions and satellite dishes, you've always had 'proper tellies', you've been in white Land Rover Discoveries, seen detached houses with bay windows, lived in a house that your mother and father own, but you've never seen real wealth. Real wealth is different from anything they could possibly imagine. You can smell it when you enter the big, hidden houses that some people live in. You can sense it as you sit down for dinner. While revolutionaries meet early, the really wealthy eat late. There is no need to rush. Being really wealthy means that you scarcely know what to spend your money on. If you live in Featherstone, or Great Houghton, or any other of the abandoned mining towns and villages across the north of England, you've read about real wealth in the tabloids, but that's just a fantasy soap opera anyway, involving transient pop stars or football players or high-flying criminals on the run. That's not reality. Real wealth doesn't exist in your community, and a semblance of it exists only in relatively small pockets in the nearby working class towns. And, even then, it is hidden from you. The world of real wealth is a hidden world, unless you are one of its members. It keeps people at bay because if people really knew about it, really saw it, they could become a threat to it. That is why people who are really wealthy always live behind sky-high walls, or even buy closed islands to live on, like the Barclay twins. It is this that keeps Britain divided and, because divided, manageable, no matter whether the Conservatives or Labour are in power. The mineworkers themselves came dangerously close to becoming unmanageable in the 1970s, with their demands for better living standards, but what happened, basically, is that they were bought off with better than average pay settlements until they could be finally crushed completely in 1985. Sometimes, if someone, or some group, provides too big a threat to the hidden world, to 'economic and social stability', they have to be crushed completely. The rulers of the hidden world have always understood this.

Despite their protestations to middle classness, there was virtually no family tradition of going to university amongst this collection of young people. Two of 25 pupils had sisters who were already at, or who were going off in the near future to, university. Scraping the barrel a bit more, two had cousins who had either been or were still there. But amongst their parents, apart from one former mineworker who had taken a part-time degree in mid-life after finishing at the pit, there was no tradition at all of higher education. Not a single one of them had been to university.

This is no surprise. There never was a tradition in these parts of the northern coalfields of university education. To talk like a sociologist, it was never a cultural norm. When you left school, you worked. There was the odd one who went to university in the early or mid-1970s, but that was so unusual as to become a talking point. Instead, the norm was that, if you were male, you went to work at the pit. With the exception of the working class grammar school boy, you didn't even consider staying on at school. And the working class grammar school boy had been separated educationally from other boys since being 11, so it wasn't as if lots of your immediate peers were doing it, and you were missing out. Hardly anybody was doing it. If you were a woman, you married a miner, had children, made the meals, did the washing, and then, at some later stage, perhaps started work outside the family home.

Partly, this motivation against further education and in favour of work, was money. It may have been a short-term, short-sighted approach — the better your education, the better your earning prospects — but people had to live short-term. You lived from week to week. You weren't salaried, you didn't have overdraft facilities at the bank and Mastercards and Visa cards. As Hoggart wrote: '....one moves generally from item to item. Wage packets come in weekly and go out weekly. There are no stocks, shares, bonds, securities, property, trade assets' [3]. If you didn't have the money, you didn't have the money. Viv Nicholson talks about her early educational aspirations in *Spend, Spend, Spend*. How she wanted to go to art school. How her teachers had sent a note to her parents suggesting that it might be a good idea. Short of the swearword, perhaps, the response from her parents was one I had heard so many times:

> 'No', said my dad. 'We can't afford it, when tha leaves that bleeding school tha's leaving and tha's going to make a wage' [4].

People sometimes think these are one-offs. They weren't. They were very far from it. I remember one lad in Worsbrough, he must have been about 20. He'd escaped the pit, and become a bricklayer. He regarded that as something of a triumph. Lowly as it might seem from the perspective of the late 1990s, lowly as it might seem to readers who are computer software designers, or architects, or heads of regional sales for international telecommunications businesses, this lad saw becoming a brickie was a mark of one-up-manship. But it wasn't enough for him. He came home one day, telling his father that he had decided to give up bricklaying and go to college full-time. His father went ballistic. The lad was a working man, his father remonstrated. A working man should work, for God's sake. What was wrong with the boy? A working man shouldn't even think about doing other things. The job might not always be pleasant, but his reward was his wage packet at the end of the week. And it should be reward enough. His father made it sound as if, in some unfathomable way, the son was betraying the community. I never properly understood it. They didn't speak for months.

What northern mining areas were left with was an absence of a higher education tradition. Education wasn't a priority. You didn't need qualifications to work at the pit. George, the retired Ackton Hall deputy, was also a governor of the local secondary school. He was blunter than I dare be:

> 'There are good schools here, and good teachers. But what they are starting with is below standard. We are fighting from rock bottom. Half of 'em can't read at 11!'

Try as they might, those charged with changing that in the 1980s and 1990s faced an uphill battle. It meant, in practice, that kids were starting from a different position from others in genuinely 'middle class' households. They could not go and get any meaningful advice from mother and father on what it's like to go to university, or which university to go to, because mother and father had never been there. Mother and father didn't know what a 'seminar' was. Mother and father had never written an 'essay'. Mother and father hadn't even, really, mixed with that many people from other parts of the country, as a student would at university. Mother and father had lived in a different world, a closed world, the world of Featherstone, or Grimethorpe, or Goldthorpe, or Worsbrough.

Talking to the kids, what was also striking was how university, and 'college', was seen purely as a mechanism for economic advancement. To be educated to a higher level for the sake of it, to develop culturally, or even to have fun, seemed to be nothing to do with it. It was all about getting a better job, purely and simply. In fact, amongst a substantial proportion, there was a marked reluctance to continue education at all but, like school, it was seen as 'necessary' to secure your economic position in the world. Gemma wanted to be a physiotherapist. She didn't want to go to college, but she thought that she would 'have to go' if she was to achieve her aim. Diana, who wanted to work in some kind of legal position, explained that: 'I might have to go. I don't have to go if I become a legal executive, and that's what I might do'. Vicky, because she wanted to be a teacher, would 'probably have to go'. The boys were much the same. The reasons for going to university were to 'get skills, get a better job, widen options'.

There was little enthusiasm amongst the boys for going into the coal industry, had it still existed in any substantial size. One said that he was 'more ambitious than that'. Ian, thoughtful and intelligent, but whose family was obviously poor through divorce and unemployment, demonstrated a realism beyond his years: 'if on the dole, I might consider it'. Another thought, with some justification,

that there are 'more options now, like going to college'. In one
sense, this is true. Far more young people now go to 'college' than
ever did in the past. And, undoubtedly, studying for A-levels, or
GNVQs, or a vocational course in health care or tourism, does no
one any harm, and might improve the chances of finding work if
the course is followed in early adulthood. The less sanguine way to
look at it is that further education colleges from the 1980s onwards
transmogrified, from being institutions that provided training and
education in an economy close to full employment, to being
sponges designed to soak up those that would otherwise be
unemployed. Featherstone High School sends somewhere between
50 and 60 per cent of its leavers every year to 'college'. In the 1950s,
and indeed in the 1960s and 1970s, hardly anyone would have gone.
Most people would have gone straight into some kind of work.
That is not to argue that what was often unpleasant manual work is
better than training or, if post-school activities were to reach this
exalted level, better than education. But this is not a situation in
which much choice is being offered. It's not training or work. It's
training because there is no work.

Whilst carrying on with education was viewed as some kind of
economic necessity rather than something to look forward to for its
own sake, there was no shortage of big ambitions. Amongst this
'elite' there was a whole gamut of professions the kids were eager
to enter: accountancy; graphic design; dentistry; law;
physiotherapy; computing; policing; nursing; teaching; travel
organising; working with handicapped children.

Yet if they were to realise their ambitions, by and large, they would
have to realise them outside of Featherstone. There is scope to be a
teacher or a policeman. You could become a nurse at a nearby
hospital. But to achieve the more ambitious aspirations would mean
moving away. Within Featherstone there is no realistic possibility of
their achievement. All that can be realised is what is already being

realised. That means a future economy of machine menders, school cleaners, machine minders. If there is to be a prosperous, rewarding future for this minor elite, it will involve commuting or leaving. For the rest, it is a future of a residual working class economy of continental shifts at packaging and pop factories.

There was, it is true, a new industrial estate in Featherstone on an opencasted former slag heap. It sat adjacent to the former pit. Four and a half years after the start of the project, by 1997 it still stood empty. By mid-1998, one building, intended for 'general industrial use', was being constructed. It was a speculative development. It is on the industrial estate, if anywhere, where new companies will come which will provide new jobs. If Featherstone is to break decisively from its economic predicament, from its entrenched economic history, it depends on this estate being a success. And it needs success. As George, the former deputy, commented on Featherstone:

'It's bloody dying. It's got to lifted up'.

Like other sites in the former coalfields, Featherstone's new industrial estate has had both central government and European money invested in it. At 40 acres, with a usually expected job creation figure of 10 jobs per acre, a potential 400 people could, at some stage in the future, find employment on the estate, depending on which businesses move in. Like elsewhere in Featherstone, it was cheap. Settling here, rather than the far more prestigious site four miles away which had attracted the inward investor Pioneer, would cost roughly £90,000 per acre as opposed to £140,000. And like elsewhere in Featherstone, another attraction is that there are lots of local people willing and able to work.

By 1997, there were indications of which kind of businesses were likely to move in. They provided for limited optimism only about the potential for the estate. There had been three serious expressions of interest, one from Wakefield and two from Pontefract, respectively six and two miles away. Clearly, the prognosis for the future was one of local relocations only. English Partnerships were 'not expecting inward investors'. There is little doubt that there will be some new employment for the people of Featherstone at this new estate, but the majority of the businesses will be companies switching their locations from a few miles away, and in many cases they will bring their own workforces with them, as the gear cutters did, and the scratch card manufacturers.

The estate is unlikely to shift the structural base of the economy from its existing dependence on small-time manufacturers and engineering. There will be no dramatic move into financial services or micro-chip design. Someone in economic development at the local authority, putting the most optimistic gloss on it, told me:

> 'I don't think you'll ever get companies like Pioneer there, but there are good companies that will move in distribution, engineering factories......not small, but medium-sized companies....one thing about the workforce in this area is that they have shown that they are capable and amenable to retrain and learn new skills'.

Though the evidence from Featherstone, as was seen earlier, is that precious few mineworkers have actually had chance to show how capable they are at other jobs.

Amongst the local population, and especially amongst the town councillors who had worked so hard to get the estate established, there was considerable enthusiasm. Harry, the 66 former winder, told me that he didn't think that the local economy would 'stay the same'. It wouldn't be 'as bad as it is now':

> *'We have the new industrial estate.....we're going to bring jobs in.....it will make a big difference.....people who've gone away will be tempted back......it is probably the best site in Wakefield....apart from the Europort'.*

Something had to done to revive Featherstone, he recognised. It was important that whatever businesses came brought jobs with them:

> *'......the service roads are being put in.....I think we'll see Featherstone start to come back into its own......young people wouldn't feel there is nothing here for them.....we are trying to get manufacturing not warehousing....we will get more people employed that way......*

> *'......that site will be full very quickly....it's what Featherstone needs, a shot in the arm......the shops we've got boarded up might start to open again...'*

John, the ex-diesel fitter in the pit who ran the security company, thought that the prospects for the estate were 'better than good'. They were 'excellent'. It would be a 'flagship for the region'. And yet his follow-up comments also revealed a desire for conservativism: a wish to see change, but not too much:

> *'The new industrial estate is not massive, but it's big enough for us and we don't want Featherstone to get any bigger'.*

Not all shared the optimism. The branch secretary of the Prince of Wales colliery, asked whether Featherstone would ever recover, was blunt and, while you wish it was otherwise, probably terrifyingly accurate:

> *'I don't think it ever will.....it has become a drugs town.....I know a lot of people who live in Featherstone....the fabric of the place has fucking gone.......it was a fucking great town........we used to go 'round on boxing day....it was one of the best days in the calendar.........the kids, they've no future.....the young 'ens are on drugs....'*

Henry, the 50 year-old factory worker, was, similarly, less than optimistic:

> *'Featherstone will stop as it is.....if it weren't for Humb Store, it would be a ghost town'.*

Alec Woodall, the local MP, was asked to comment following the closure of Ackton Hall in 1985. His words echo with poignancy in the late 1990s:

> *'The only hope the town has for survival is to get new industries to fill this massive gap. If we do not get new firms, I fear for the future of Featherstone. It will die'*[5].

Thirteen years after Woodall said this, there were no new firms of any substantial size in Featherstone. All it had that was new was the smattering of engineering and concrete firms on the redundant pit site. And all of them together employed hardly any miners.

The prospects for the future in some mining towns and villages were far bleaker than they were in Featherstone. After all, Featherstone had some established factories, a new industrial estate, a collection of 'retail outlets', and was close to motorways. Some had none of these.

In Great Houghton, for instance, whilst close to it were new enterprise zones, the mood in 1998 was one of considerable pessimism. Barbara, the wife of an ex-miner in her sixties, explained to me that:

> *'what we are in danger of doing is not bothering.....the youth have seen their dads out of work, their brothers out of work.....it's easy for them not to bother...I don't know what lads of twenty must think....they must think it's a no-hope place....if you've managed to get an interview you've succeeded, never mind a job. You keep 'em down that long until they think there's no hope'.*

Leaving Featherstone remains a possibility for the 'elite'. But it might not be easy to do. Miners didn't like to leave their home town, even after they were out of work. That reluctance has been inherited by their sons and daughters. The overwhelming majority of the kids, asked if they would be prepared to leave Featherstone, said they would rather stay. Only seven, significantly or otherwise all girls, expressed a definite desire to leave. The ties felt were ties to family and friends. The known world is a more comfortable world. It's a long-standing thing. Nobody comes. And nobody goes.

Peter's dad is long-term sick. Only in his forties, he might never work again. He used to work for a 'clean up the environment and rehabilitate the long term unemployed' agency — there are loads in ex-mining areas — but he's been on the sick for over a year. His elder sister welds three wires together every day at Pioneer. Peter told me: 'I would like to stay here if I could.....But I would move if necessary.....I'm happy with the house we live in....I've been in this house since I was born, so I'd rather stay there'.

Sarah's dad is an electrician, though she didn't know which company he worked for. Her mother is a cook and a waitress at the Top 'Ouse. She lives in a council house: 'Yes, I'd be prepared to move, but not far off for if the family needs you or owt like that'.

Mark's dad is a former miner. They own their own house. Mother and dad are still together. They're doing ok: 'I wouldn't want to move far away'.

Paul's dad is a self-employed engineer. He used to work for a company doing the same thing. In fact, it's the same company he works for now, just that as we moved into the 'enterprise culture' he became self-employed. His brother has done well, escaping into a posh-sounding telephone-banking operation in Leeds. But his brother hasn't left Featherstone. He drives in every day. So would Paul: 'I would move if I had to for a job, but not if I didn't have to'.

The known world is a comfortable world, but it can be a limiting world. You might aspire to great things, but not achieve them if you are in the wrong place. The Kennedys would never have made it if they had lived in Featherstone.

Unlike some of the boys, and nearly all the adults I talked to, the seven girls expressing a desire to leave — half of all the girls I talked to — seemed fully aware of Featherstone's limitations. Both Kirsty's parents work. Her dad is a foreman on a building site. Her mother works in a bakery: 'I want to leave. Featherstone is boring. I want to live abroad. I wouldn't want to go to university'.

Harriet lives with her mother. Her dad left about three years ago. He still lives in Featherstone, but she doesn't see him very often: 'we don't get on right well'. Harriet's father drives an ambulance. Her mother works as a non-teaching assistant at a school. Harriet spends her leisure time visiting friends in Featherstone. She'd like to leave: 'I would like to go somewhere where there is stuff to do'.

If the social 'elite' stay in what is, essentially, a parochial and economically-limited town, they may not achieve their full potential. If they leave, the town itself will probably suffer as its skilled youth flee. The truth is, as with most mining and ex-mining towns, only a very few will, in the end, leave and substantially diminish their links. There is a certain magnetism that holds people to places like this, and forces them back after escape attempts have been made. You have to be truly determined to really get away.

For every elite, of course, there is a mass. Most of us are in it. If you want to meet the non-elite, the mass, of Featherstone's youth, you can find them at the youth club.

There is only one youth club in Featherstone. It is run by a very earnest and well-meaning man in his mid-forties. He cares about the kids. You wonder where he gets his stamina from, to keep on, relentlessly, caring, in the face of their constantly rude and uncultured behaviour. But care he does. You can tell. He does a good job. From talking to the kids and observing them, you can tell that not many people have ever paid them any real attention throughout their entire lives. That is why they are rude and uncultured. It's not their fault. Conversation between them and their parents has been clipped, limited. Messages are passed. A meal is ready. A particular television programme is on. A footballer, in a match being shown on television, is off-side. But conversation, discussion, dialogue, has been pretty rare.

One youth worker at the club painted the scene:

'the main thing that's lacking is social skills. You take them on a bus trip and they get hyper. They're not used to it. They're not used to people being concerned about them. They look at you funny......Many of them don't go to school. Even kids who've had a job pack them in after two weeks....because they can't be bothered turning up'.

This mid-week night in 1997, there were about 20 kids in the place, ranging from about 13 to 20. The boys were quite loud. Their vocabularies were limited, even taking into account their ages. They would shout when talking would have sufficed. Shouting is, of course, a form of demanding attention. You cannot easily be ignored if you shout. The really confident do not need to shout. They can be quiet, and still get their way. But, if you are used to being ignored by those you so desperately wish would not ignore you, you shout. You point. You make all kinds of noises. You use obtrusive body language, shifting your laying-down position rapidly in your chair, and throwing things at people.

The girls were less unruly. They didn't shout in the same way. They didn't have to shout between themselves. They didn't have to shout to attract the boys. Their sexual attractiveness to the males ensured that they were always given at least some attention. After all, if you could 'get going' with one of these, your esteem would rise amongst your male peer group.

A contrast with the 'elite' was the attitude towards school work. Anyone who tried hard, or was successful, at school was condemned as being a 'swot' and a 'puftah'. You would be excluded from membership of this gang if you were a swot. It ran the attendant risk of being seen as a Jessie. Real men weren't interested in school work. Real men were hard, and did manual work. They lifted heavy objects, climbed under machines, hands covered in black oil.

There was virtually no overlap between the school 'elite' and the boys and girls at the youth club. This is a very small town — everybody knows everybody else, and everybody lives next to everybody else — but only one girl was on both the school council and at the club. The working class had already divided itself. Perhaps this is what they had meant at the school when, despite having mothers who were cleaners and fathers who mended machines, they described themselves as being 'middle class'. When I asked the kids at school about leisure activities, no one mentioned the club. Maybe you were middle class if you didn't go to a club as rough as this one. The 'elite' told me that the club was 'too rough'. Peter said that 'trouble causers go there. People who aren't bothered about school'. Harriet said that she 'daren't go to it'. The earnest and well-meaning man in his mid-forties, who worked in all the youth clubs across the borough, with its near half million population, described Featherstone's youth club as being the 'worst'. There was a 'drug problem and an underage drinking problem' in Featherstone:

> *'There are lots of 11 and 12 year olds just left to do their own thing. In the last two to two and a half years, the drug problem and the underage drinking problem has got worse. Quite a few of them use methadone, and I am talking of kids 13 upwards, though most of the abusers are 15 or 16'.*

Sometimes you have to go to rough places. You have to go to them if you want to know the truth. You can have the cosy world, watching television on a comfortable sofa behind curtained bay windows, sipping a cup of tea and chatting politely with your husband, your wife, your sister, any time you want, or at least they tell me that most people can. But it's not a complete world. The complete world is harsh and rough, unforgiving and unforgivable in its inequity, its decadence, its tragedy.

I asked the kids in the club about their ambitions. One 15 year old, leaving school in two weeks, wanted to work in a bank. He was loud. He had to impress the crowd. The louder he was, the more attention he might get. If there was a chance of that, he had to pursue it. Were he to achieve his objective of securing a job in a bank he would, no doubt, become 'middle class'. But you were left doubting whether he would. Being loud might gain you some credibility at the 'worst' youth club in the borough. It might not have quite the same impact in the interview room at the bank. His father ran one of the pubs on Featherstone's main street. Asked if he had ever considered being a publican, he didn't know what the word meant. A young woman wanted to be an air hostess. It would provide an opportunity to travel. My thoughts were suddenly arrested. In the club at Featherstone, she looked quite good looking. I thought, for a fleeting moment, that I was at a beauty contest. I had once known, I remembered, Miss UK. She lived in one of the pit villages I knew well. Her father was the manager of a pit. You were doing all right if you were a manager at the pit. You could have a big car and holidays abroad. Sometimes, people were a bit jealous. They would say "'e's fucking coining it in'. I had known this woman when she was spotty and gauche. I had known her when she had the most God-awful to look at boyfriend, with greasy black hair and yellow teeth. She used to stand at the bar in one of the pubs. When she blossomed, later, she was quite beautiful. I would linger at the bar a bit longer. Fame was brief. She ended up doing the 'catering' in a pub she ran with her husband. Serious glamour is like a comet in mining communities. It comes, it causes a stir, it lights up the sky, it quickly goes. But plenty try to catch hold of the comet's tail. Ask Viv Nicholson.

Another girl at Featherstone's youth club, who would leave school in two months' time, wanted to be a hairdresser. Less ambitious, probably more realistic. One lad wanted to be a 'singer or a cook'. He knew what he liked — singing and eating — so he knew what he wanted. I thought he had real spirit. The earnest and well-meaning youth worker told me later just how many of even the most modest aspirations were so often dashed. I was here for one night. He'd watched them, listened to them, counselled them, year after year. The girls would not become air hostesses. They would not travel the world. Instead, they would end up in early motherhood, cocooned from outside reality in a small, stone terraced house, going out occasionally to the shops, but rarely going elsewhere. On Featherstone's high street, any day you go there, nearly all the young women you meet are pushing prams. The boys.....well, the boys would drift along, in and out of low-skilled, low-paid, no-hope jobs. If they are lucky, they might get a job at Humb Store as a packer, or as a syrup operative at the pop factory. After 10 years, they might get a gold watch. Others might drift into criminality, maybe out of boredom, or desperation, or because their mates are doing it. Some would end up in early fatherhood, then early relationship break-down, then early abandonment of a child which would be brought up by a mother and a series of transient step-fathers. Reality is not kind to the youthful mass in Featherstone. Fantasy is better. But fantasy, anybody's fantasy, can exist only in short bursts. Otherwise it wouldn't be a fantasy, it would simply be normality. And, too often, the only way that is seen to fuel the fantasy in Featherstone is to engage in various nefarious practices. Drugs. Burglary. Anything you shouldn't be doing, really.

There was no fantasy to descending fast, in a small cage, cramped together with too many other sweaty men, deep, deep, into the earth. Yet, somehow, there wasn't then the need, or perhaps it was simply that there wasn't the opportunity, for the same intensity of fantasy-seeking. The pit, the club, rugby, your family, had to be enough. You didn't have much of a choice.

The clock cannot be turned back. But there is no doubt whatsoever that, in the 1950s, 1960s and 1970s, almost all of the young men in the youth club would have ended up at the pit. A combination of factors would have seen to that. First of all, there wasn't much else for men anyway. Secondly, this particular cohort would not have had the wherewithal to do much else. Harry, the 66 year-old winder, knew all this too:

> *'I despair when I see young lads of 20, and they say to me "I've never had a job"....we wouldn't have the problems we do now with young people if they were going to the pit 8 hours a day'.*

Nobody in the club expressed any interest in going to university: 'no way' came the unequivocal, and unanimous, response. The old, working class belief that studying is somehow not what a man should do was still strong here. Studying is what puftahs do, who don't want to get their hands dirty.

It was all right for a girl to study. She wouldn't want to climb under machines, she wasn't strong enough to heave things about, she wouldn't want black grease on her delicate hands. Yet this caricatured masculinity no longer secures a stable, viable place in the world. It did when the pit was there, but it doesn't now. You won't make much money getting your hands dirty unless you own the business itself. For those unable to make the transition away from the macho culture of grease and manual work, what is left is economic insecurity and low pay. Trapped there, you are trying to compete against the third world. And the only advantage you have is that markets and supplies are on your doorstep, whereas the third world is thousands of miles away.

When I ran into Bob, the 45 year-old worker at Humb Store, in the Top 'Ouse later, his view was a grown-up version of the idea dominant in the youth club: 'it's a qualifications-dominated world. But that's not what really counts'.

His father had a run a scrap yard, yet he had been only 'semi-literate'. He had known a multi-millionaire who couldn't read or write. The really valuable skills in society, he assured me as he took another drink from his pint of bitter, were about knowing how to survive, about living on your wits, about knowing when to buy and sell. Not about having a degree. And of course, in some ways, he was right. Learning how to survive and prosper, economically and emotionally, is not something you can learn from a book. If you can, you have to combine the two: get some qualifications and learn to survive. Otherwise you might end up at the packaging factory on a continental shift, not sure whether it is day or night, not really sure whether you should be sleeping or working. Just like Bob.

Quite a few of the kids in the youth club were the sons and daughters of one-time mineworkers. I asked them what they did when they weren't here. 'Get pissed', was the most common response. 'Where?' I continued. 'At the cricket field'. At least, that was where they had been getting pissed, until they were moved on by the security firm hired in recent years by the parish council to keep order in the town. 'Get stoned', was also a common reply. Cider was their preferred tipple. They got it from 'the Paki shop. She waits while there is no one around and puts it in a carrier bag'.

All across West and South Yorkshire, the police have tried to clamp down on the selling of alcohol to under-18s. They send letters to off-licence proprietors warning them that random checks will be carried out. Then they send cadets in, trying to buy alcohol. But it has only a limited effect. As Eric, who represents Conisbrough on Doncaster council, told me, the kids threaten to smash the shop window if they don't get what they want.

Getting pissed and stoned is all right, but it has to be controlled. And you have to do something else as well. You can't spend your entire life pissed and stoned. Fantasy has to come to an end. You are Miss UK one day, and cooking meals in a pub the next. You have to earn a living. But it was difficult to see how some of the young men here would find a place in the modern world.

The night had been coloured by some open, though mild, sexual activity. Girls sitting on the knees of uncouth, loud, young men, occasionally kissing lips around which the boys were trying to sprout bristles as yet one further indication of their intense masculinity. It was still, I thought as I looked at them, even after all these years, even after the pit had gone, even after liberal legal reforms and gay pop stars, it was still such a terrible crime to be a 'Jessie'. Here was an element of continuity with the past that looked like it might never end. As long as I could remember, to be thought of as a jessie was a terrible condemnation. You weren't a real man. You were a bloody jessie. Even now, in the late 1990s, you had to try desperately hard to make sure that no one thought you were a jessie. You had to have a girl on your knee. You had to smoke in the most aggressive way possible, pulling hard on your cigarette until the burning bit became long and pointed, resembling the end of one of those red-hot pokers you would push and prod the coal fire with that were once so common in Featherstone. You had to shout, you had to be heard. You had to be hard. Otherwise, somebody might think you were a jessie. And that must be the worst thing in the world to be. A jessie. 'There aren't many virgins here', the earnest and well-meaning man told me. Obviously. And certainly no jessies.

They talked openly about illegal drugs. Many frequently — so they claimed — smoked what they referred to as 'weed'. Many claimed to know others who were on heroin. Asked where you would get heroin, they replied 'just ask anybody on the street'. I confess I didn't try it.

I asked the kids where they got the money from for cider, and weed, and whatever else they took. They looked at me as if I was a complete imbecile for even having to ask the question. 'Nick things', they replied. Wasn't that obvious? How else do you get money?

Sex comes earlier than it did for their grandparents and granddads, probably earlier than it did for their mothers and dads. This school year, out of 70 girls, there were five teenage pregnancies. I was told at the school by one group of girls that

> *'some girls are always going on about how many times they have done it. And they are always asking how many times you've done it'.*

I wondered how they met their partners, how the world was reproduced. Dave the deputy's son said that his girlfriend was in his class but he'd also met her 'in the street'. So much easier, I thought, than answering introduction ads in the press. When asked how long he had been seeing her he said, 'nine months, but it's serious'. He said it with such gravity. It sounded like a disease. But, then again, they were only kids. Time would teach them that what is serious one day ceases to exist the next day. Like the pit.

The world of mining communities was never idyllic. Far from it. It was a world of hard work, money shortages, chronic illness, premature death. But, at least after nationalisation in 1947, it was a relatively stable world. If you wanted work, you could get work; if you wanted a house, the council would see to it that you got one. You could go drinking with your mates. The women could play bingo and 'cal'. It wasn't a glamorous life, but you could get by and have fun while you did it. There was no heroin, and no crack cocaine, and little crime.

If you spend a day now in the slightly bigger of the former mining towns that is closest to Featherstone — perhaps to visit the market selling cheap clothes and counterfeit designer sports wear on a Wednesday, or to get served beer on a Thursday night by topless barmaids — what will strike you above all else, as you walk around the square in the middle of town, as you sit in a cafe, as you call in the pubs, is poverty. It's evident in the clothes people wear: old overcoats, and old shirts, and old jackets that people haven't changed for years. Not because they don't want to change them. Not because they're out of touch with fashion. Simply because they haven't got the money to go and buy another.

And alongside the poverty you will see illness and you will see people who look old before their time. You can tell how old people are by the ages of their kids, and by the clothes they wear. You just know that they are far younger than they look. I sat in a cafe one ordinary Thursday in 1998. There were only 15 or 20 people in there altogether. All the women had young children. At least three of the children had something noticeably wrong with them. All of the grown ups, without exception, were smoking. When they had put one out, they lit another. They smoked as they went to the counter to order food. They smoked as they carried their food back on trays. They smoked before their meal, and they smoked after their meal. They smoked as they drank their tea.

You walk around, and you want to help them. You want an economic, and a social, and a cultural, revolution. You want to remember them, as they were, full of pride and hope for the future. You want them strong, and confident, knowing that their day is still to come, but come it will, as they used to believe. But you know it isn't. And you know that you can't really do anything about it.

And what you don't want is to see their lives shattered, the world they lived in torn apart. You don't want it, because once you were there with them. You know that they go from day to day, from street to street, because you've seen them, calling in occasionally at houses and shops that have been there for a hundred years, and you know that nothing, really nothing, will change to make things better, more prosperous, less parochial. I remarked on this once to an older man who had lived in the locality all his life. He took his time before answering me, thinking about my words. Then he fixed me with his now watery, but still steely, blue eyes. 'What do you expect them to do?' he said, riveting the position deep into my psyche. I suddenly realised, of course, that I hadn't a clue.

NOTES

1. *Vibration White Finger. Litigation Against British Coal.* A briefing from Thompsons. Undated, circa 1996.

2. George Orwell, 1937 *The Road to Wigan Pier.* Martin Secker and Warburg, London. (1969 Reprint). pp 176-177. Emphasis in text.

3. Richard Hoggart, 1959 *The Uses of Literacy.* Aspects of working class life, with special references to publications and entertainments. Chatto and Windus, London, p111.

4. Vivian Nicholson and Stephen Smith, 1977 *Spend, Spend, Spend.* Jonathan Cape, London.

5. *Pontefract and Castleford Express*, 11 April 1985.

Epilogue

For all the 1980s and most of the 1990s, as the contraction of the coal industry continued with pits closing relentlessly week after week, the Conservatives were in government. The Conservatives were commonly blamed for the decline, even if they themselves blamed 'market forces'. In the Conservative lexicon of the time, market forces could not be argued with. Market forces were supreme. Except that it wasn't market forces, and everyone knew that it wasn't market forces. Because the market was rigged.

By the time Labour returned to office, in May 1997, most of the coal industry itself had already gone. As mining areas had traditionally been Labour-voting, many had high expectations of Labour. They certainly expected more help than they had seen from the Conservatives.

And Labour did appear to place more emphasis on helping the situation in mining areas. Within five months of taking office, the new government established the Coalfields Task Force, in October 1997. Nine months later, in June 1998, the Task Force's report was published. In the foreword to the government's response to the report, which followed in December 1998, no less than four cabinet ministers - John Prescott, David Blunkett, Peter Mandelson, and Chris Smith - stated that it marked 'our commitment to repair the damage done to coalfield communities over the last 20 years' and the start of the government's 'long term commitment to regenerating the coalfields'.

A mix of measures was announced. The central financial incentive was an additional £354 million of government money to be spent over three years.

Two new institutions were created as well, the Coalfields
Regeneration Trust, and the Coalfields Enterprise Fund.

The Coalfields Regeneration Trust was established as an
independent charity. Over three years, it would have £52 million to
spend. Its aim was to make sure that 'pit villages' - small places,
like Featherstone, where there had been little economically other
than coal - benefited from assistance, as the big industrial estates
and enterprise zones had done. Its publicity material referred to
credit unions, and one-stop-shops, and community chests, and
sports facilities.

The Coalfield Enterprise Fund was yet another attempt to stimulate
the small business sector within the former mining areas, this time
with the emphasis on supporting 'small firms with high growth
potential'. The government would be providing £15 million for this
over three years.

There was to be further organisational change, too. Regional
Development Agencies were to be set up across Britain. In the
former mining areas, as elsewhere, they would 'lead economic
development and social and physical regeneration in the regions
and provide a greater degree of co-ordination to existing and
regional spending programmes'.

And in West Yorkshire, not too far away from Featherstone, one of
the Regional Development Agencies - Yorkshire Forward -
pioneered a 'millennium village' at Allerton Bywater, a former
mining village. Allerton Bywater would become 'the most
innovative and environmentally friendly place to live in the region'.

With its plan for 'improved leisure facilities', and 'training
opportunities' and 'improved community learning and study

resources', it is not clear that 'innovatory' is the right word to use, though the scheme is certainly another well-intentioned project and is likely to significantly change Allerton Bywater.

With a range of new housing planned, and proximity to Leeds, a prospect is the transformation of Allerton Bywater into a commuter village. The scheme is only commencing at the time of writing, so it is too early to tell.

Labour also pledged to offer some assistance to housing in mining areas. Another £28 million would be forthcoming, according to the report, over three years.

For the Coalfield Community Campaign, however, Labour's measures were welcome but insufficient. The Campaign's response in October 1999 to newly-announced regeneration efforts involving offices and workshops to be developed as part of 'Networkspace' was reported in a local newspaper as being:

> *'The money shows the Government is committed and moving forward, but all the other recommendations by the Coalfields Task Force seem to have been lost. There are still areas of concern which have not been addressed such as roads which could be built to improve access to businesses. Only one of these has gone through and that was up in the north east'* [1].

Networkspace sounded pretty high tech. Really, it was a partnership between a private sector property developer and English Partnerships, a government supported development agency.

Regeneration measures take time to have an impact. The Coalfields Regeneration Trust (CRT) itself was not launched until September 1999. In its very first phase it was still looking for projects rather than implementing any. As with the Coalfield Enterprise Fund (CEF), it is far too early at this stage to assess the extent of its effectiveness in bringing about worthwhile regeneration.

In its focus on incorporating social and community aspects to the regeneration process, however, for a national scheme the CRT did at least represent something new. Its priorities included 'support for community facilities, community transport, welfare and debt advice' and assistance for 'community enterprise'.

The CEF, though, was of the same genre as had gone before. Small business sector stimulation was common to many past regeneration efforts, and even the emphasis on high tech companies had been the subject of previous attempts.

Barnsley had seen an 'innovation centre' established in the late 1980s, for instance, with assistance from the local authority, the European Commission, and the job-creation arm of British Coal. Small businesses doing something new, something innovatory, would be set up here and would provide a dynamic element to the local economy. As a centre for developing small businesses, it saw some success. Yet four years after its establishment, an academic appraisal I was involved in concluded that

> '.....there was only one company up and running which could lay claim to being a genuinely innovative firm: it has to be said that progress to a high technology local economy via this route would take a long time'.

Perhaps the CEF will target high tech companies more successfully, and help to bring about more of a 'modernisation' of the local economies of the coalfields.

While Labour had placed a new emphasis on coalfield regeneration since taking office, there had been a plethora of attempts under the Conservatives - some of these were central government efforts, others were initiated at the local level - and these should not be overlooked. Labour's approach was a continuation and a re-focusing of regeneration efforts, rather than being something completely new.

Under the Conservatives, there were enterprise zones set up in West Yorkshire in 1991, for example, and later in South Yorkshire, North Nottinghamshire, the former coalfield of North East Derbyshire and what was the north east coalfield; there was the creation of British Coal Enterprise in the mid-1980s, an arm of the then nationalised coal industry devoted to job creation; there was a Task Force, extra money for Training and Enterprise Councils in mining areas, and large numbers of regeneration partnerships [2]. Most of them had some beneficial impact. Sometimes it was too modest to make a huge amount of difference. Amongst other things, the Task Force paid for women in Doncaster to be trained in supermarket check out skills so that they could get jobs at Asda. Men were given training to become builders or warehouse staff. The West Yorkshire enterprise zone provided the bulk of industrial employment in the locality, though most of the biggest companies on it had either already been situated there prior to its designation as an enterprise zone, or had relocated from very nearby. The biggest employer on the zone, for instance, moving into it in October 1990, was a men's outfitter, providing 370 jobs. But upon setting up on the zone, the company closed one factory in the town in which the zone was situated, and one three miles away, where the company were occupying the former baths of a redundant pit. The company had moved its factories from one place to another, but there were no new jobs.

As the coal industry declined in the 1980s and 1990s, an army of consultants grew, both inside and outside universities, presenting economic evaluations and 'action plans' for ways forward. Outside universities, some of the consultants made fortunes. People produced reports on 'capacity building', new roads were driven across South Yorkshire, workshops set up from which small businesses could be run. It was all worthy, and it was all honourable, even if some of the consultants had very little experience of, or personal involvement with, the coalfields. As the 1990s progressed, the 'action plans' 'continued, though the academic evaluations themselves faded away, at least from the academic journals. Like everything else, the academic world is affected by fashionability. And fashionability, in whatever sphere, never lasts for long.

Fashionability did attach itself in the 1990s, however, to something various academics identified as 'social capital'. It was a simple idea really, as most things which are analysed by academics are, but it had a direct bearing on the validity of the 'economic' and the consultants' evaluations of regeneration schemes. It demonstrated how, by themselves, such economic evaluations, with their focus on the number of hectares of land brought into industrial use, or the number of training places taken up, were inadequate, especially in the context of a mining area.

'Social capital' is about co-operation, trust, friendship, self-discipline. It is about relationships between members of a community, be that at the local or regional level. It is about social cohesion, and the moral code which governs behaviour within a group of people. Unlike capital investment, which is based on physical products paid for by somebody's money, or human resources which, in the 'conventional' sense, are developed through education and training, social capital exists as a reflection of ethical and behavioural norms within a community. A recognition of the concept of social capital reflects an acknowledgement that psychology - individual or collective - may have as strong a bearing on the economic prospects for a locality or region as have the numbers of people with NVQs and degrees, or the level of capital investment per employed worker. To acknowledge the existence of social capital is to step outside of that which is normally quantified and that which is normally recognised.

And 'social capital', some academics argue, is a 'factor of production', like human labour, and like machines, and raw material. And factors of production are needed before anything can be done. As one of them wrote, social capital:

> *'... has major consequences for the nature of an industrial economy that society will be able to create. If people who have to work together in an enterprise trust one another because they are operating to a set of ethical norms, doing business costs less'* [3].

'Social capital' is pretty similar, really, to Littlejohn and Warwick's 'local cultural capital' referred to in the introduction to this book. Their local cultural capital relates to the behavioural norms specific to a local community. For them, it found expression in the solidarity which existed in mining communities, in the 'sense of a shared glory and pride'. Alongside this, the more negative aspects of life in mining communities, 'hardness, ugliness and danger', were noted, but it was the former attributes that provided the communities' strengths.

And, even then, ideas on 'social capital' and 'local cultural capital' are not new. *Coal is our life*, back in 1956, was really at least partly about the moral code common to mining areas. Dennis, Henriques and Slaughter painted a picture of a self-policing community with norms of behaviour which could not be transgressed by any of its members. They did not use this particular example, but the constraint on where swear words should be used was noted earlier. Swearing was reserved for the pit or the pub, providing the company was all male; swearing in front of a woman was taboo. Crime, too, was frowned upon and, in particular, stealing from people you lived next to, or people you worked with, or drank with, was regarded as the lowest form of human activity.

When the local economies of mining areas were destroyed, the 'social capital' was destroyed too. The spirit that had held places together was drained, quickly, as if it was going down a plug hole. It may well be possible, over time, if enormous effort is made, to rebuild the economies of mining areas on new lines. Call centres might provide a contribution to replacing the jobs lost, though it is likely to be people who would never have found work, or wanted to find work, in the mining industry who might find employment in them. Others will commute to nearby cities - though only the young and fit and the skilled - and find an economic future. But rebuilding social capital, rebuilding the spirit, may take a lot longer. And it may well be too late.

NOTES

[1.] *Barnsley Chronicle,* 22 October 1999.

[2.] Many of them are examined in R.Turner, 1993 *Regenerating the Coalfields. Policy and Politics in the 1980s and early 1990s.* Avebury, Aldershot.

[3.] Francis Fukuyama, 1995 *Trust: the Social Virtues and the Creation of Prosperity.* Hamish Hamilton, London.

Index

LEARNING AND SOCIETY

About the series

As advanced industrial societies move into the 21st century, they will continue to experience profound and widespread changes. These will embrace their economies, labour markets, technologies, communications, social policies, the organisation of communities and family structures, the conservation of the environment and the responsible and sustainable use of natural resources. At the heart of these changes, as we shift to what some commentators have called the post-modern world, will be global financial and economic forces, driven by the information revolution, whose effects will be characterised by uncertainty, risk and indeterminacy.

Learning has a vital contribution to make if people are to come to terms with these changes, and to understand and control them. This means that lifelong learning has to rise to the top of the social agenda of governments world-wide. The challenge this poses cannot be overstated, especially in the United Kingdom, where too few people still achieve their potential through the current educational system.

The Learning and Society series is one outcome of the partnership between Sheffield Hallam University and the Northern College. The aim of the series is to provide an opportunity for those involved in research and development work that links lifelong learning with the processes of social and economic change, to publish on a wide range of theoretical and practical issues that will inform public policy and educational theory and practice. The series will include research monographs, accounts of new projects and initiatives, collections of papers, and studies in the history, policy and methods surrounding the learning process and its impact on society.

The first volume in the series, Exits and Entrances: Political research as a creative art by Lewis Minkin represented a major contribution to the important question of how we conduct intellectual enquiry and the importance of creativity in that process. The second book, Higher Education Learning from Experience, by Colin Raban and Maggie Challis was very different, and reflects upon how higher education should regard learning from work and life that mature students bring to their academic studies, and how this should be appraised and accredited.

In this third volume, Coal Was Our Life, Royce Turner provides a provocative and controversial account of a West Yorkshire mining town made famous in a pioneering sociological study of the 1950's, where the closure of the local pits has caused social and economic devastation. It is a moving story of how real people have tried to come to terms with circumstances they could not have imagined fifteen years ago; how they survive, how their lives have changed, and asks hard questions about what hopes they have for the future. This is one of the most important essays on working class life to have emerged in decades, and is a fitting addition to the Learning and Society series.